THAT GREAT LUCIFER

Sir Walter Ralegh, with his son Wat, aged eight.
By an unknown artist.

By permission of the Trustees of the National Portrait Gallery

THAT GREAT LUCIFER

A PORTRAIT OF
SIR WALTER RALEGH

By
Margaret Irwin

1960
CHATTO & WINDUS
LONDON

Published by
Chatto & Windus Ltd
42 William IV Street
London, WC2

★

Clarke, Irwin & Co Ltd
Toronto

To E. J. I.

Printed in Great Britain
By T. & A. Constable Ltd
Hopetoun Street, Edinburgh

CONTENTS

★

CONTENTS

ILLUSTRATIONS

★

PREFACE

*

This is not a novel, or a fictional biography. There are no imaginary scenes or conversations in it; and Ralegh's own words are quoted continuously. But it is a portrait of him and some of his contemporaries rather than a comprehensive life; and it would be pretentious to add a bibliography. The sources are mostly evident from the text, or in my few footnotes. I had not intended to use these, as they are generally the hall-mark of a work of original scholarship, which this book makes no claim to be; though I have worked on it for six years, and read on the subject many years longer. I only began to put footnotes when quoting from legal opinions by experts which I would not have discovered in my general reading; and to these I have added a few others. Of all the books I have read on Ralegh, I found Edward Thompson's life of him the most inspiring and liberal-minded.

Ralegh's own works I have read, casually but continuously, ever since I bought a facsimile of his minute 'Instructions' to his son—the strangest paradox of this paradoxical man, for it belies himself as though intended to be read in reverse as in a mirror. Then, as 'a reward for *Royal Flush*', John Buchan gave me a 1st Folio of the *History of the World*, printed in 1614 in Ralegh's lifetime, which I had already known in later editions; from then on I had his *World* as my own, to enter at will. And a few years ago when I sailed to Trinidad and up the Amazon for 1,000 miles, I took as my most vivid guide-book Ralegh's own work on his voyage for 500 miles up the great sister river of the Orinoco.

But I did not think of venturing on this book till Ian Parsons persuaded me and, when it was first finished, helped me enormously in correcting and compressing it, in a masterly work of editing. I also thank A. D. Peters for his final criticisms, as illuminating as they were encouraging.

M. I.

BOOK I

RALEGH AND ELIZABETH

"You have lived like a Star,
at which the World hath Gazed"

RALEGH'S JUDGES

A*

CHAPTER ONE

'A Bare Gentleman'

SIR ROBERT NAUNTON'S
'FRAGMENTA REGALIA'

THE year 1587 was a dangerous cross-road in some of the
greatest lives in Europe. It was the last year of the precariously balanced Elizabethan peace. The English Queen
had contrived to spin it out on a cobweb-thread of diplomacy
that had danced to and fro with every breeze and glittered with
the dewy innocence of her protestations, ever since she had come
to the throne twenty-nine years before, and all Europe had laid
bets that she would be at war and defeated within six months.
But her gossamer thread still swung and never snapped, until
now at long length her rival, Philip II of Spain, discovered that
his patience was exhausted and swore to launch his Armada to
invade England and dethrone her Queen.

By then the English Government itself egged on his decision,
for its patience was also exhausted by the constantly recurring
danger of plots against the Queen's life, in favour of the Catholic
Mary Queen of Scots. After nineteen years of them, Elizabeth
had at last been induced to put to death her prisoner, cousin, and
heir to the throne, in the February of 1587. The execution of
Queen Mary horrified Europe and clinched King Philip's warlike
decision. It also cleared his path by removing the chief obstacle
to his plans for invasion. The Spanish Sovereign was supposedly
Mary's champion, but he had had no wish to free her to make
her Queen of England and thus, with her ally France, a Catholic
power that would rival his own. Her shocking death released
him from this awkward obligation; he could now avenge it by
wrenching the English throne from the heretic and murderous
Elizabeth, and claim it as his own inheritance, through his
ancestor John of Gaunt. So the armies and huge ships of Spain
and Portugal, all named after saints, gathered together for the
long deferred 'Enterprise of England', and the powers of prayer
and sacrifice prepared to aid them in a terrible retribution. The

11

Pope sent his blessing on the Crusade and the promise of a million gold ducats—but not to be paid until after the Crusaders had landed in England, for 'we are sorry to say it but we have a poor opinion of this Spanish Armada and fear some disaster'.

Within two months of Mary's execution, the Pope was proved in the right by Sir Francis Drake's surprise attack on Cadiz harbour, where his small squadron destroyed over thirty of the great galleons, and vast quantities of the stores there collected in readiness for the 'Enterprise'. 'Just look at Drake!' exclaimed the Pope in what seems an unsympathetic spirit of 'I told you so'. Drake modestly called it 'singeing the King of Spain's beard', and raced on to singe it again at Cape St Vincent, Lisbon and the Azores. His action marked the climax of his career, and halted the Spanish Armada for that year.

Yet still Philip believed it could set sail in 1587; and England still expected the invasion in that very summer or autumn; and Elizabeth still tried to swing back again on to her thread of safety by protesting against Drake's action and promising to keep the peace she had clung to so tenaciously throughout her long reign.

But for the rest of her life she would never know peace again.

These were the major roads that crossed each other and led to the 'Invincible Armada''s attempt to invade England in the following year.

Other, apparently minor, roads also crossed, and caused a clash that seemed of merely private and personal importance at the time, but which was to have tragic results on the three most glorious figures of the reign: the young Earl of Essex, his fifteen-year-older rival, Sir Walter Ralegh, and their ageing Queen, Elizabeth herself. For it was in the spring of 1587 that Essex, a tall, fair, impatient youth, came to Court, and into headlong collision with the Queen's new Captain of the Guard, Ralegh.

Robert Devereux, second Earl of Essex, was an impoverished aristocrat on his father's side, descended from Edward III, from the Bohuns and Plantagenets and most of the ancient Norman nobility who had been ruined or killed off in the Wars of the Roses. His mother's much newer family was more useful to him, for Lettice, née Knollys, was a granddaughter of Anne Boleyn's sister, and therefore cousin to the Queen. And Lettice herself, after marrying the Viscount of Hereford and then the first Earl of Essex, had now been married for nine years to Robert Dudley, the magnificent Earl of Leicester, who had been ever since the beginning of her reign the Queen's paramount favourite and so the most powerful influence at Court. He was in fact, or had been, the nearest to a husband the Queen had ever known. But by 1587 this elderly attachment to 'Sweet Robin' or her 'Eyes' as she nick-named him, was loosened, and the light of her Eyes out-shone by the suddenly soaring star of Sir Walter Ralegh.

Sir Walter's knighthood was of only three years' standing; he was related to none of the influential nobility, and had started life as 'a bare gentleman', the youngest son of a plain Devon squire, a churchwarden of East Budleigh, his coat of arms deeply carved on the massive pew, to which every Sunday he led his wife and those of their numerous family then at home, for hours of reading from the new Bible—a crime punishable with burning alive in the memory of even the youngest, Walter; so that while still doing his lessons on a horn-book (since paper was too scarce and dear to be wasted on children) he may well have been more impressed than bored by the long quiet readings which were later to make so deep an impression on his own prose.

His father owned a farm and a few ships, and had shown his independent spirit by lending one of them to his cousin Sir Peter Carew when he rebelled against Queen Mary's Government in protest at her marriage to Philip of Spain, and attacked her ships as well as his, in flagrant piracy on the high seas. Mr Ralegh's farmlands had a more respectable history for, though lately diminished, some had been granted to his family by William the Conqueror. His son Sir Walter made no boast of that, but set store by the fact that he could count on the support of 'more than a hundred gentlemen of his kindred'.

His uncle Champernoun was the Vice-Admiral of the West, in command at Plymouth of a post held in the family for more than half a century, and one very helpful to sailors on the windy side of the law. His elder brother of full blood and some of his Carew cousins had been knighted as 'the finest seamen' of their day; his three elder half-brothers, the Gilberts, had won renown as navigators and explorers. Sir Richard Grenville was his cousin; so also, more distantly and less genteelly, was Sir Francis Drake. On all sides of the family—and they were many, for his father had married three times and his mother twice—he was related to the most famous sea-captains (or infamous pirates) of the West Country, who were alternately backed by the Queen's Government for making profit, or repudiated for making trouble. Heroes or ruffians, they scarcely presented the most decorous credentials for the highest court positions. The Captain of the Queen's own Guard was personally responsible for her safety, and therefore constantly in attendance on her and able to win her attention; it was moreover traditional that the post should lead to some of the greatest offices in the State.

Yet Walter Ralegh, not then even knighted, had been almost unknown when he came to Court five years before at the age of thirty. He had been an adventurer of all sorts, a freelance soldier and sailor, and occasional scholar at will, in the casual amateurish manner of the Elizabethan gentry. He had left his home in the thatched farmhouse by the sea very early for Oxford, and was at once reputed 'the ornament of the juniors' at Oriel, especially in oratory and philosophy. The juniors recorded less favourably that he once casually borrowed a gown he never returned; and gave a caustic flick of advice to a good archer but a coward who wanted to avoid a duel—'Challenge the fellow to a shooting match!'

After only a year at Oxford, and before he was seventeen, he snatched at the chance to fight as a mounted volunteer in the religious wars that were making an international cockpit of France. Ralegh served under a cousin with the chivalric name of Gawain Champernoun, who had married the daughter of the famous French Huguenot, the Count of Montgomery. The private company raised by Champernoun could expect no sanction from their Queen, and in defeat no quarter from their foes; since the Spaniards hanged their captives 'not as Frenchmen but as heretics', the French hanged theirs 'not as Spaniards but as murderers', and the Papists of both nations hanged the English not as Englishmen but as Protestant volunteers; to make it quite clear they wore scrolls round their necks as they swung on the gallows to say they had fought without the consent of their Queen. Punctilio in national neutrality was strictly observed.

'There are no such things as Wars of Religion,' Ralegh wrote long later, 'only Civil Wars.' And 'by Civil War no nation is ever bettered.' Yet he went on fighting for six years for the Huguenots, in the battles of Jarnac and Montcontour and in the following retreat, and saw them smoking their enemies out of caves in Languedoc by letting down a chain with lighted straw bound round a stone, so that the besieged came rushing out 'like bees smoked out of their hives'. The campaign was crushed, and the Huguenot leader beheaded on the scaffold, in fulfilment of his ill-omened banner, which showed a severed head on a black ground, and the motto, 'Let valour end my days.' Ralegh returned to spend a couple of years in London as a member of the Middle Temple, though without studying law.

He lived in lodgings in Islington in an obscurity that the gossips called 'turbulent and irregular'; his friends were 'boisterous blades' but 'had wit'—of necessity, for he had a short way with bores. One evening in a tavern when 'a bold and impertinent fellow and perpetual talker' interrupted all others with his 'noise like a drum', Ralegh leaped like a tiger upon him and sealed up his beard to his moustache so as to shut his mouth. He was jailed for a week for fighting with the son of Sir John Perrot (half-brother illegitimately of the Queen, and later Lord Deputy of Ireland) and bound over to keep the peace— which he did not. Such impatient rages and lack of worldly wisdom sound like those of an outrageous schoolboy; but he was also writing verses approved by the leading author of the day, George Gascoigne, his first great literary friend, a swashbuckler and noted connoisseur who was then also 'marching among the Muses for lack of martial exploits'.

The two soldiers out of a job, together with Martin Frobisher, a huge stout man with no culture but a great navigator, would go down to Limehouse and sit for hours with Ralegh's elder half-brother Sir Humphrey Gilbert in his house by the docks. There as they watched the ships sail down river, Ralegh, so much the youngest of the four friends, planned with them the discoveries and conquests they themselves would make, and not only at sea.

Gascoigne was an adventurer both in life and letters; a Cambridge scholar, member of Gray's Inn, M.P. for Bedfordshire, and holding some minor post at Court. He had also won fame as a soldier in Holland under the talkative young William of Orange, now called 'the Silent' because he had kept his counsel when he saw through Catherine de Medici's plans for the Massacre of Saint Bartholomew. These humdrum details are nothing compared with Gascoigne's literary career, wherein he was so brilliant an originator that he is sometimes called the First of the Elizabethans; as Ralegh, twenty years younger, is called the Last of them. Gascoigne's 'mind was a very opal'; he tossed off a 'Hundred Sundry Flowers' of song, and half a dozen new forms of literature that at once caught on; English plays in blank verse, a Greek play he had translated for the London stage, comedy and short stories in prose, all these novelties making their first appearance in England; and as a side-line several 'dainty devices' and masques for his friend and patron Lord Leicester, to entertain the Queen on her ruinously magnificent visit to Kenilworth. Gascoigne had then just finished the first English satire in blank verse, 'The Steel Glass', and paid the budding young poet Walter Ralegh the high compliment of printing the latter's verses 'In Commendation' of it.

This is the first printed verse we have from Ralegh, when just twenty-three; more pithy than poetic, and, as often in his letters, he was too eager to speak his mind to mind mixing his metaphors. 'Spiteful tongues in canker'd stomachs placed,' is odd anatomy, more suited to the 'hot boiling ink' that he had poured on his adversaries' 'barren scalps' as a freshman in the furious Oxford debates that were apt to end with the smashing of college windows and furniture, and a penalty from the Proctors of twenty-four hours in the stocks. His crude rhetoric seems harsh in a tribute to the urbane Gascoigne, whose demurely humorous refrains, thrummed out to his lute—'Thus if you sup or dine with me'—or—'For so my wife taught me to say'—are more modern in tone than any until the impromptu rhymes of the cavalier poets in the next century. In violent contrast, Ralegh's praise of his friend's new form of verse is chiefly an attack on the critics who will certainly fail to

'esteem
Such stately steps as they cannot attain;
For whoso reaps renown above the rest,
With heaps of hate will surely be opprest'.

The grimly explosive last couplet is remembered for Ralegh's own later proof of it.

His mind, more versatile even than Gascoigne's, was to shine in stronger and more varied colours than his; but with the hard brilliance of a diamond rather than an opal. His humour flashed out in dangerously 'cut-throat jests', which he took for granted would amuse his friends as well as enrage his foes. Gascoigne must have despaired of ever making a courtier of his carelessly outspoken young friend. And as for Ralegh's idol, Gilbert, so fiercely, fanatically in earnest, it was hard to believe he had been trained as a page in the service of the subtle princess, Elizabeth, and had encountered the punctilious bonhomie that Philip of Spain had painfully forced on himself in his sacrificial mission of matrimony in England.

Sir Humphrey Gilbert was fourteen years older than his half-brother, Ralegh, and of much more consequence. He had been at Eton, Oxford and the Court, and been knighted on active service. His family's ancient and noble seat at Compton Castle near Torquay had been a second home to the young Walter in his holidays. Their mutual mother was 'a woman of noble wit and good opinions'. She had dared to visit a prisoner condemned to be burned for heresy in Mary Tudor's reign; and still more remarkably had acknowledged herself beaten in argument. 'I was not able to answer her—I, who can read, and she cannot.' Her fearless spirit of enquiry was inherited by both these sons; though not her clemency and humility.

Humphrey also owed his early start at Court to their mother's birth as a Champernoun and her relationship to Mrs 'Kat' Ashley, née Champernoun, Governess to the Princess Elizabeth. But the black-browed young man was too uncompromisingly direct and often too harsh to achieve real success as a courtier— or even, some said, as a Commander: a grand fighter both on land and sea, he had not the power to win men to him that his half-brother Walter possessed. They gave him the worst of all reputations: that he was unlucky. Worse still, he had begun to believe it. Not so Walter, who was later to endanger his own career by his furious assertions that Humphrey Gilbert was far fitter for supreme command than the incompetent Lords chosen by the Queen's Council.

Both of them were now out of work and under a grievance. Their large family was getting poorer, their land less, and Walter's birthplace, his beloved home of Hayes Farm, had had to be sold. They must make a fortune and speedily. To make money was then the mainspring of adventure; commerce and colonization were the prosaic reasons for voyages of discovery that read like poetry. Patriotism was yet another motive, though the word was then seldom used.

The brothers were determined to put their country back where she used to be, in the middle and most important part of the map. She had been pushed out of it by Spain's acquisition of America, which had made England a mere far-western outpost of Europe; but that could be turned into a point of vantage, from which England could harry other navies and outstrip them in the race for 'rich and unknown lands, fatally and it seemeth by God's providence, reserved for England'.

So Gilbert wrote with Ralegh's help, in urgent attempt to convince the Privy Council that there was a North-West Passage through the Arctic Ocean to Cathay and India; then that North America was 'of all other unfrequented places, the most fittest and commodious for us to meddle withal'. As a still better notion, he told them 'How to annoy the King of Spain . . . fall upon the enemy's shipping, destroy his trade in Newfoundland and the West Indies, and possess both regions.' Gilbert's motto, appropriately, was 'Why not?'

The Privy Council observed punctilio by modifying this aggressive wording against an officially neutral power; in the patent they at last issued, the two Devon brothers were given leave to discover and annex 'any remote and barbarous lands', but only such as were 'not already possessed by Christians'. Gilbert and Ralegh paid little attention to the wording. The Queen's face had to be saved as usual, but they would have agreed with Mrs Fairchild that 'the Roman Catholics are *called* Christians, but...'

What mattered to the brothers was that they had at last raised the necessary cash, chiefly by private subscription from their friends, and had now won their long awaited leave to use it. Ralegh in the meantime had tired of waiting and swung off on another of his 'rogue' forays all on his own, this time to a campaign in the Low Countries, to keep his hand in as a soldier before turning sailor. As soon as the fleet was ready he was back in Plymouth to be joint leader of it and captain of the ship *Falcon*. George Gascoigne had put every penny he could raise into the expedition, and intended to embark on it himself. All was set for him to sail with his friends, when suddenly he died. 'It is now time to go to bed,' he had lately written in a Lullaby of singular resignation, telling 'youth be still', and himself to 'welcome pain, let pleasure pass'—and then 'Go sleep and so beguile thy mind.' But he went before the time. His mantle fell on Ralegh, who showed his gratitude by acknowledging him his leader 'among the Muses' as well as 'martial exploits'. He took his motto, 'Iam marti quam Mercuris', fulfilled it, and so made it famous.

Spain clamoured for the expedition to be recalled when it was known that Ralegh was to be one of its leaders, and ordered her ships to be ready to attack it. The expedition was unlucky from the start. South-westerly gales drove it back from the Azores, and the damaged ships had to be refitted and set out all over again, into the still worse storms of winter, and the dangers from the Spanish fleet, now fully warned of their intentions. Gilbert, dour and irascible, quarrelled with one of his captains, Knollys, who finally deserted.

Then Ralegh was nearly killed, and lost many men, in a desperate fight off Cape Verde. The victorious Spaniards sank one of the ships with all hands, and the rest straggled back yet again to the Devon coast; all except Ralegh's, which sailed on for six months alone, in search of some sea-prize or victory or above all the discovery of some strange country. He was only forced back at last by storms, and with his supplies down to starvation point. No sooner did he land at Plymouth than he engaged in another fight, legal this time, for he and Gilbert charged Knollys with desertion, and as Knollys was a kinsman of the Queen, like Ralegh's former adversary Perrot, this again showed him no respecter of persons. The two brothers were also in trouble for having snatched a boat-load of oranges and lemons from a Seville trader before they had sailed; the Council had commanded them to return it, but fresh fruit was useful against scurvy, so they had chosen to ignore the command and to pay fines instead. This detrimental entry was the first mention of Ralegh in the Council Book and has been considered highly characteristic of him by moralists ever since.

He and Gilbert had lost all they had put into their sea venture; so, amphibiously, they turned soldier again, this time in Ireland, where Gilbert had already held command and won his knighthood. Now Ralegh followed him there with a captain's commission, obtained probably from Gascoigne's patron, Leicester, and a troop of a hundred men, to help put down yet another rebellion of the 'native Irish', prompted and strengthened this time by the foreign powers with whom England had, officially, to keep the peace. He attacked his new job in a hurry, or rather a fury, of impatience. America was waiting for him, and to him America was everything; but first he had to clear up this mess in the treacherous Irish bogs where everybody quarrelled, English as well as Irish, and Ralegh as angrily as any. His bad temper glittered like phosphorescence on a stormy sea. He hated the soft-spoken native kerns who shook a 'glib' of shaggy hair over their eyes to conceal their thoughts; and at night swarmed yelling out of the woods 'like hags and furies of hell, with flakes of fire fastened on poles' ends', to 'burn between 700 and 800 thatched houses in a market town',[1] and leave behind them 'above 500 men's bodies'; then vanish like smoke into the forest again. To fight them was, in Ralegh's words, to 'fight as one beating the air'.

The dirt was disgusting (it was thought unlucky to scour the milk-pails), the food revolting, of hard oat-cake, and on feast-days 'flesh half-cooked without bread or salt'[2]; and the native usquebaugh, a raw spirit mixed with raisins and fennel-seed, made everybody drunk, English and Irish, men and women alike, though Ralegh, never a drinker, could not abide it. Indigestion may have played a part in his ferocity, which was clean contrary to his behaviour in all other campaigns.

But, as his admired exemplar Humphrey Gilbert insisted, this was not a campaign, but a foul stab in the back from Spain and the Papacy, who pretended an official peace with England, but had stirred up the Irish to rebellion, and had now begun to help them with money and arms and even large forces of men. The Irish havens would make the best vantage points for attack on England, 'and if the Spaniard might be master of them, he would in a short space be master of the seas, which is our chiefest force'. So Ireland had now become England's Achilles' heel, or rather the serpent coiled around it, and there could be no hope for their own island until it was cut away.

Stories of Captain Ralegh soon flew like wild-fire over Ireland, bringing terror to the enemy, for he was as ruthless as he was

[1] Letter 1577 from Sir Henry Sidney, father of Sir Philip Sidney.
[2] Don Francesco de Cuellar. *Narrative of the Spanish Armada*, 1588.

reckless. The wholesale massacre of the prisoners at Smerwick is the worst to be held against him now, though he acted under orders. The prisoners were chiefly Spanish and Italian jail-birds, released only in order to invade Ireland and help her to rise against the English Protestants; for as the President of Connaught groaned to 'Wise Walsingham' (who wished Ireland 'buried in the sea')—'It is now a quarrel of religion.' The new Deputy, Lord Grey de Wilton, observed punctilio by ordering the massacre of the prisoners not as Papists, but as enemy agents in time of official peace; just as English sailors taken on the Spanish Main were slaughtered or enslaved in the galleys. Ralegh, as one of the captains who carried out their commander's order at Smerwick, would have given a still more practical answer; that only imbeciles could expect a small force of English to keep six hundred dangerous foreign prisoners in a country already aflame with revolt. But nobody at the time questioned the necessity for the massacre. The poet, 'Gentle Spenser', Lord Grey's secretary, didn't even mention it.

Ralegh's cruelty, swift and relentless, has left no such shuddering horror round his name in Ireland as has that of Cromwell in the next century. And other stories, of his genius for guerilla warfare and his dare-devil courage, threw a brighter though sometimes lurid glow around him. He had braved his way into a chieftain's stronghold by a ruse, and with only eleven men had captured him and more than three hundred followers. He had rushed back alone into a horde of enemies to rescue a wounded friend; for his followers were all his friends, and would go on with him to the end, knowing that he would stand by them till then. He proved it by holding a ford single-handed against a small army, 'standing with a pistol in one hand and his iron-shod quarterstaff in the other', until his handful of an escort had crossed the river.

The men under him loved him; those above him hated him even worse than did his enemies. His brilliant strategy and his gallantry won him no high promotion. He quarrelled hotly with his superiors and criticized them with a plain-speaking that seems amazing now, but was not so uncommon then in the army. He charged the Lord Deputy himself and the commanding General, the Earl of Ormonde, with making Ireland a 'lost land —not a commonwealth, but a common woe'. He 'disdained' his own appointment under them 'as much as if it were to keep sheep'.

If only Sir Humphrey Gilbert had been made Lord General, then 'all the unbridled traitors of these parts would come in and yield themselves to the Queen's mercy'. In his passionate praise of his half-brother he burst out, 'Would God the services of Sir Humphry Gilbert might be rightly lookt into! Who with the third part of the garrison now in Ireland, ended a rebellion not much inferior to this in two months.'

Here was family feeling with a vengeance, and literally so. These Devon men were all relatives and as thick as thieves. The Lord Deputy made a dignified protest to prove his 'grounded experience and approved reason' as superior to Captain Ralegh's; but had finally to fall back on, 'For mine own part I must be plain: I like neither his carriage nor his company.' He refused to give Ralegh a new command in Ireland; and so there he was back in London and out of work again. He was now nearly thirty years old, and as penniless as when he had left Oxford as a boy; for the 'militia' in Ireland was too poorly paid even to 'yield him food and raiment'. But he 'was one that it seems Fortune had picked out of purpose . . . to use as her tennis ball': so Sir Robert Naunton wrote in amazement at the way 'she tossed him up from nothing, and to and fro to greatness. . . . Not pulled up by chance', Naunton insists, except by seizing his chance to use his 'natural parts'. The lowest ebb in his career gave him his greatest opportunity; and a more surprising adventure than any yet was now to begin for him.

The Queen had been impressed by some of his strictures and wished to hear more of his opinions on Irish matters. He was called to confront the Lord Deputy in person before the Privy Council and the Queen herself, and put up a pretty cockfight for them. 'He had much the better in telling of his tale,' Naunton tells us with an evident chuckle, adding that 'he had gotten the Queen's ear at a trice, and she began to be taken with his elocution and loved to hear his reasons to her demands.'

That the elocution was frank to the point of boldness, and flavoured with a deep West Country burr, gave it piquancy for her among the polite, precise accents of her Civil Servants, none of whom however could flash out such hard, clear and incisive answers. There was sound sense in them too; he was even so original as to understand something of his enemies' minds. Instead of moaning like some of the councillors that 'the real cause of the mischief was the Devil, who would not have Ireland reformed', he told them that the rebel Earl of Desmond was himself feared like the Devil by the lesser chieftains; and that a discriminating leniency towards these 'small men' would win many over. And his main objection to the Earl of Ormonde, head of the Butler family, as Commander-in-Chief, was that no great Irish family would stand the rule of another; the Geraldines 'will rather die a thousand deaths, enter into a million of mischiefs and seek succour of all nations, rather than they will ever be subdued by a Butler.'

But Ralegh showed no such power to see his private opponents' point of view, nor they to see his. They were astonished and dismayed at the Queen's gracious, even delighted reception of the rough, not to say rude soldier. She 'loved a soldier', wrote Naunton; but to his superior officers he was rather a 'rogue' free-lance, who had fleshed his sword only on sleeveless errands in foreign wars and near-piratical sea-fights, before these obscure minor campaigns in the dripping bogs and backwoods of Ireland.

CHAPTER TWO

'The Best-Hated Man in the World'

SIR ANTHONY BAGOT

THAT character-part was now suddenly metamorphosed into the rôle of the superb courtier. 'He was no slug', was the gossip Aubrey's piquant understatement. His dragon-fly wings flashed open on the instant in disturbing brilliance; they swooped from one royal favour to another, then alighted on the duty highest and most intimate of all for his 'Eliza-conse-crated sword'—that of defending her consecrated person as the Captain of her Yeomen of the Guard. He was there at the door of her chamber, ready to be called within by her, to give advice, or maybe entertainment.

Other posts of hard work and profit, as well as honour, had already crowded fast upon him; he was appointed to direct enquiries into the Navy, and given a commission to clear the seas of Portuguese privateers; he helped found a company for Eastern trade; was M.P. for his county, knighted, made Lieutenant of Cornwall and Vice-Admiral of Cornwall and Devon and, to crown these, Lord Warden of the Stanneries, which brought him control of all the tin-mining down in the South-West.

As a free gift the Queen gave him the rich Monopoly of wine licences, and the export of broadcloth; also some fine estates in England and vast wildernesses in Ireland, which he managed to improve rapidly; lastly, in order that he might royally enter-tain distinguished foreigners, the princely Durham House in the Strand was specially withdrawn from the Bishop's See of Durham for his own private use.

Bishops had been broken in to this sort of eviction; Dr Cox of Ely had at first refused to give up Ely Place in Holborn to Sir Christopher Hatton, and got short shrift, in her shortest letter, from his 'Governess of the Church'. 'Proud Prelate, you know what you were, before I made you what you are. If you do not immediately comply with my request, I will unfrock you, by God! Elizabeth.'

So Ely immediately complied, and was graciously permitted to walk in his gardens and pick twenty bushels of roses a year. And now in his turn Durham complied; but instead of roses had the spectacle of Ralegh's withering tobacco plants, grown in Ireland, brought up river to be dried and cured in the Bishop's grounds.

Others had very happy memories of Durham House. 'I well remember his study there,' wrote the delightful Aubrey, 'which was a little turret that looked into and over the Thames and had the prospect which is as pleasant perhaps as any in the world and not only refreshes the eyesight but cheers the spirits, and (to speak my mind) I believe enlarges an ingenious man's thoughts.'

He was speaking Ralegh's mind too, for there came to flow through it that rhythm of 'all the rivers of the world', to which he has compared the thoughts of men. He was at the height of peaceful prosperity, now in 1587, sitting with his friends in his pleasant turret above the Thames, watching the ships below sail down towards the ocean; he had climbed fast to it since he had watched them from his brother Humphrey's window overlooking the Limehouse docks.

But it was a much lower and more humble place than a Bishop's Palace that he wanted most to possess, and that was the home of his birth and childhood, the reed-thatched old farm-house at Hayes Barton by the Devon coast, with its walls of homespun cob and wide stone kitchen hearth where he had crawled as a baby among the dogs and the outstretched boots of seafaring men, their deep voices growling and grumbling far above him. They were the voices of his earliest friends, shaggy ruffians with rings in their ears and long knives in their leathern breeches; when he was old enough to run down through the long meadow to play and paddle by the sea, there on the pebbled beach they told him stories of floating mountains of emerald ice, of stifling jungles that hid cities built half of gold, their lords all in jewels and bright feathers, their naked slaves with mouths painted black and ears stuck through with claws, 'like hounds of death'. A menace worse than any such monsters was that of capture by the King of Spain and the Inquisition, to be burned alive or to die rotting slowly under the long whips, as slaves in their stinking galleys. These were the dragons that he

25

must one day fight; the New Worlds across the Western ocean were the fairyland that he must find and conquer.

So he tried to recover that birthplace of himself and his earliest dreams. But Hayes Barton had been bought by a Mr Duke, who had wished to add it to his already vast estates. Ralegh wrote to offer him 'most willingly to give you whatsoever in your conscience you shall deem it worth', because 'of the natural disposition I have to that place, being born in that house, I had rather seat myself there than anywhere else . . .

> At Court the xxvi of July 1584
> Your very willing friend
> W. Ralegh.'

It is an oddly guileless letter for a man reputed to be a hardened fortune hunter; he leaves the price unconditionally to the seller, ignores any question of a business deal, and lays his guard open by telling frankly how much the place means to him.

He might hunt fortune, but he never guarded it; never learned caution, nor suspicion; nor thought who might want to do him a bad turn, nor why. If they did so behind his back, then 'my tail is good enough to answer them'. In this case, as in others, his pride showed how vulnerable he was. The rich country landowner, Mr Duke, took his own pride in refusing the eager request of the new Court upstart (and who in God's name was this *Sir* Walter Ralegh whom nobody had heard of two or three years ago?).

More than three hundred years later some rich Americans, who had never heard of Mr Duke, wished to transfer the simple farmhouse bodily to Virginia, to do honour there to Sir Walter Ralegh; but found its cob walls more immovable than even their massive stone foundations, or the giant 'King beam', a tree-trunk eighty feet long that ran the whole length of the house. So Hayes Barton has been left rooted in the soil from which it had grown, its small stone-mullioned windows, one of them framing the Ralegh coat-of-arms, still letting in the salt sea breeze that had blown in on the infant Walter's cradle in the upper chamber of the west wing, where he had looked, even from his birth, 'towards the sunset'.

His appointment to the Queen's Guard was without pay, except £14 a year for the Captain's uniform of 'tawny medley at

13/4 a yard, with a fur of black budge'. Ralegh preferred on occasion to wear silver armour. His splendid clothes had quickly become legendary. There was the story that he first caught the Queen's attention by spreading his fine new cloak before her 'in a plashy place' so that she should not muddy her shoes; another told how he used the famous diamond on the hilt of his dagger to scratch on a window, for the Queen to see, 'Fain would I rise, yet fear to fall', and that she capped it with, 'If thy heart fail thee, rise not at all.' There was later even a rumour that some of the innumerable pearls on his cloak were loosely sewn, on purpose, so that they might scatter in careless largesse to the crowd.

Such legends were typical of the scornful extravagance, and the arrogance, which infuriated his fellow-courtiers. All very well for him to pose as the 'silent lover' who dared not whisper his devotion to the remote Moon-Goddess he worshipped from afar; it was plainly seen on Earth that this same Queen took pleasure in his 'strong natural wit and better judgment, and bold and plausible tongue. . . . The truth is,' Naunton slyly added, 'she took him for a kind of Oracle, which nettled them all.'

The Oracle cared nothing for that; he showed his 'better judgment' most injudiciously by bowling over all contrary opinions like ninepins, so fiercely and impersonally intent, and only on the subject of his talk, that he never even saw his opponents except as dummies that obstructed it.

'A tall, handsome and bold man, but,'—as Aubrey is often quoted, 'his naeve' (or flaw) 'was that he was damnable proud.'

His irony was in defence of his pride; but could pierce as sharply as his wit. The worst smart of all came from his indifference, even ignorance, of the wounds he inflicted; since his wit, irony and pride were so instinctive as to be all but unconscious.

The worst danger to be feared was his influence over the Queen. 'He loved a wench well', so Aubrey tells us, relating several scandals in proof of this, and of how well the wenches loved him. Whatever the nature of the Queen's love for Ralegh, the proofs she gave of it were strong enough to cause alarm as well as jealousy. 'See, the Knave commands the Queen', cried a low comedian pointing at them together; and the Queen frowned, but showed no denial of it. She had promised to finance Ralegh's recent colonizing expeditions to America on condition that he did not go himself, for she could not bear him so to risk his life, nor indeed that she should lose his company. The condition made him as unpopular as did the promise; who was he to waste the public money on such hare-brained adventures as a 'New England towards the sunset'? He had too many schemes and could talk too well on all of them; he could do everything at once and all too easily and carelessly.

He wrote poems of course, as did every fine gentleman; and he squandered them like the legendary loose pearls from his cloak, for he lost the bulk of his poems and would not put his name to them in the anthologies; but that too was gentlemanly. What worried the other gentlemen was that they were apt to be disturbingly enigmatic, sardonic; the language simple and direct, yet the terse monosyllabic words that could pay a charming compliment to his friends could also stab like sword-thrusts—and whom did they stab? One could never be quite sure. They were generally voted to be 'most lofty, insolent and passionate'.

He was so clever in so many ways, and so sure he was right, that he must be as untrustworthy as he was influential. Even the powerful Elder Statesman, William Cecil Lord Burghley, found it advisable to beg him to intercede for his wild young son-in-law, Edward de Vere Earl of Oxford, when he was in trouble with the Queen over a duel with Sir Philip Sidney. Ralegh did so, successfully, but gave a far too frank opinion of de Vere to Burghley, so that his good deed won him no gratitude from either. And things had come to a pretty pass when old Cecil himself, the Queen's chief adviser throughout her reign, must entreat a plain Devon squire to use his influence with her on behalf of a seventeenth earl!

The snobbery covered real anxiety. Ralegh played 'Sir Oracle', and not only to the Queen. He seemed 'able to sway all men's fancies, all men's courses'. His first attempts at a colony in North America failed, yet no one could shake his certainty that his countrymen could be persuaded to cross the huge Atlantic into an unknown wilderness, to plant there 'an English nation'. Early in this very year of 1587 he had actually induced one hundred and fifty householders to hazard not only themselves but their wives and families also, to sail out there under Captain John White to form a self-governing community on their own land, a new scheme that seemed madder than any plan of exploration and conquest.

That expedition too was doomed to fail, but Ralegh's relentless persistency drove him on to make an English empire overseas. He put £40,000 of his own money into it, a fortune far larger then, at the old value of money. 'He can toil terribly,' said old Burghley's son, that equally astute statesman, Robert Cecil, in unwilling admiration.

He even used his position as leader of fashion to sway men's fancies. Until England would go to America, he would bring what he could of America into England. So he planted that rare new delicacy, the potato, but couldn't give it the importance that it was to acquire later in Ireland, where it was to spread from his own estates all over the country and sway the course of her history.

He brought the new Indian weed tobacco into fashion, to the annoyance of the old privateer, Sir John Hawkins, who had introduced it into the country nearly twenty years before, but never thought that a barbarous heathen custom would catch on among the English nobility and gentry. Hawkins' own trading in black slaves, kidnapped from the African coast, seemed more respectable, and certainly of far greater future profit.

Yet the slave trade was to be stamped out, and by the next century tobacco would become the chief source of English revenue, rising in three more centuries to over six hundred million pounds a year. The young scientist from Oxford, Thomas Hariot, whom Ralegh had engaged as his 'tutor' in mathematics and astronomy (he was later to be the first to see Halley's comet through his new telescope that magnified fifty times), advertised tobacco as a soothing medicine whose virtues 'would require a volume' to relate. But the virtues of a new medicine are dull compared with the vagaries of a new vice. It was Ralegh's example as a connoisseur of exotic taste that made tobacco a social necessity. Every man wanted to smoke when they saw him snap open his heavy gold tobacco case, ringed about with small coloured candles, carelessly flourish his long silver-mounted pipe in conversation to emphasize some point he was making, then lean back and negligently puff a smoke-ring in silence to emphasize that his opponents had made no point.

There was great joy in the story that a new servant had dashed a pail of water over him, thinking his master was on fire, or else possessed by a devil that blew smoke out of his mouth, as was all too likely. Growing rumours of his magic and atheism, coupled with the 'loathsome and devilish practice of tobacco-drinking', were later to add to King James of Scotland's superstitious fear and hatred of him; and so to help him towards the scaffold. For all that, he took a last pipe in the hour before he stepped out to die.

His present sovereign lady showed her eagerness for any new fad by trying a pipe herself. She even paid up a bet to him, rather wryly, when he boasted that he could tell her the weight of his tobacco smoke and she, snatching at what looked like an easy win, betted against it. So he weighed a pinch of tobacco, smoked it, rapped out the ashes and weighed them, and the Queen handed over the cash, crowing with laughter and exclaiming that many unlucky alchemists had turned gold into smoke, but Ralegh was the first to turn smoke into gold. There she was prophetic, though few saw it at the time. Serious folk said this silly new habit would not last; there was no money in smoke, and it would all end in smoke—like all his mad projects that were burning up the nation's wealth and his own too. But that was right; it showed he too would not last, he would never get anywhere, nor keep anything. All his show and splendour, his fine houses and estates and jewelled clothes and new-won wealth, flung away as fast as he got it, yes and his Sovereign's favour, so they hoped and prayed, would be burned up and wither away like fairy gold, and everything, everything end in smoke.

And so Sir Anthony Bagot marked another danger point in 1587 by writing to Sir Edward Dyer that Ralegh was 'the best-hated man in the world: in Court, city and country'.

The flat contrary was true among his own countrymen of Devon and Cornwall and especially his sailors, and the army of his servants; for all of these were spellbound by him as a leader, yet also laughed with him in the homely intimacy of the West Country accent that he shared with them and never troubled to change. His Queen and goddess herself could mimic and mock it for all he cared; he still 'spake broad Devonshire to his dying day'.

It was the cockneys who hated 'his bloody pride' and made

street songs of it. They resented the royal grants of Monopolies or 'Patents' that added to the price of various goods. Many other courtiers held some, and some made far more out of them than Ralegh did, but *he* spoke in Parliament defending them; that showed you 'the gentleman with the bold face!' He also defended the poor in Parliament, and stopped the plans to tax them in the same way as wealthier men. But few can rightly value a negative benefit. The taxes that he prevented were not there, and so were forgotten.

And the Londoners would never care for nor hear of the gratitude to him of 'the rude and barbarous multitude' in the West Country, the commonwealth of tin-miners who made their own laws and held their courts on Crockern Tor in the midst of Dartmoor, where long ago a huge table and seats had been roughly hewn out of stone, like the prehistoric bridges and sacred circles on the Moor.

There Ralegh, the Lord Warden of the Stanneries, sat with his 'stannators' and the tin-miners, like a chieftain of the Stone Age, often in the driving rain and mist that made the Moor a lost wilderness. He worked to improve their laws and redress their grievances, and the commonwealth found its spokesman to tell how deeply they were 'beholden to your kindness. Your ears and mouth have ever been open to hear and deliver our grievances, and your feet and hands ready to go and work their redress.'

Their vision of him was very different from that seen by the Earl of Essex when he came to pay his court to the Queen, and at once fell foul of her Captain of the Guard.

CHAPTER THREE

'Such Competition of Love'

THE EARL OF ESSEX

Essex was not quite twenty, and young even for that; he was tall as Ralegh, and fair as Ralegh was dark, his bright hair and new-sprouting wisps of beard rather untidy and his dress careless, his hands delicate as a woman's, and his eyes those of a dreamy yet excitable boy. He stooped with his head thrust forward, and his portraits scarcely show the beauty which won a fame that was largely due to his extraordinary personal attraction. Eager, volatile, now gay, now moody; refreshingly, when not disconcertingly, impulsive, he charmed both men and women to spoil and forgive him, and to love him.

His pride was as great as Ralegh's but of an entirely different nature. It was the pride of an aristocrat who knew himself to be, on his father's side, of bluer blood than the Queen's, and did not as yet realize how much he was a pauper. His first sight of the resplendent dress of her new Captain of the Guard may have helped him, angrily, to do so. Who was this bold swarthy fellow with a broad Devon accent, but superb clothes and bearing, that *he* should be in command of the most coveted, most confidential and influential post at Court? A soldier of fortune was all that he was; and where had he looted those jewels? From the Queen's favour chiefly, so Essex soon learned to his rage. This new favourite had pulled himself up by his shoe-strings, and now wore jewels on them said to be worth 6,600 gold pieces. Even his thick, neatly pointed black beard caused envy in those whose hair grew straight and straggling; Ralegh's 'turned up naturally' without the aid of tongs, at the corners of his mouth, so that one never knew whether or no he were smiling in derision.

And vanity was the chief measure of Essex's pride. He could be childishly touchy, hot-tempered and bad-mannered. Ten years earlier when presented as a little boy to the Queen, he had refused to take off his hat or let her kiss him; ten years later he was to show himself the same spoilt child by turning his back on

her in a rage, and when she boxed his ears and told him to 'go
and be hanged!' he swore she was 'a King in petticoats' and that
he would not have taken such an insult from Henry VIII himself.
That was towards the end of their impassioned friendship; the
beginning was soon to flare up in quarrels almost as violent. But
from the moment of his arrival in the spring of 1587 Elizabeth
was charmed with this new pet, possibly rather a puppy but then
he was still such a child; yet had already proved himself a man
and been knighted for his courage in the tragically heedless
charge at Zutphen where his friend Sir Philip Sidney, 'that
inconsiderate fellow' as Elizabeth bitterly complained, had 'got
knockt on the head'. The finest flower of England's chivalry, who
had wooed Essex's elder sister Penelope in such poignant sonnets,
lay dead on a wasted campaign; and Elizabeth hated waste.

This lad had had the sense to keep alive, and so much alive,
eager and high-spirited, that he gave new life to herself. In his
ruddy hair and quick passions she could see a reflection of her
own stormy childhood as the red-headed 'bastard' of Henry VIII;
perhaps also of the son that she might have borne to her Sweet
Robin the Earl of Leicester. But he was only Leicester's step-son,
and the son of 'That She-Wolf', as Elizabeth called her cousin
Lettice ever since she had taken Leicester for her third husband.
Yet in sending him to Court Leicester hoped to reawaken the
Queen's favour and provide an antidote to Ralegh's.

Essex awakened it for himself with a success even quicker and
more spectacular than Ralegh's, for it was as early as May that
Sir Anthony Bagot wrote of the Queen, 'Nobody near her but
my lord of Essex; and at night my lord is at cards or one game or
another with her till the birds sing in the morning.' It was an
extraordinary friendship for a woman of fifty-four with a youth
of twenty. Elizabeth's emotions would never be only maternal;
nor Essex's filial; if indeed his were ever that. She was to show
tenderness in forgiving his tantrums even when dangerous to
herself; but there is never a sign of any tenderness in his feelings
for her. Her glittering façade made her seem invulnerable to one
who kept his adolescent egoism to the end of his life.

Egoism was indeed a strong factor on both sides of their relationship; vanity was her self-interest in it, as ambition was his.
But what excited and disturbed it more was the queer heady
fascination that Elizabeth exerted in her dealings with men. 'I

B   33

was never beautiful,' she once admitted, 'though in my youth I had the reputation of it.' In old age her last portrait was to show real beauty; the eyes there are no longer alert and keen as a hawk's, while looking at nothing before them. They are dreaming under the tired lids, whose exquisite long curves can at last be seen; the fine head is no longer held erect as a stag's, but content to rest on her thin hand; while Time and Death stand as friends behind her to give her release from her crown.

That was not to come for many years; for the present she was still keeping up her reputation without the reality. But reputation has great power, especially over a young man, and especially in England, where people begin to believe in a woman's charms when advertised for thirty to forty years. Essex had seen her when ten years younger, but then his childish gaze, clear from all suggestion, had seen a rather alarming unreal face painted red and white like a china dish. Since then he had heard of her, even from her enemies abroad, as 'Semiramis' and the 'English Cleopatra'; had heard of the many lovers, some of them great princes, that she had kept panting in pursuit of her for years on end, and of her mockery of them.

Catherine de Medici's son had been kept dangling for eleven years while she flirted with him or, alternatively, asked her councillors 'what compensation do I get in the marriage articles for his enormous nose?'

She had been excommunicated, but could laugh at the Pope and say they ought to marry.

She told her most dreaded enemy, Philip of Spain, what she thought of the Inquisition; 'Why cannot Your Majesty let your subjects go to the Devil in their own way?'

As for her looks, even at this day, the foreign visitors were so dazzled by the shining robes and gauze ruffs, like transparent wings, that shimmered round her spare form that they declared, even at home, where there was no point in flattery, that one would think her to be under thirty, if indeed one could think of her age at all, or of herself as a woman, and not as part fairy, part devil, part goddess. That last was how most of her subjects thought of her, and especially the crowds in street and country-side who found in their adoration of her a substitute for the Mariolatry of which they had been deprived since the change from the old religion. They had a Virgin Queen instead of the

Virgin Mary. A yet older religion that lingered deep in their legends and festivals, their games and songs, linked her with another 'Our Lady', Queen, not of Heaven, but of 'Elphame', the Fairy Queen who was also the Moon Goddess, Hecate or Diana. As Diana she was sung in countless poems, and had chosen to be painted, with the goddess's crescent moon and huntress's bow as her emblems.

'She can be old or young as she pleases,' it was said of Hecate; and so people felt of Elizabeth.

The half-conscious worship of the crowd was expressed freely by the courtiers; they could gaze at her in genuine admiration when she was past sixty, yet 'as beautiful as I ever saw her'; they could also exploit their admiration to their own advancement. Essex found them all professing their passion for the Queen, writing love poems, exchanging trinkets and tokens; raised to glory by a friendly joke or trifling present from her, or a nickname that was not too teasing, but terrified of a snub or a pout ('she pupped with her lips' was a danger signal) or of a jeering comment on their clothes. A happy young fop wrote in triumph of his new frieze jerkin, 'the Queen loveth to see me in it and saith, " 'tis well enough cut". I will have another made liken to it'; but added a shuddering memory, that she had 'spat on Sir Mathew's fringed cloth and said "the fool's wit was gone to rags". Heaven spare me from such gibing!'

They never knew where they were with her, what she would say or do next. To woo her attention had all the excitement of a desperate gamble where they played against each other for the highest stakes in their cut-throat 'competition of love', as Essex called it, and all would have agreed, especially the Queen, for it was the machinery of her whole policy, flirtation its fabric, and personal jealousy the spur to her courtiers' ambition and to English enterprise. Even the playful 'toys' and 'tokens' they exchanged with her could touch a tender and deep significance; as when she sent Sir Humphrey Gilbert, who was known to have 'no good hap at sea', an 'anchor guided by a lady', praying, as Ralegh wrote to him in affectionate friendship, that it would bring him luck on his next voyage.

Ralegh's friends at Court were all his rivals. Essex's immediate jealousy of him was shared, and violently, by many others. Even Essex's step-father the great Lord Leicester had been shaken

from his indolent security as reigning favourite to show anxiety
lest the obscure soldier, whom he had helped to advance, was
now supplanting him in the Queen's affections. Leicester had
been in disgrace lately in Flanders and must have found it
rather galling when Ralegh, his former protégé, reassured him
on this point; 'The Queen is in very good terms with you . . . you
are again her Sweet Robin.'

Lesser and newer favourites such as Sir Christopher Hatton
and Sir Thomas Heneage showed their alarmed anger at Ralegh's
royal progress in surprising ways; Hatton, not merely a good
dancer but a judicious Leader of the House of Commons, proved
himself as a politician by sending his Sovereign (to whom he
owed £56,000) a little bucket, in complaint of being 'destroyed
by Water', her punning nickname for Sir Walter; and received
in return from her a dove with olive branch, as a promise of no
more 'destruction by Water'. There were long elaborate letters,
jewelled bodkins in threat of suicide for love, enamelled rainbows
in further assurance against 'Water'; and some challenges to
duels to give reality to the fantasies.

But then fantasy was a very real part of life to the Elizabethans.
In their portraits, rose-trees grew twining round their silken legs
as they took root while a poem was written; hands reached down
from the clouds to pull their desires up to the heavens; hellish
storms and seas raged around them as they stood on ships split
by lightning, encompassed by flaming masts and drowning faces,
while their demeanour remained unruffled in the heroic calm
of loyal devotion. In everyday life bleeding hearts pierced by
arrows were the general wear; puns grew far-fetched though
quite solemn; ladies were unkind and 'young gentlemen as sad
as Night for very wantonness'.

One young gentleman, however, refused to play the game of
tender reproaches. Essex's flattered excitement as the Queen's
new chief companion was spoilt from the beginning by the sight
of that hard-bitten experienced adventurer, Sir Walter, at the
door of her chamber; and all that he had since seen and heard
of their close friendship worked his rage against him up to a
pitch of frenzy. The Queen, he considered, had slighted his
sister Lady Dorothy Perrot; years ago, Ralegh had fought a duel
with Perrot and been imprisoned for it, so the royal snub to the
Perrot family was doubtless due to Ralegh's vengeful influence.

'See the Knave commands the Queen'; he had heard that tale, and a deal more. On a hot evening in July he attacked the Queen to her face on her desire 'only to please that Knave, Ralegh, for whose sake I saw she would both grieve me and my love'. By Essex's own account in a private letter, he did this deliberately within Ralegh's hearing so that he, 'standing on guard at the door, might very well hear the worst that I spoke of him'. She answered angrily that there was no cause for him to disdain Ralegh, but he insisted that he *had* 'cause to disdain Ralegh's competition of love'; he would 'describe unto her what he had been and what he was, and spoke my grief and choler as much against him as I could'.

But 'it seemed she could not well endure anything to be spoken against him', and the youth's hectic rage burst out against Elizabeth herself; he swore he 'had no joy to be near about her when I knew my affection so much thrown down, and such a wretch as Ralegh highly esteemed of her'. She had tried to 'drive me to be friends with Ralegh, which rather shall drive me to many other extremities'.

His present one was too extreme for even Elizabeth to meet, for she kept silent. Essex planted his final goad: 'What comfort can I have,' he demanded, 'to give myself over to the service of a Mistress that is in Awe of such a man?'

Still the Queen 'made no answer but turned her away'.

So the angry young man turned too, and strode out through the door, brushing against the Captain of the Guard who stood there insolently shining in silver armour, and perhaps even laughing at him within the mask of his upcurled beard. Essex took horse and rode away down the cross-road of his envious ambition that was to lead to 'many other extremities', and finally to the scaffold—both for himself and, long later, for Ralegh.

But he could see no further than his mood of the moment, which he relieved by at once writing the foregoing account of his quarrel to a sympathetic friend; and then by riding off again to the coast to take ship for the Dutch war, which would make Elizabeth welcome him home 'if I return; if not, *una bella morire*' would make her sorry.

There is no corresponding account of the quarrel by Elizabeth or Ralegh, though there is a cryptic little verse by him, playing on the word 'disdain', which may well be his curtly contemptuous dismissal of the youth's loud-mouthed accusations. But the clues in it are now obscure. One longs to know what he and his Queen made of that scene to each other; did she laugh, or he triumph, that she was known to be 'in Awe of such a man' as himself? That 'she could not well endure anything to be spoken against him'? Even Elizabeth might be embarrassed to declare or to deny the truth of such charges to the smiling black beard of her Captain of the Guard. She may have only told him to take a pipe, since she enjoyed watching him with it, and could let her agitation disperse in a comforting cloud of smoke.

Essex's hopes of winning her repentance by his brave deeds in Flanders, or else by his 'beautiful death', were quashed by her sending after him and hauling him back from his ship like a runaway schoolboy. Yet before the year was out she made him a Knight of the Garter and Master of the Horse, an appointment held ever since the first month of her reign by his step-father Leicester, and bringing him £1,500 a year as well as several lesser emoluments.

But it could not 'drive him to be friends with Ralegh', whom he tried to challenge to a duel, prevented by the Privy Council, in the following year. That was the year of the Armada.

CHAPTER FOUR

'How We May Annoy the King of Spain'

PAMPHLET BY SIR HUMPHREY GILBERT

ENGLAND had first been threatened with invasion by a Spanish Armada only six months after Elizabeth had come to the throne, a brilliant and unpredictable young woman of twenty-five, whose legitimacy and religion, morals and policy were all in question. To the Roman Catholic Great Powers then paramount in Europe, her sole chance to keep her kingdom and even her life lay in abject submission to her former brother-in-law, the 'Very Catholic King', Philip II of Spain.

Yet she had contrived to wriggle out of all his ambiguous suggestions of marriage to himself or, still more ambiguously, to one of his satellite allies. He did not state what were his personal feelings for Elizabeth, and took great pains that others should not know them. He covered up his tracks even in his letters of proposal to her through his ambassador, de Feria, expressed in so contradictory a fashion that this hot-tempered little Spaniard from Seville, himself passionately in love with his English fiancée, was driven nearly distracted by the sluggish, tortuous methods of his half-Flemish King, brought up in North Castile where coldness is held to be the supreme virtue of a gentleman.

Whatever Philip felt for her could scarcely have been indifference; as he proved with a recklessness that flatly contradicted all else known of him. Pique, and a sudden passion for personal revenge on the insufferable young woman who had flouted him, helped drive him into the one precipitate action he ever made; and the most disastrous to him. No sooner did he realize that Elizabeth would refuse his offer of matrimony than he transferred it to the sixteen-year-old French princess, Isabel de Valois, who was already betrothed to his fourteen-year-old son, Don Carlos. A tragic scandal followed; Carlos' unbalanced and ungovernable behaviour had already caused some anxiety, but had begun to improve in his eagerness to be worthy of his lovely and gentle bride, whose miniature he wore on a hidden chain round his neck. When she was snatched from him by his father, he showed the mad fury of a jealous boy, became increasingly violent, and finally was put in prison, where he died, no one quite knew how. Most people believed that Philip had secretly ordered his son's death, and the Pope made awkward enquiries.

The 'Very Catholic King', the most religiously orthodox monarch in fact as well as title, was singularly unlucky with his Popes (he had even been forced into war with one of them); the superstitious, and Philip among them, thought it was due to the unhappy portent of his birth at the very moment when the Imperial Army of his father, Charles V, was engaged in the sack of Rome, in burning churches, murdering Cardinals, violating nuns, and imprisoning the Pope himself. It had not of course been the fault of the Emperor, who had also been the most religious monarch of his day; as he frequently explained, he had not even been in Rome at the time, and his troops were a mixed lot who had got out of hand. All the same it had cast a shadow over the birth of his heir, Philip; all the joy bells had been turned into penitential psalms, and Philip was prone to think he himself had had to do penance ever since, especially in matrimony.

His first and best-loved wife had died in childbed at sixteen. His second, Mary Tudor, an elderly virgin, had humiliated him by false hopes of childbed that cheated him into over a year in her rain-and-beer-sodden island, where the coarse shouts of the populace taunted him with impotency (he who had had as many bastards as he could respectably acknowledge); where the wiles of her young half-sister the Princess Elizabeth had tricked him into a furtive and frustrated wooing of her; upon which she still presumed until this day, taking no account of his displeasure. She had allowed her country to become openly heretic, and had even weathered the Pope's excommunication of her, which had greatly strengthened Philip's hand; but she professed to believe he would never really raise it against her.

'As for the King of Spain,' she told a French Ambassador, 'my enmity and his having commenced with love, you must not think that we could not get on together at any time I choose.' So she preened herself on the undoubted fact, so bitter to him, that he had rescued her from prison, restored her position at the English Court, and persuaded Mary Tudor to appoint her as her successor to the throne. Of gratitude to him for all this there was not a trace; only of gratified vanity. At least he could be grateful to God that he had escaped the fate of having her as his third wife.

But he was ill requited for it, for the third wife whom he married instead, Isabella of France, was made so unhappy by Don Carlos' mysterious death that it helped, it was said, to cause her own, in childbed, just three months after that of Carlos.

That ended the alliance of Spain and France and their plan for a united invasion of heretic England. The Duke of Alva, Spain's greatest soldier, had no immediate opportunity to launch his new-summoned armadas against her, nor to use the maps of English harbours in East Anglia which he had scanned with Philip to discover the best landing places for their flotillas to attack from Flanders. But the idea of the 'Enterprise of England' had come to birth, and grew.

And there was at last, by his fourth wife (his niece) the birth of a fairly normal son and heir to Philip; though he was not nearly as intelligent and charming as the two little daughters by Isabella, to whom Philip was devoted, and wrote fatherly-friendly letters about the jonquils and nightingales in the gardens of his new mountain palace of the Escorial.

As he grew older, slower, more stiff in his joints and set in his ways, he shut himself closer and closer into the Escorial, which he had had built in the shape of a gridiron in memory of the martyr St Lawrence. The palace was also a monastery and a church, and the tomb of his greatest ancestors. It would be his tomb also; and he was more at home in it than anywhere else. He slept at night, briefly, and worked all day, and more, in two small rooms like monks' cells whose windows opened into the chancel of the church, so that he could hear the Mass chanted day and night. The rooms smelt of damp stone and stale incense and thick curtains. He worked harder than any of his secretaries, reading many documents that could well have been left to them, and scribbling endless notes in the margin.

A born Civil Servant, who believed in paper as devoutly as in God, he would have revelled in forms in triplicate. His remoteness from the vast sweep of lives that he ruled over, so meticulously, fed his pride in a curious way. It pleased him to think that from this narrow room, with no breath from outside of the torrid or icy air that swept down from the Guadarrama mountains, he was governing and transacting all the major business of his country, and of many others. Elizabeth's airy diplomacy might swing on a cobweb thread, at the apparent mercy of every wind that blew; but it was Philip's greying head, like a pale spider in his dark and airless corner, who spun the web of power-politics that enmeshed the world.

So he believed; and with some reason, for his Empire was the greatest since that of ancient Rome. More than half the Old World was his; and all the New World in the West. That last had been decreed nearly one hundred years before by the Borgia Pope Alexander VI to be the rightful property of Spain and Portugal.

The decree came naturally to be questioned, especially in England. The privateer Sir John Hawkins had published a manifesto to prove the right of English ships to the freedom of the high seas, and of undiscovered countries. He had been knighted at Plymouth by Philip himself when on his conciliatory mission of matrimony to England; and for many years continued to prove how useless was any conciliation of the stubborn and thankless English. His name in the Spanish archives, oddly transformed to 'Juan Aquines', produced always an outcrop of scandalized comments in the margin in Philip's minute, almost illegible scribble.

The fungus growth of tiny notes sprouted up thicker and thicker, almost all to do with disaster and, if by Act of God, then expressing pious resignation. An Atlantic gale that swallowed up one of his great ships entire, together with all hands on board and the loyal commander who had been his 'friend', could scarcely ruffle the stifling calm of his seclusion. Only indignation against England could stir the stuffy air with a faint but threatening breeze.

'The study of Novelties was inserted as it were by Nature in the English'; so he wrote, and by Novelties Philip meant 'seditions, conspiracies, treasons and the like, which had fixed a dwelling place for themselves in that Island'. 'And at sea', he should have added, for it was the recurrent names in his papers of English sailors, from Hawkins onwards, that the King first looked for, and most dreaded to find.

His pale protuberant eyes probed down into desperate appeals for more and ever more help for his new colonists, who as well as his mariners lived in constant dread of any sail sighted afar off, lest it should prove to be English. The Governor of Biscay himself had been kidnapped in his own port of Bilbao. Philip made a note of it; also that he was shocked by Sir Richard Grenville's capture of Spanish frigates off Cuba; and even more shocked by the casual fraternizing that followed. In contrast with the Spanish Government's formula of cruelty to captives, the English sailors had caroused with their conquered enemies in 'banqueting houses covered with green boughs', and organized together a rip-roaring hunt of mountain bulls. This unorthodox open-air entertainment, far too breezy for the Escorial, produced a note of censure on friends as well as foes.

The names increasingly feared in the reports were of 'those sons of Neptune,—Drake, Frobisher, Sir Walter Rawly'. Drake's was translated appropriately as El Draco, the Dragon, with the sub-title 'The Master Thief of the Unknown World'; and soon had that of Ralegh coupled with it as a formidable second. In his very first voyage 'to annoy the King of Spain' it was Ralegh, though a young and hitherto untried sailor, who had adventured on in his solitary ship for six months after his fellow-captains had abandoned the luckless enterprise. That had shown his relentless force of purpose; and as soon as he won power and money at Court he proved that same purpose to be still, as it would always be, the mainspring of his life. It was of more enduring value to England, and therefore of danger to Spain, than even Drake's fulfilled ambition as the greatest destroyer and robber of the Spanish navies. But Ralegh's hope, to bear fruit far beyond his lifetime, was to be the creator of an English Empire in the New World.

In his first year after coming to Court he sank what money he could on a two-hundred-ton ship, the *Bark Ralegh*, and two Dutch fly-boats for stores; and had four pinnaces built to his own plans, seven vessels in all. 'The rumour of Ralegh's fleet so vexed the Spaniards' that their reports enlarged the number to sixteen; but added the crumb of comfort that the Queen had refused to let him sail with it himself. The Ralegh touch was shown however by their boarding of a great Spanish galleon from a raft, made impromptu out of boxes which sank as they came alongside; and a vast booty was seized of pearls and gold, cochineal, ivory and hides. The Spaniards held Ralegh responsible for the expedition, not merely financially, though he had been forced to let his cousin Grenville take his place; but it was still 'under the order of Sir Walter Ralegh', translated into the surprising form, 'Guatteral'. The Spaniards gave up trying to cope with his name after he had outlived his fellow-captains, and referred to him simply as 'that old pirate'.

They were all Devon men, and all kinsmen; all stood by each other, took on each other's commands at a moment's notice, but over crews who knew them all; and they ground each other's axes as firmly and harshly as their own.

The notes against Ralegh's name show the Spaniards and their King to be curiously baffled by him. They recognized him as the greatest gentleman of all the sea-robbers, who treated his foes not only courteously but cordially—a good deal more so in fact than he often treated his English 'friends'. He gave his captives the lavish hospitality due to honoured guests, and in so frank and friendly a fashion that by the end of the evening they were all talking with the casual intimacy of old comrades who could after all see eye to eye on international affairs. Don Pedro Sarmiento de Gamboa, Governor of Magellan, who had been captured by two of Ralegh's pinnaces, the *Serpent* and the *Mary Spark*, was released without any ransom and given safe conduct to travel home through hostile parts of France, all through Ralegh's kind influence.

Sarmiento reported to Philip that he was assured that Ralegh was 'very cold about these naval preparations for war and is trying secretly to dissuade his Queen from them. He is much more desirous of sending to Spain his own two ships for sale, than to use them for robbery.' Philip replied, quite quickly for him, how highly he would esteem, and reward, any help from Ralegh. But when Sarmiento believed that Ralegh was concerned in a plot to murder Elizabeth, Philip smelt a rat—for the *Serpent*, with her sister ship the *Mary Spark*, might well be sent to a Spanish harbour as a feint, to do what damage there they could. Old John Hawkins had played Philip the trick of keeping his confidence for years, and his pay as a spy, by pretending that he would help him to dethrone Elizabeth—and all the time he had been telling her the whole transaction and laughing over it with her. No doubt Ralegh was playing the same game, though he had not received any Spanish pay for it. So Philip very politely pointed out in a message to Ralegh that it would be awkward for him to raise suspicion in his own country by selling his armoured ships to Spain, and told his ambassador that he 'need not mention' Philip's own suspicions of Ralegh—and of his Queen, who was probably as much in the plot to double-cross him as Ralegh. It all sounds highly improper, but diplomacy had not then begun to be respectable.

Philip's cold eyes explored the increasing evidence of English intrigues, insults, injuries and, most infuriating of all, the impudently friendly and specious letters of the English Queen; but they never changed expression, nor could ever shut in sleep, so his exhausted secretary believed, as his own blinked helplessly at two in the morning over a letter that the King had just written and handed to him. Jerking himself awake, the wretched man snatched at the ink-stand in mistake for the sand-castor, and poured the ink all over the carefully composed, interminable screed. Even then the King's eyes only bulged a little more, but did not flicker; his flat comment fell heavy as lead: 'It would have been better to have used the sand.'

He would never lose his patience personally, and with a servant. But the time came at last for him to do so with the heathen 'Queen Jezebel', as Elizabeth was called when she executed Mary of Scotland, made her a martyr for the Roman Catholic Church, and so herself thus gave the final signal for the 'Enterprise of England' to start.

The papers now on Philip's gold-inlaid table were all of draft plans for the greatest Armada that had ever set out to conquer a nation. A hundred and thirty armed ships, some of them the largest ever made, would sail up the Channel and embark the Duke of Parma's expeditionary army from the Netherlands, sixteen thousand strong and all tried veterans, and land them on the south coast of England. There would be well over thirty thousand men in all, with two thousand five hundred guns. The great Admiral Santa Cruz, who was to have led them, died worn out by all the preparations and, worse, the delays to them; but the Duke of Medina Sidonia, a country gentleman of the highest rank in Spain, would do instead. He 'begged to be excused'; he had never been to sea nor in a fight, and wrote persistently that if he were put in charge of the Armada he was certain it would turn out badly. His protests were ignored; after all, there were other disturbing letters on the table—if Philip had ever permitted himself the weakness of being disturbed.

But his equanimity seemed unruffled as he read of Drake's swoop on Cadiz harbour, and his destruction of the ships and stores collected there. Nor when, for good measure, on his way back he seized the King's own East Indiaman, a mighty galleon with treasure on board worth £114,000. Elizabeth turned the knife yet further in the wound with her official protestation of how deeply shocked she was by Drake's actions, all done against her orders. It arrived at the same time as the private, but soon public, report that she had, all the same, pocketed her own share of Drake's booty, worth some forty thousand. The Venetian Ambassador in Spain said tactlessly: 'Everyone is amazed to see how cleverly that woman manages in everything.'

But this time she could no longer manage appeasement.

On July 12th, 1588, the Armada started for England, on the very day that Philip had set sail for his marriage to Mary Tudor thirty-four years before. And the English weather now was just as it had been then—appalling. Medina Sidonia's letters complained of outrageous tempests, torrential rains, and 'such summer seas as had never been in living memory'. (But they *had* been; Philip remembered them.) In this hellish climate, wrote his reluctant Admiral, there was 'no difference between winter and summer, save that the days be longer'. (How much longer, Philip also knew; they had seemed endless.)

Reports of action at sea seemed doubtful and perplexed; Medina Sidonia still begged to be relieved of his command; gave confused reasons for a necessary retreat; thought later that, 'weather permitting', they would return to the Channel; if not, push on to the North Sea. Then the storm clouds shut down on them, and the fog of war obscured all news.

There came a report from Paris of triumphant victory. The 'Invincible Armada' had vanquished the enemies of Spain; fifteen of Drake's ships were sunk, and 'the great dog Drake' himself a prisoner in chains. The rejoicing bells rang out the glad news throughout the land; hymns of praise and thanksgiving were chanted in Church services.

Only the Pope remained unconvinced, and went on praising Drake's courage; 'Have you heard how he has offered battle to the Armada? Do you think he showed any fear? He is a great captain.' Once again the Papal 'hunch' was right. Other messengers in sackcloth and black came riding to the Escorial, silencing the gaily clad cavaliers who were shouting triumphant tidings through the streets. These dark riders brought later news.

Note. The account of the Armada in the following chapter is an attempt to show it as it was seen by the Elizabethans, rather than in the light of later research. It is taken mainly from the writings of Ralegh himself, whose duties enabled him to consider the action from various angles. Moreover his practical and scientific experience, especially in shipbuilding, give him an authority above that of most of his contemporaries.

CHAPTER FIVE

'So Great and Terrible an Ostentation'

RALEGH, OF THE ARMADA

'GENTLEMEN, *no war!*' Elizabeth had continually rapped that out at the Council table as she thrust a sweet from her comfit box into her mouth, and wished she could so stop all the bearded mouths opening wide as oysters round her in fulmination against Philip, and refusing to swallow the indigestible fact that now England stood alone against Spain.

Elizabeth knew how few friends, even passive ones, England had now. She knew the appalled indignation throughout Europe aroused by her execution of Mary. She could even share it. The continual plots to kill herself and make Mary Queen, whether with or without Mary's connivance, were no moral justification for a judicial murder. When you keep a fellow-Sovereign and rival claimant to your throne in prison, it is only to be expected that she will plot to get free by any means, even by a foreign invasion and the death of her jailor. If only, Elizabeth had wistfully said, they were 'two milkmaids with pails on their arms', she would gladly forgive Mary. She was apt to wish she were a milkmaid. But the sentimental touch had no effect on Parliament; both Houses were unanimous in their petition to her as 'the natural Mother of this land', who owed much more to them than to a remote cousin; and one that 'whilst she shall live, our enemies will hope and gape after your death . . . and our ruin and destruction . . . therefore it is meet to cut off the head of that hope'.

And so after all Elizabeth's 'Answers Answerless' to her 'faithful Commons', all her delays and contradictions of orders, the head was cut off. Even then she tried to double on her tracks, disclaim responsibility, find scapegoats for her own torturing sense of guilt. A secret assassination in prison would have been more convenient, even more honest; but her servants were such 'nice' and 'dainty' fellows, they would not agree to it. The age had grown too respectable for such old-fashioned crimes. Political murder must now be legalized—and God, or the Devil, only knew what that would lead to.

Her bitterness was vented on all her Council, even her eternally loyal old friend Cecil, Lord Burghley, whom she refused to see for weeks; nor would she attend to any public business, nor go out, nor give a glimpse of herself to her people, who were showing their thankful relief by public rejoicing and psalms of praise. Some relief she too had felt at first; for so many years this deed had been urged on her by her people; and she alone, on her sole responsibility, had held out against it in spite of increasing dangers to herself, and to them. Mary's partisans had held a dagger at England's back all through her reign; had been her most deadly because most intimate danger. But the sudden removal of a danger can have a worse effect than the danger. The deed was done, there was no more to be done. Elizabeth had come to:

'that dull calamity,
To that strange misbelief in all the world,
And all things that are in it.'

The French might shriek for war against her in the Paris streets, but the French King, Mary's former brother-in-law, would not fight to avenge her, and was probably relieved himself. Nor would Mary's own son, the young King James, 'that false Scotch urchin' as Elizabeth had called him five years before, when he showed himself a double dealer at sixteen. And though his Scots nobles clamoured for revenge, they had clamoured earlier to put Mary to death themselves. 'As for my son, I cannot answer for him' Mary had written to Philip of Spain on the last night of her life. James had protested to Elizabeth against his mother's impending doom, warning her with the example of her father, Henry VIII, whose otherwise spotless reputation had been 'prejudiced' only 'in the beheading of his bedfellows'. The unfortunate reminder enraged Elizabeth; and James, alarmed, hastened to make it clear that what really mattered to him was the hope of his future accession as King of England. How foolish he would be, he wrote to Leicester, 'if I should prefer my mother to the title'. Now that she was beheaded, it would be still more 'fond and inconstant' in him to fight for a dead mother than for a live one. He asked instead for compensation for the hurt to 'his honour'. An English dukedom, with lands and money attached, would help him to forgive his mother's murder. It was refused; but in any case her death was a gain to him, and the astute, but gauche, youth made another gaffe by showing his delight to his friends—to their disgust.

It seemed to Elizabeth that the only person to suffer from Mary's death was herself. Her reputation was blackened for ever; her self-esteem shattered. The 'physical despair' that Belloc has described in her at the end of her life, was foreshadowed now. In killing Mary she had killed her own spirit. Essex's coming to Court later that spring was the first thing that began to revive her, for certainly she snatched at his fresh companionship with the desperation of one clutching at life.

A far better shock-treatment was given by new danger. Philip of Spain was as cynical about Mary's death as the rest of her 'allies'. Mary's faithful champion and would-be rescuer, as she had believed him to be till the end of her life, considered, as her son had done, that her death was chiefly important for clearing his own path to the English throne. He had threatened war for years to set her free; but not until she was dead did he really set in train his attack on England.

Every nerve in England was being strained to meet it, with, in result, the final cure of Elizabeth's nervous breakdown. However good reason she had had to wish to die, she now found 'for my people's sake I desire to live'. The danger brought back her youth, and the first desperate but gloriously defiant summer of her reign; for now, as then, her dockyards resounded with the crackling noise of sawn timber and shouted orders, to answer the threat from Spain's.

Ralegh had rushed back to them from a flying visit to Ireland to see to his estates, the best managed in the country, and to show himself there as Mayor of Youghal. His shipbuilding plans were the most advanced of his own day. He and the old buccaneer Hawkins, and the great mathematician, Ralegh's friend and tutor Hariot, made plans for improved warships on the modern lines that had proved seaworthy in Atlantic storms. They were built to fight, and not merely to carry troops, like the earlier English galleons and those still chiefly used by the Spaniards. With deeper keels and lower castles on the upper deck, the English ships could now sail faster, and were no longer top-heavy and apt to drift in a wind. They would be at a bad disadvantage if they tried to board the enemy's high-built galleons for hand-to-hand fighting, but they were to avoid that. The captains had determined on a new form of strategy to match their new ships. They would carry more heavy guns of longer range, so that they could fire from a distance without coming in reach of the enemy's grappling irons; or of the devastating downward sweep of fire from their towering 'castles' that could rake the English decks from above, and make a shambles of them in a few minutes, so that the English sailors could get no chance to board the floating monster. As for hand-to-hand fighting, a Spanish man-of-war could carry well over five times as many soldiers as an English one. It was 'on record that one Devon man could chase eight Dons up a narrow street', but such odds were not to be tempted on an open deck.

Apart from the 'little ships' of private owners, most of them too little to help much, there were only thirty-four in the Queen's Navy, with six thousand men. Ralegh built and equipped three of them to his own plans and at his own expense: the *Roebuck* and *Ark Royal*, and the *Ark Ralegh* for the supreme Commander of the Fleet, Lord Charles Howard of Effingham, who flew his flag in it. But Ralegh himself was not given a command at sea. The West Country was thought the chief danger point, as a likely place for the Spanish troops to land, and Ralegh's influence in the West was so great that he was chosen as the best commander to organize—and improvise—the militia there. He strengthened old fortifications and created new, formed a Home Guard, and rode over the country, and up to London and back at incredible speed, for 'extraordinary consultations'—some all too extra-ordinary; for the Queen and her Council kept demanding that the Lord High Admiral should 'keep an eye upon Parma', and station more of her ships at the east end of the Channel, to lie in wait for the Duke's expeditionary army from Dunkirk.

All Ralegh's powers as her 'Oracle' were needed to prevent a still further, dangerous dispersal of her small navy, and to get the main part of it concentrated at Plymouth. From thence they sallied out to attack Spanish ports and so draw off the Armada; but the English weather was unkind to them too. A full gale drove them back to Plymouth to wait, and wait, for the enemy's move. At last came news of it, from the rocks of the Lizard.

On a July night, by the light of a gibbous moon, a vast and

shadowy crescent of towering ships was sighted, slowly rolling towards the Cornish coast. Gradually its full length could be discerned; it was a serpent seven miles long. The English fleet warped out of Plymouth harbour and pursued them up the Channel towards Dunkirk, their new long-range guns causing constant damage and worse still, dismay. The magnificently decorated galleons ahead of them lumbered heavily on at an average speed of about two miles an hour, as unwieldy, Drake jeered, as gaudy women great with child. They too carried long-range guns, but they were not mobile enough to use them to advantage, and besides their whole strategy was based on the boarding and grappling of Mediterranean warfare.

But they could not get to grips with these new fast English ships that chased and worried them, bit at their heels again and again, and wore away, scot free.

And Medina Sidonia still stuck strictly to the orders he had had on paper, and would not risk a major engagement until he had made his rendezvous with Parma. But it was the English who accomplished their rendezvous, with their squadron posted at the east end of the Channel to 'keep an eye upon Parma'; and now with their fleet united could move in to the main attack. As the Armada lay at anchor in Calais Roads, Drake sent his fire-ships filled with explosives among them, to their horrible panic and consequent destruction. The Spaniards cut their cables, many of their ships clashed together, some sank, some fled out to sea; the rest sailed on, still in search of Parma. But there was no rendezvous. A neap tide at Dunkirk prevented Parma's transports coming out for fear of grounding in the shoaling water, and Medina Sidonia had to turn and engage with the enemy again, without his powerful ally.

Then followed 'that morrice dance upon the waters' when, as Ralegh himself has told, the Spaniards' enormous and 'Invincible Navy', strengthened with the greatest Argosies of Portugal, Florence and other allies, 'were by thirty of Her Majesty's own ships of war, and a few of our own Merchants . . . beaten and shuffled together, from the Lizard in Cornwall, first to Portland —from Portland to Calais—and from Calais, driven with squibs from their anchors, were chased out of the sight of England, round about Scotland and Ireland, where, for the sympathy of their barbarous religion—hoping to find succour and assistance,

a great part of them were crusht against the rocks, and those that landed . . . were broken, slain, or taken, coupled in halters to be shipped into England. Where Her Majesty . . . disdaining to put them to death, they were all sent back again to their countries, to recount the worthy achievements of their "Invincible and dreadful Navy . . . an Army and Navy unresistible".
. . . With all which so great and terrible an ostentation, they did not, in all their sailing round about England, so much as sink or take one ship, bark, pinnace or cock-boat of ours, or ever burnt so much as one sheepcote of this land.'

So much for the necessity of making him stay on land to recruit and command an army against the invaders! 'Not so much as one sheepcote' must have had its bitter as well as triumphant taste for Ralegh in writing it. But there is not a trace of it in the generosity of his praise, which declares the whole victory due to 'the wise, valiant and most advantageous conduction of the Lord Charles Howard'.

Also to Sir Francis Drake. Unlike Martin Frobisher, who abused Drake publicly as being only 'out for spoil', Ralegh went out of his way to point the contrast of the stupendous Spanish failure with one of Drake's recent exploits when he 'with only eight hundred soldiers landed in their Indies and forced Santiago, Santo Domingo, Cartagena and the Forts of Florida'. And now he shared the chief honours of the Armada's defeat with his Lord High Admiral, his cheerful rubicund face grinning in agreement as Howard modestly proclaimed, 'We plucked their feathers little by little.'

Ralegh had ridden up to London the moment the Armada had passed Plymouth, and with it the danger of a Spanish landing down West. He urged that he should then join the fleet, in however mean a job might be chosen for him. The Queen only gave way when she heard that the Armada was stranded off Gravelines, and sent him with a message to the Lord Admiral to attack, board, and sink the enemies' ships, if the fire-ships failed to burn them.

But Ralegh and Howard had no intention of following the fighting orders of 'the Lady' and the ignorant land-lubbers in London. The wind was doing the job very nicely, and they did not give a rush for the old-fashioned prejudice that considered it unsporting to use long-range cannon except as a preliminary to the hand-to-hand fighting on deck. It would be the act of 'a madman rather than a man of war', wrote Ralegh in hot contempt of the Council; and later in his *History of the World* he declared, in his incisive prose, that the Lord Charles Howard had been wiser 'than a great many malignant fools that found fault with his demeanour. The Spaniards had an army aboard them, and he had none; they had more ships and of higher building and charging; so that had he entangled himself with those great and powerful vessels, he had greatly endangered this kingdom of England. . . . But our admiral knew his advantage, and held it; which had he not done, he had not been worthy to have held his head.'

The 'malignant fools' may have been partly responsible for the modest understatement on the medal, struck in honour of the victory, attributing it entirely to the weather, under the direction of the Almighty. 'God blew with His winds and they were scattered.' One critic at any rate felt that the English seamen might also have been mentioned; their ceaseless dogging and chasing of the Spaniards, and raking their decks with fire, had helped to victory as well as a lucky wind; and Edward Fenton, with considerable restraint, remarked to old Cecil that the 'result might, without undue arrogance, have been in part attributed to their own skill and courage'.

The same pleasure in belittling an achievement is shown by those who argue that Elizabeth ran no immediate danger when she insisted on riding bare-headed in a steel corslet to review her land army in person, accompanied only by the Earl of Ormonde and Lord Leicester, Lieutenant-General of all the land forces in England, and won such glowing fame as 'the Virago of Tilbury'. But her advisers knew well there was danger, so soon after the Catholic plots against her life, in her thus adventuring herself 'to armed multitudes, for fear of treachery'. So she told them in her speech to the troops, and why she would not heed the advice. 'I do not desire to live to distrust my faithful and loving people. Let Tyrants fear: I have always so behaved myself that, under God, I have placed my chiefest strength and safeguard in the loyal hearts and good-will of my subjects; And therefore I am . . . resolved in the midst and heat of the battle, to live or die amongst you all . . . I know I have the body of a weak, feeble woman; but I have the heart and stomach of a king—and of a King of England, too, and think foul scorn that Parma or Spain, or any prince of Europe, should dare to invade the borders of my realm; to which, rather than any dishonour should grow by me, I myself will take up arms—I myself will be your general.'

Her speech ended with a tenderly warm and grateful tribute to Leicester, who had well earned it, as 'my Lieutenant-General in my stead, than whom never Prince commanded a more noble and worthy subject'; and with her confidence that 'by your obedience to my General, by your concord in the camp, and by your valour in the field, we shall shortly have a famous victory'.

It is a vivid picture of her, however absurd some squeamish modern tastes may find the gleaming corslet over a vast far-thingale (but the mid-Victorian ladies who first climbed the Alps in crinolines had none the less courage for that, and possibly more), her flamboyant head 'of a colour nature never saw' bare to the wind off the river, riding into the very midst of her raw new troops; her voice, loud as her father's shout when she chose, ringing across them to their furthest ranks, with all the gay confidence of a huntsman's call.

Her impulse to get in the closest touch possible with her people, and stir their hearts to pride and hope with her living voice, is a refreshing contrast to the methods of her prime adversary of Spain, who preferred to crouch over his desk, cramped as a hermit-crab in its shell, and choke his warriors with paper.

England's victory had begun even while the Queen was inspiring her people to it; and proving greater than either she or they had thought possible. Not only Spain but her ally Ireland was now quelled, for surely it would 'breed some diffidence' between them, that her Irish friends had slaughtered the ship-wrecked Spaniards as fast as they struggled up through the surf, one chieftain alone 'killing eighty with his gallowglass axe'; and eleven hundred bodies lay strewn on a single Irish shore.

Such unkindness from their friends 'were to be pitied in any but Spaniards', wrote Carew from Ireland to Ralegh (who addressed him in his letters as 'Noble George') and added happily, 'The ancient love between Ireland and Spain is broken.' Noble George spoke too soon, for Philip of Spain was not the man to let a few instances of eleven hundred or so murders by his Irish allies prejudice his future hopes of attacking England through, and in conjunction with, Ireland. The winds that had scattered and destroyed his Armada could not penetrate his airless cell in the Escorial, nor his enclosed and deadened mind. With the pride of a true hidalgo (and being half Flemish Philip was more Spanish than the Spaniards), he bore his defeat 'patiently, and thanked God it was no worse'. How right he had been to distrust those deluding thanksgiving cermonies which had now all turned into weeping and gnashing of teeth! Just as the rejoicings at his birth had done, when news came of the Sack of Rome. And just so had the joyous bells and church processions proclaimed a son to him by Mary Tudor of England, who had been burdened only with an evil tumour. None of these had been his fault, but God's will, and 'it is better not to speak of it'. He had sought as always to forestall disaster by expecting it; but one wonders what 'worse' he could have expected.

He swore revenge; but never won it before he died horribly, heroically, five years before the death of the woman who had conquered him. His confessor later told William Cecil's son, Thomas, that in his agony Philip had avowed that 'whatever he suffered from Queen Elizabeth was the just judgment of God because, being married to Queen Mary . . . he could not affect her. But as for the Lady Elizabeth he was enamoured of her, being a fair and beautiful woman'. Death-bed confessions are held suspect in history; but it was believed at the time.

While Philip prayed night and day, in unison with the monks whose penitential chants echoed through his narrow window into their church, Elizabeth drove in a triumphal car drawn by white horses to a splendid thanksgiving service at St Paul's. Her people, fired by her speech to them, thronged round her in an uproarious welcome of praise, attributing the victory even of the fire-ships to her divine inspiration: 'Dux foemina facti'. They forgave her the agonizing uncertainty of her long refusal to execute Mary of Scotland, or to declare war on Spain, and forgave even her fleet's short supplies of ammunition, for no one could have foreseen the appalling amount used in the nine days' fighting in the Channel.

The captains grumbled furiously of course. They said, and truly, that they could have destroyed not merely the half of the enemy's fleet, as they had done, but the whole of it; instead of following it like good quiet sheepdogs, with never the bark of a gun, since their ammunition had run out. But so had the Spaniards'; as well as their provisions and, worst of all, their water. For all the storage space on their huge galleons, it was their supplies that ran out first, by a long shot. And so not a shot was fired on either side during the long pursuit of the Armada up the East Coast as far as the Firth of Forth. Thereafter it passed on alone round the north of Scotland and west of Ireland.

No one in fact in those days could have expected a sea-campaign to last one-quarter as long; and the English Exchequer was even more in debt than usual, but with none of the modern expedients for getting round that difficulty. The sailors might blame the Government, the Council and the Queen; but what everybody in the nation at large remembered about her was the living ringing voice that so many had actually heard, and others heard tell of—a voice like a cheer, and great as Old Harry's—it had spoken to them, prayed for them, declared herself one with them, as they were now at one with her. Never had they been so happy in their devotion to her, nor she in her love for them. The country went mad for joy, the bells pealed out, the bonfires blazed, the banquets lasted all night.

One especial prize she had promised herself, to thank and honour the man who had been her closest friend and lover and her help-mate in trouble, long before she had come to the throne. In this latest danger he had worked desperately and success-fully at the land defences of the whole country, never sparing himself, and achieving in so short and flurried a time what few younger men could have done. She would now reward her sweet Robin, Earl of Leicester, by creating for him a new office of Lord Lieutenant of England and Ireland. Such power had never before been given to a subject, and her most politic advisers, old Cecil and the Leader of the House, Sir Christopher Hatton, did their best to dissuade her, but to no avail. She had already made out the patent for it when Leicester, already tired out, was taken suddenly ill and died.

The rejoicings all went on as before, and she had to attend them and go on showing her joy; but the spring of it was broken for her. These very feastings after the strain of overwork may have helped to kill him, for he was self-indulgent and the doctors had tried to insist on a more careful diet, and Elizabeth had written teasingly that he must be sure to eat no more than the shoulder of a wren and drink only the twentieth part of a pint of wine with plenty of St Anne's sacred water. Now their long gay comradeship was over, and their furious quarrels and reconciliations, their secrets of love and marriage, shared by no one else. Only they knew the truth about each other. He had done lessons with her in childhood; had been imprisoned with her in the Tower by her sister, Mary Tudor, and had helped her there with money raised by selling his estates; had ridden on a white stallion to her as she sat under a tree in Hatfield Park, to tell her that Mary was dead and she was Queen of England; and she had created him her Master of Horse on the spot. 'His youth, stature and florrid beauty had recommended him' to the post, and to many other posts increasing in glory and power; and she could still see him as that young man on the white charger, as well as the ageing, balding man with a paunch, and a whitish beard enhancing the purplish red of his face. He was only a few months older than she, but had not the wiry whipcord strength to make him wear as well.

Now he was dead, everyone else seemed very young.

CHAPTER SIX

'An Anchor Guided by a Lady'

THE young men were quick to come into their own. Leicester's widow Lettice, 'That She-Wolf', cousin of the Queen, having flagrantly 'deceived' three husbands hastened to make a fourth of her lover Christopher Blount, as young, violent and hare-brained as her son Essex, whom he was to follow blindly, and in doing so help bring them both to the scaffold.

As if to replace Leicester with his stepson, the Queen turned more and more to Essex for consolation and amusement, disturbed and enlivened by flashes of angry annoyance, at times serious. She enjoyed having a lion-cub to tame, but not when he stood roaring across her path.

Yet another boyish Blount, Charles, elder brother to Lettice's Christopher Blount but very unlike him in his 'sweet face and most neat composure', had won Elizabeth's friendship and the favour of a gold queen from her chess-board which he tied with a red ribbon to his arm and flaunted in his triumphs on the tilt-yard. Essex's jealous rage burst out. 'I see every fool must have a favour!' he exclaimed, and challenged young Charles to a duel (strictly illegal), got wounded by him, and scolded by the Queen, who swore 'God's death! it was fit someone should take him down and teach him better manners!'

She insisted they should make friends, and they did so, all too well, with the tragic results that attended most of Essex's friendships—though Charles was to avoid the final tragedy for himself. He fell in love with Essex's elder sister Penelope, Lord Rich's wife, whom Sir Philip Sidney had loved in vain and made immortal in his exquisite sonnets to her as 'Stella'. 'You teach my tongue with one sweet kiss', Sidney had written, and that it seems was all he had ever won from her. But Charles Blount, later Lord Mountjoy, became her accepted life-long

59

lover, and through her all the more closely and intimately bound to her adored young brother Essex.

That irritable lord, humiliated by his defeat in the duel with Charles Blount, and baulked by the Privy Council of his duel with Ralegh, was determined to outdistance his greatest rival; and this time on the showier field of active service.

Ralegh was spoiling to get to sea again, above all to lead an expedition himself to carry out his schemes for new English colonies in North America. So far these had proved unlucky. His brother, Sir Humphrey Gilbert, already near ruined by his investments in them, had led the first of them, and claimed the New Found Land as the first English colony in North America. His presentation of it to Elizabeth I was enacted there in 1959 before Elizabeth II. But Gilbert never presented it to his Queen, for he was drowned on his way home.

Ralegh's cousin, Sir Richard Grenville, had led the second, together with Thomas Cavendish, the second Englishman to sail round the world. Also with them were Ralegh's young friend and mathematical tutor, Hariot, and John White, who could draw maps and paint in water-colours—one of our first artists to do so. These 'Seekers of New Lands and Finders of New Knowledge' were the harbingers of the dawn of the New England; and the Queen herself had given the sanction of her unofficial title to its name: 'Virginia'. It was so that they christened its first site, on Roanoke Island.

Ralegh paid out huge sums for further supplies and reinforcements for the colony, drawn from his private Monopolies, which people thought the Queen awarded him merely for his own luxuries—jewels on his shoe-strings and the like—whereas he gave every penny he could spare to his precious colony. But it, too, failed, for the pig-headed fools, in spite of their scientific and artistic leaders, managed to fall foul of the Indian aborigines; and were thankful to be picked up and returned home by Drake's fleet on its way back from the West Indies.

The fate of the third colony was the most mysteriously desolate of all, for the artist John White led a hundred men up-country through the forests, from Roanoke Island to Chesapeake Bay, and none of them was ever heard of again. It was called the 'Lost Colony'.

Ralegh prepared a yet greater expedition to go out the next

year and rescue it, under Sir Richard Grenville, since again the Queen refused to let him lead it himself. But the next year was 1588, the year of the Armada; and neither Grenville nor Ralegh could be spared to look for Lost Colonies, or such 'Eggs in Moonshine', as their joint cousin Humphrey Gilbert had once described other men's wild-goose chases, but not his own.

The threat had passed by, but not the Queen's fear of it. There was no more to be got from her for Virginia. She had given her name to an

'undiscovered country
From whose bourne no traveller returns.'

It was a wild-goose chase on which too many fine men had died. Ralegh, Gilbert, Grenville, they had laid their eggs in moonshine and, to her, they were all addled. Her token or 'toy' that she had told Ralegh to send Gilbert, of an anchor guided by a Lady, had brought him 'no good hap at sea'; his next voyage had proved his last. The quiet heroism of his death in a desperate storm, as he sat reading a book on the deck of his tiny frigate, to calm his mariners' spirits, has given his name a tragic glory for ever. 'We are as near Heaven at sea as on land,' he told them. His turbulent spirit then at the last knew rest. Presently his comrades on the consort ship saw the lantern on his deck extinguished, and 'in a moment the Frigate was devoured and swallowed up by the Sea'.

'He is won with a world of despair,
And lost with a toy.'

Those strange lines of Ralegh's may hold an echo of his 'true brother's' fate. Gilbert had been his first and greatest friend; never his rival.

To Elizabeth, the least romantic of ladies, whose page Gilbert had been when she was a disconsolate princess, Gilbert must have seemed an 'inconsiderate fellow' to get drowned in an eight-ton boat in the Atlantic gales when there was a bigger and better ship at hand.

At the present moment, the Armada had just been conquered, and England set free for the first time for thirty years from the immediate fear of invasion. To Ralegh it meant the signal to go ahead and strike while the iron was hot, to seize the American colonies and make a new world for England. To Elizabeth, a woman, and nineteen years older, it meant 'Go slow. Keep what you've got. Seize nothing—except privately, and then don't admit it.'

To the end of her reign, fifteen years later, Elizabeth would never admit herself officially at war with Spain. She would not listen to Drake and Ralegh; she took what they could bring her in the way of plunder from the Spanish fleets and pretended to hide it beneath her farthingale (where formerly other secrets were believed to have been hidden), but acknowledged her perquisites chiefly by the granting of further Monopolies; these drew down further obloquy on her servants, and finally, though she did not yet foresee the danger, on herself. The Armada had prevented Ralegh's attempt to rescue his Lost Colony, and after that, the Queen would give him no further chance to do so. His vision of Virginia faded yet again into the sunset.

But suddenly he got another chance at sea. While the Queen's attention was newly occupied with Essex, her 'Water' managed to slip through her fingers; he won her leave to sail with Drake on an expedition of reprisals for the Armada. Their plan was to force the Tagus and sack Lisbon from their ships. Essex was forbidden by the Queen to join them, but refused to be done out of his chance of leadership in this vengeance after victory. He rode off in disguise, again pursued by the Queen's couriers, but this time they were too late to catch him before he got on board the *Swiftsure* with his friend the military commander Sir Roger Williams, and urged him, successfully, to set sail on the instant. Essex was jubilant, the Queen infuriated, the naval leaders, frustrated by his presence, were blamed for it, threatened by her with the whole cost of the campaign above the initial sum (barely £20,000), and with hanging.

Essex, as highest in rank, claimed a high share in command; with the backing of the military commanders he made hay of the naval plan, and insisted on marching overland to invest Lisbon. His experience of war on land, though slight, gave him a better chance than at sea, where it was non-existent. Yet even so his land campaign failed, and with heavy losses.

Drake and Ralegh, in spite of their rage at the botch made of their plans, managed to clear the seas of the enemy's ships and burn two hundred of them in the Tagus estuary alone.

The Queen rewarded Ralegh with a gold chain, by way of a slap at Essex, who urged Sir Roger Williams' claim to deserve one just as much. Her opinion, already frankly expressed to Drake, was that Williams deserved a halter.

But Essex was still her 'white boy', as old Sir John Perrot in Ireland put it; and even more so since her fondness had been frightened by his running into danger; and her anger at it wiped out by joy in his safe return. And the next piece of Court gossip to be treasured among the letters to Francis Bacon's brother Anthony, who ran a private intelligence service, tells us that Essex was now so paramount at Court that Ralegh had retired to Ireland.

It was a poor substitute for the high seas; but since Essex's bungling of the attack on Lisbon, Elizabeth insisted that the fleet must now stay at home to guard her shores against Philip's further attempts at invasion. It was also the best way for her to keep Essex at home. And the best way to keep him there in a good temper lay in Ralegh's absence. So she made no objection when Ralegh asked leave to go and attend to his vast and unruly Irish estates.

The see-saw on which he and Essex sat so precariously had swung Ralegh down for the moment; but he was nonchalant about it to his cousin George Carew, and sent him the cheerfully impudent message, 'The Queen thinks that George Carew longs to see her; and therefore see her.' Straight on top of it the letter ends with a sudden change to warmth and tenderness, 'Farewell noble George, my chosen friend and kinsman, from whom nor time nor fortune nor adversity shall ever sever me.'

CHAPTER SEVEN

'The Boys will Laugh'

RALEGH had enormous work to do in Ireland and did it with his usual force. Both English and Irish had been encroaching on lands to which they had no right. He turned them out of their unlawful possessions, but at the same time gave them fresh opportunities of livelihood by setting them to work on a host of new schemes. As Warden of the Stanneries he had become an expert in mining, and now reopened the long disused and forgotten Irish mines. There used to be exquisite gold in them, unearthed in quantities in prehistoric days and now all but worked out; but there was still a little silver and plenty of tin.

He replanted trees in those forests that had been destroyed in the guerilla warfare of his early Irish campaigns, and long before them; he drained the unending bogs and made them fit to grow pasturage for cattle, and even crops, many of them a strange new experimental sort. The peasants, as always in Ireland, were contemptuously, or at best tolerantly, amused by the strange whims of the high and mighty English chief who had a fancy to make them plant whole fields of a dull root with an Indian name, as if anyone in Ireland, however starving, would ever grow or eat anything so outlandish as his new-fangled 'potatoes'. Yet they took root there, both in the soil and in men's habits, far more quickly than in England; easier to grow than any crop, they saved the people from famine again and again; became the staple food of Ireland, and in time changed her economic history.

Still more outlandish were his fields of another Indian plant called tobacco, grown, not to eat, but to burn and puff through the mouth; and what profit could there ever be in that? No matter, he was an English lord, and as mad as they make them, but he paid for the work.

He rebuilt Lismore Castle, that had once been the seat of King John, and the centre of a great town with twenty churches

Robert Devereux, 2nd Earl of Essex, from a portrait attributed
to Sir William Segar.

By courtesy of the National Gallery of Ireland

and a University; and made it not merely a strong fortress on a strategic bend of the Blackwater, but one of the grandest Gothic piles of architecture ever raised to look down on its glimmering image in the wide-flowing river below. It was as powerful as it was beautiful, and the Lord Deputy of Ireland was frankly scared by what he took to be a challenge to his own sovereignty of Ireland. Ralegh answered that he did not care, 'as I can anger the best of them. And if the Deputy be not as ready to stead me as I have been to defend him—be it as it may!'

He was not himself as fond of the magnificent Castle of Lismore as of the 'litell house' formerly granted him as Mayor of Youghal; for that, he said, reminded him of his earliest home, the farmhouse at Hayes Barton in Devon, which he had tried, too eagerly, to buy from the rich landowner Mr Duke. It was strange to find one so like it at Youghal, up at the top of the little straggling street of fishermen's huts; a homely, red-brick, wood-beamed Tudor manor house, rare indeed anywhere in Ireland. He made his home chiefly there, and planted his new-fangled flowers, the yellow scented wallflowers and Azane cherries brought from the Azores. They now grow wild over the crumbling grey stone walls that tower above the churchyard and garden of 'Ralegh's house', as it is still remembered, though the very name of the old-fashioned little port is like a sleepy yawn of forgetfulness.

Ralegh did not go to sleep there, like so many other English in Ireland, nor acquire their taste for the native dress and customs, and especially their usquebaugh. His energy did not abate a jot, whether on land or sea; for he took his ships down to guard the shores of Devon and Cornwall, re-formed the fortifications at Portsmouth, arranged ransoms for captives in Barbary, and annoyed the Privy Council by his naval attacks on such foreign vessels as were helping the Spaniards' war against England by carrying Spanish goods under neutral colours.

Yet he found time in Ireland for his most peaceful achievement there, and that was his greatest new friendship, with the poet Edmund Spenser, whose civil service work in the rebellion had been rewarded with Kilcolman Castle.

Generations of Englishmen, who had set out to subdue Ireland, had themselves subsided into surrender to a dream that had held sway for centuries before the nightmare of the English guerilla campaigns. They went to fight in forest warfare, as native to the inhabitants as to wild beasts; they stayed to live at ease in a milk-mild climate, among people who were mostly tall, handsome and 'active as the roe-deer', royally yet casually hospitable. Their dances were gay, though their songs were sad; their stories long and marvellous, but often funny, and above all there was never any hurry. A man might do as he liked, dress as he liked, fight whom he liked; sit all day in 'flowery groves' beside the many 'spacious rivers full of fish' (it is the English Spenser's praise); or, if he wanted more active sport, join with his friends in a raid on some annoying neighbours and make 'the shady woods resound with dreadful yells'. After which they had leisure to observe, with an earlier poet:

> 'The leaves were gay and green
> And pleasant to be seen.
> They went the trees between
> In cool array.'

It was Spenser who gave the most grimly realistic account in prose of the brutish horrors in Ireland, and what is worse, propounded the most realistic remedies, in recommending that 'loose, wandering persons', such as his own trade-fellows, the bardic minstrels, should be 'taken up'; and that Ireland needed most of all to learn the 'intellectual' way of life. Yet even he found there his escape into fairyland when he wrote his *Faerie Queene*, the purest romance in English; and, unfortunately for itself, the longest. That also was due no doubt to the influence of the lingering sad twilights, the mirage-like reflections, and all that another Anglo-Irishman, George Bernard Shaw, inveighed against four hundred years later, in the land's 'torturing, heart-scalding, never satisfying dreaming'.

For four centuries earlier than Spenser's day, the land had conquered the proud Anglo-Norman families who had come to conquer it. They had even forsworn their noble and ancient names 'and took Irish surnames and nicke-names', as Sir John Davies indignantly mentioned in his 'Discoverie of the True Causes why Ireland was never entirely subdued'. True, he also, and sympathetically, pointed out that the English laws gave 'no benefit nor protection' to the Irish, so 'how was it possible they should be other than outlaws and enemies to the Crown of

England?' From an English Attorney-General of Ireland, at that time, this sounds fair enough. He gave indeed more blame throughout to his own countrymen from England, both to the rulers, in their lack of understanding of the natives, and to the settlers in going native. They broke English law in adopting the Irish language: but wasn't it plain sense to make your neighbours and servants understand you?—and in wearing the national dress: but surely still plainer sense to be practical and comfortable? Did ever an English lawyer know how to go lightly through bogs and thorn-thickets without wearing either the open-toed brogues and tight trousers, or else bare knees, rough frieze skirts and saffron-dyed shirts?

But it was in sheer defiance that they wore them when forced reluctantly to visit the English Court, even that of Henry VIII, the first English sovereign to be styled King of Ireland instead of Overlord. He had started the present troubles in a wholesale way by hanging the Earl of Kildare and five of his uncles together at Tyburn; it upset the 'Home Rule' through the great Norman-Anglo-Irish families, especially the Fitzgeralds of Kildare, a system already grown fairly unsystematic, but better than nothing. And precisely nothing was what Henry gave the Irish instead for government. Also nothing for religion and education, when he abolished Roman Catholic rule there. The Pope had as yet meant little to a Celtic race, whose Christianity had started independently of Rome, and in a more liberal spirit, combining Biblical with heathen classical lore in happy innocence. But Henry also abolished their monasteries and wandering friars; founded no University nor schools in their place; and forced on them instead the Bible and Prayer Book in English, a language more foreign to most than Latin had become. So that he all but extinguished the dim afterglow of that light which Irish saints and scholars had once spread through Europe's Dark Ages.

In Henry's favour it must be admitted that he did not fuss too much over details like surnames and dress. But later the English tried to tighten up the law against national dress for State occasions; and for the first time did so in Ireland itself, at a special Parliament of nobility and clergy in 1585. It proved a mistake, though the Lord Deputy Sir John Perrot provided, at his own expense, 'Gowns and other Robes fit for that place and their degrees, which they embraced like setters'—but evidently only for the fun of new clothes at a gift, for they soon wearied of them, and the principal Lord of Ulster besought him that his chaplain should go through the streets beside him 'clad in the Chief's Irish trouser, "for then" (quoth he) "the boys will laugh as fast at him, as they now do at me". Whereat the Deputy could have smiled', writes Sir Edward Cecil. 'Yet casting a frown upon his countenance,' Perrot read Tirlogh Leynogh a solemn lecture on 'contempt of order and decency', and on the seemliness of the new long robes that kept tripping him up. If 'any idle or ill-affected person' laughed at them, the cause was his 'ill wearing of the same, from his want of civil custom'.

It was a pity that Sir John, that gigantic genial bastard of Henry VIII, could *not* have smiled; and one wonders if it were Sir Edward Cecil's hint as a prudent civil servant that cast the frown upon his countenance instead, and made him give an admonition so crass as applied both to a high chieftain and to the corner-boys of the Dublin streets.

> 'The little worm of laughter,
> That eats the Irish heart,'

was among the most dangerous of their weapons; but the burly Sir John was the right man to have countered it with a gust of Falstaffian laughter.

More dangerous than clothes, language, even laughter, was religion. 'These people call themselves Christians,' wrote their Spanish ally, Don Francesco de Cuellar, and inconsequently disputes their claim to be so called, because 'the great majority of their churches and monasteries have been demolished by the English'. But that gave good cause to sour him, for when his galleon from the Armada was wrecked on the Irish shore he sought holy sanctuary, only to find the monks fled to the woods, the chapel and hermitage turned into drinking-places for swine, the images of the saints destroyed, and in their place twelve Spaniards hanging 'by the act of the Lutheran English'.[1]

Nor were the native Irish much better, for they slaughtered and plundered most of their wretched 'allies' as they crawled up from the sea, and Cuellar was only saved by a young girl 'most beautiful in the extreme', who however took her share in robbing

[1] Don Francesco de Cuellar, op. cit.

him by snatching his 'relics of great value' to hang around her own neck, explaining that she was a Christian, which, he caustically observes, 'she was in like manner as Mahomet'. Cuellar was an impressionable Latin, and thought 'most of the women very beautiful, but badly dressed, in chemise and blanket and a linen cloth much doubled over the head'—the origin of the Galway petticoat, cloak and mutch cap that some remember as the most beautiful feminine dress except that of a nun. But compared with the stiff formality of sixteenth-century dress it must have seemed unbearably sloppy.

Still more so were feminine morals. Ireland was as yet a long way from becoming the most Puritan of the Catholic countries; the women were cited as the most drunken and unchaste in Europe, 'except only in Bohemia', also, rather oddly for such Bohemian living, the best-looking, and the most intelligent and enterprising. They took a shockingly prominent part in politics, the chieftains' wives being often more active, dominating and warlike than their lords.

*　　*　　*

'Desperation begetteth courage,' as Ralegh wrote long later, 'but not greater, nor so lively, as doth assured confidence.' Now that the rebellion of 'Monster', as he always spelt Munster, had been quelled, and Spain's Armadas doubly defeated, England seemed to have cut away the serpent coiled around her heel. This new assured confidence set him free to catch a glimpse of Ireland, though not as she had been, for Ralegh never caught that as clearly even as Spenser did, who wanted to make a History of the Antiquities of Ireland. But he could enjoy with him the salmon- and trout-fishing in the 'spacious rivers' praised by his friend; the swans gliding downstream; the pale sunsets that seemed to last for ever. Above all they shared their poetry; and wrote superb yet sincere compliments of each other's; of which one line in particular shows the quality of their friendship:

'Neither envying other, nor envied.'

Ralegh's inability to write poetry except when it was urged out of him by the force of some sudden passion, made him the most spontaneous of all poets in the opinion of the reflective Spenser, who called him, 'Thou that art the Summer's Nightingale'. Yet Ralegh's poetry did not have to be personal. He had written a gravely admiring, almost envious tribute in 1587 in his Epitaph on Sir Philip Sidney's recent death, which was so ironically in contrast with the end of his own life.

> 'There didst thou vanquish shame and tedious age,
> Thy rising day saw never woeful night,
> But pass'd with praise from off this worldly stage.'

Ralegh's tribute was as honest as it was poignant; he had never been an intimate friend of Sidney's, and did not pretend to it. He had not in fact had a poet for his close friend since George Gascoigne had been his patron twenty years before. Now it was Ralegh's turn to play patron to his Gentle Spenser, and he snatched at the chance with a grateful delight for the escape that he must often have needed, into the clear, precise, dream-world of *The Faerie Queene*. In return, he at once recognized the 'news value' of this endless romance, which Spenser should have started publishing from the moment he began to write it, when everyone was worked up about the danger from Mary Queen of Scots (Spenser's false Duessa) and eager to acknowledge the legendary Champion of England, King Arthur, whose Welsh blood now flowed through the veins of Elizabeth Tudor, Spenser's Gloriana.

But it was not too late, Ralegh urged, for nobody in England could take in anything until long after it had happened. And anyway Duessa's friends and Gloriana's enemies still lived on. So he wrote two superb sonnets as preface to the poem, one of them inciting 'meaner wits' to learn of Elizabeth from Spenser's 'angel's quill', how to 'Behold her princely mind aright, and write thy Queen anew'. It was an excellent advertisement; but the other sonnet was in the grander manner, showing in sonorous hyperbole how Spenser so out-shone Petrarch that 'Oblivion laid him down on Laura's hearse'; and even, half in joke, how Homer himself 'did tremble all for grief, And curst the access of that celestial thief'. He pulled the celestial thief away from his never-ending dream, and took him back with him to the bustling, practical, ghastly-bright Court of Gloriana and boosted him there and all his anti-Papist propaganda, until he managed to secure a pension of £50 a year for him, to the horror of the old Treasurer, Lord Burghley. 'All this for a song!' he exclaimed, and never knew that the song would live on when he was forgotten, except by historians.

*   *   *

Ralegh's end of the see-saw rose sky-high when Essex's dropped to the ground with his marriage to Sir Philip Sidney's widow, the elusive Frances Walsingham. Elizabeth could overlook it when Essex got her maids of honour with child, but not when he dared to marry one. Her sexual, and especially marital, jealousy has been called almost pathological; the 'almost' seems an understatement, for she was, in this respect only, a little mad. The tortuous emotional crises she had undergone since before her adolescence had given good reason for this. The amazing thing is that she could retain in general a far more than normally vigorous mind, with sense of humour and understanding; and show it as abnormal only in this one respect: that, as she herself had been deprived of marriage and children, so she wished to deprive others. It was an unpleasantly painful neurosis, especially to those others.

She could enjoy the dazzling simulacrum of love and possible marriage, but the reality of it, in others, shattered it for herself. It cracked the false mirror in which she could preen herself as Queen of Love and Beauty, and showed the grey truth of a lonely old woman.

Once only, and long before that truth had become absolute, she had cried her grief at it aloud in terrible foreknowledge of herself, at the birth of Mary's son. 'The Queen of Scots is delivered of a fair son—and I am a barren stock.' This admission to herself held more bitterness than her open accusation to Mary, many years later—'You have in various ways attempted to take my life, and to bring my kingdom to destruction.'

That frankness in enmity is only the reverse side of her capacity for friendship. She could express in half jocular cameraderie her indignation to Philip II, and even give a wry grin to her threat to Henry III, the decadent King of a divided France—'Your realm, my good brother, cannot abide many enemies. Give not the rein, in God's name, to wild horses;'—thus showing the danger of his placing herself as the Grey Mare among them.

And in her earlier relations with Mary of Scotland, her enmity showed the earnest candour of friendship when she urged her much younger cousin against her marriage to Bothwell after her husband Darnley's murder: 'For the love of God, Madam, use such sincerity and prudence that all the world may judge you innocent.' That came from the heart, of her own experience with Leicester after his wife Amy's death.

But her candour broke down to Mary's son in her apology for 'that miserable accident' of his mother's death; she may have been half forced, half tricked into abetting it; but in excusing it she sank to her basest hour.

She could indeed feel sympathy for her rival for the Crown; but none for any woman who dared her rivalry in marriage. The falsity of such emotion must be balanced by the truth of Elizabeth's friendships, and so it is only fair to say something of them. A few women were her lifelong friends; she had shown staunch loyalty at great risk to herself when, as a girl of fifteen and practically a prisoner, she had demanded of the Council that they should release her governess 'Kat' Ashley from the Tower and 'be good unto her'.

When old, she wrote to another 'Good Kate' in sympathy for her sorrow at her child's death, begging her to take this message from her as God's 'silly vicar, yet a loving sovereign', i.e. to 'let nature not hurt herself'. And to 'Mine own dear Crow', her pet name for her beloved Lady Norris, who had been bereaved of a son, her warmth of understanding glowed out in a long letter, broken off with a single word that tells more of her than all the rest that she wrote 'on this unsilent subject'.

Her friendship was shown at its tenderest to elderly mothers in their griefs; to faithful servants in their sickness; she sat beside old Cecil as he lay dying and fed him with her own hand; and was at Christopher Hatton's bedside all the last night of his life. She took pains too for the youngest. Though she wrote very few letters herself, there is one to 'Boy Jack', her godson Harington, to give him the pride of her own vile handwriting, and added a clerk's fair copy to save him the trouble of deciphering it.

But the most moving example of that double act of friendship is in her last, tremulous, all but illegible scrawl, two months before her death, to Charles Blount, Lord Mountjoy, together with a fair copy by Robert Cecil, 'lest you cannot read it'. It says nothing of the nervous depressions of her last illness in this her seventieth year, but laughs with a gay confidence at his

72

doubts of himself in his arduous service in Ireland, which indeed, so she tells him, 'has more need of bits than spurs. No louder trump may sound your praise than we have blasted, in all our Court and elsewhere.'

And like the blast of a young fellow-soldier's trumpet, the old woman's letter ends with the brave shout of a Latin quotation: 'ad Tartara eat melancholia'—in effect, 'To Hell with Melancholy!'

Yet it was melancholy which killed her within the next few weeks, for the doctors found no other cause of death. She could not conquer it for herself, but she could for a friend. Friendship was her true emotion and showed her face clear.

But in the case of love she put on a mask disguising her real capacity for feeling behind a glittering, or a terrible, façade. That last was to confront first Essex, and then Ralegh.

CHAPTER EIGHT

'Every Hair of my Head Stareth'

SIR NICHOLAS THROCKMORTON

THE love of Ralegh and his Bess Throckmorton caused his first great fall from fortune; and lasted to the end of their lives. 'God hold me in my wits,' she wrote on the day he died. God held her in them and in love of him for the twenty-nine years that she had to survive him, in the memory of his words to her in the face of death: 'I chose you and I loved you in my happiest times.'

They had certainly been his most fortunate. His rival Essex was married, disgraced, and banished from Court; and Ralegh summoned back to it, and again in favour. The Queen, flicking her returned prodigal on the cheek with her sharp-ringed hand as she granted his request for Spenser's pension, demanded playfully, 'When will you cease to be a beggar?'

'When Your Majesty ceases to be a benefactor,' he replied as gaily, and unabashed. Once again they were on the chaffing terms of their former easy intimacy. Yet this casual piece of banter has been solemnly recorded as an instance of his shameless greed; though on behalf of an impoverished friend who was also one of the greatest poets England ever had.

True, Ralegh also got something for himself: the charming and not very large Manor of Sherborne in Dorset, which would make a peaceful home for him and his family when he was able to rear one. It was time to do so, for he was just on forty, and moreover had fallen deep in love, unluckily with one of the Queen's Maids of Honour, the orphaned daughter of a once highly eminent statesman, Sir Nicholas Throckmorton. On the face of it nothing could seem more suitable, though Bess had inherited little more than her father's stature, good looks and talent for easy letter-writing. She was tall and slender, her hair golden, her eyes wide and blue, her features rather irregular but showing charm and humour, like her letters, which read just as though she were speaking them, their wildly erratic spelling emphasizing their individual tone, sometimes laughing or picturesque, but always frank and direct. She and Ralegh had of course, like others at Court, to try to keep their love a secret from the Queen; particularly important at this moment in the spring of 1592, when after five years of waiting and disappointment he had just won back to the peak of his old high favour with her. And he had proof of it, more precious to him even than Sherborne.

He had started a new sea venture, at his own great expense, and infinite labour in persuading other adventurers to join him, in fitting out a fleet of thirteen ships to seize the Spanish silver fleet and attack Panama. At last he had persuaded the Queen to let it sail under him; and so, at last, he had won his supreme ambition and was to be, for the first time in his life, an Admiral in sole command. Then her favour tacked on to a contrary course, flattering but infuriating. Once again she could not bear to let him take the risk; he was too rash and careless and would 'get himself knockt on the head'; besides she needed her Oracle after his long absence in Ireland to stay and help her with his counsel. The utmost he could win from her after all his persuasions was that he should lead out the fleet and then hand over his command to Frobisher; and even this concession was only because it was known how the sailors loved him, while Frobisher was unpopular and would have trouble in starting the expedition.

It was while he was at sea that rumours were eagerly spread by his enemies that he had got Bess Throckmorton with child; and some, far worse for him, that he had secretly married her before he sailed. The supposition that he might have done this in order to stave off the worst of the Queen's anger is incredible; since all knew it was the very way to increase it. The Queen had shown she could sometimes overlook seduction (in Essex's case more than once); but that she regarded marriage as a far more criminal offence, and against herself. It was this worst offence that Ralegh committed, whether or no he first seduced Bess, which is not unlikely from the other scandals about him, particularly those heard and repeated by Aubrey, who would have been amazed by one modern accusation of Ralegh, that he was sexually cold. On the contrary, Aubrey describes with gusto his 'getting up one of the maids of honour against a tree in a wood', and how she kept protesting, 'Nay, sweet Sir Walter, Oh, sweet

Sir Walter!' until 'as the danger and the pleasure at the same time grew higher, she cried in the ecstasy, "Swisser Swatter! Swisser Swatter!" She proved with child'; and Aubrey adds approvingly, 'I doubt not but that the hero' (as he generally calls Ralegh) 'took care of them both, as also that the product was more than an ordinary mortal.'

She could not have been Bess Throckmorton, for Aubrey tells us that this was 'his first lady' after coming to Court, and as he had come there eleven years before his love-affair with Bess, he was unlikely to have waited so long before proving that he 'loved a wench well'.

The Queen's fury with Ralegh and Bess exceeded anything she had shown even with Leicester and Essex. Ralegh was summoned to return to London on the instant, abandoning his fleet forthwith to the unwelcomed leader, Frobisher. As soon as he landed he was arrested and clapped into the Tower, and learned that Bess was imprisoned there too, in a separate cell and with no means of communication, a bleak way of spending a honeymoon; but 'very properly so', in the opinion of some historians, who seem to echo Robert Cecil's shocked expressions on Ralegh's 'brutish offence' in getting a Maid of Honour with child and possibly even marrying her clandestinely, as he certainly did openly later on.

Yet it is now admitted that there is something odd and 'most obscure' about the whole business. If Bess Throckmorton were with child by Ralegh in July 1592, why was one never born (nor miscarried) until two years later, when they had their eldest son, 'Little Wat'? And the Queen's rage against them both is thought extraordinary, even for her. Having punished them with imprisonment for several weeks, her resentment against Ralegh lasted for five years, and against Bess for her whole life; hardly to be explained only by outraged propriety; or even by a fiercer jealousy of Ralegh, as of someone still more indispensible to her, than of Leicester or Essex.

It so happens that there is indeed another reason for it; one that stares us in the face—once we have noticed it. For the oddest thing in history is the way people get into their own close compartments, and fail to connect with each other, even their nearest relations. We know that Bess's father had been Sir Nicholas Throckmorton; and know too a fair amount about him, in quite other connections. Yet we can so easily forget to notice his most important connection of all; to wit, with his daughter and his future great son-in-law. So naturally we miss his connection with the Queen's undying implacability against his daughter. To see it, one must look back quickly at Sir Nicholas Throckmorton himself; and a curiously interesting person he turns out to be, foreshadowing not only his Bess but her husband.

Sir Nicholas had everything to recommend him at the start of his career with Elizabeth, who was his fourth Tudor sovereign. He was bold and handsome, with excellent brains, still only a year or two over forty, and a staunch Protestant, with every reason to give eager welcome to the new young Queen, as there was for her to welcome his services.

Her 'best' stepmother, Catherine Parr, was his first cousin, and had had him in her household after marrying Henry VIII, so that Elizabeth must have known him in her childhood. Her little brother, King Edward, whom she loved, had liked him and made him a Knight of his Privy Chamber, and Treasurer of the Mint in the Tower. Her elder sister, 'Bloody Mary', whom she loathed, had failed to execute him for treason after Wyatt's rebellion, when the London streets clanked with corpses of condemned traitors hanging in chains at every corner.

But Sir Nicholas actually won an acquittal, a thing then unheard of in a treason trial, by his magnificent defence, unequalled by any until nearly half a century later when it was surpassed by his son-in-law's—unavailingly, for by then the course of justice had receded. It had not very far to recede; Throckmorton's jury were imprisoned for over nine months for daring to acquit him, and then had to buy their release with the enormous fine of two thousand pounds. It remained an awful warning to future jurors never to give a verdict of Not Guilty against the wishes of their sovereign. So there again Sir Nicholas strides out of his special compartment in history, to help destroy his future son-in-law, the very man of all others in whom he would have welcomed a kindred spirit.

Throckmorton was kept in the Tower for a year in spite of his legally proclaimed innocence; watched Mary's moon wane, and then the splendid sunrise of Elizabeth; rushed to her side, advised her to make his close friend William Cecil her Secretary of

State, and saw himself as the coming man. He served her in France and then Scotland as her Ambassador, his chief job to write letters home. From then on we see him chiefly through them, as vivid as his daughter's later, and still more vigorous—so pithy, fresh and forcible that they have been constantly quoted ever since, but often without the memory of who wrote them—the frequent fate of a good letter-writer.

Many remember, but only as the saying of someone unknown, Throckmorton's early description of Lord Bothwell, later the lover of the Queen of Scots, as 'this glorious rash and hazardous young man' whose 'adversaries should both have an eye to him and also keep him short' (whether of cash or of a head is not quite clear). Many also have been entertained by Throckmorton's furiously frank consternation on hearing that Robin Dudley's wife, Amy Robsart, had 'had her neck broken with other appurtenances', in order to clear the way to Dudley's marrying the new Queen Elizabeth. This all Frenchmen and women were saying openly to Throckmorton, 'which every hair of my head stareth at, and my ears glow to hear. One laugheth at us, another threateneth, another revileth the Queen, and some say, "What religion is this, that a subject shall kill his wife, and his Prince not only bear withal, but marry him?" ' His shame was so great, he told William Cecil, that he 'wished himself dead'.

It is hardly the language of diplomacy, even to his great friend whom he had helped to power. But how he obviously enjoyed dashing off these indiscretions to his cautious colleague, cheerfully calling the King of Denmark 'a dissolute and impudent Prince' whose wineglass held three litres, adding as ingenuously as a converted choirboy, 'though he be a Protestant', and blatantly putting down in black and white how he quite understood his Queen's veiled intentions that he should 'nourish and entertain the garboil in Scotland'.

He was not fond of nourishing garboils. He jibbed at the practical suggestion that he should connive at the murder of the troublesome Bothwell, along with his grand-uncle the Bishop of Moray; and wrote with tiresome punctilio that he was sure it would not be agreeable to Queen Elizabeth's 'princely nature, nor to her godly mind, to consent to any murder'. He even made conscientious objections—in spelling that vies with his daughter's, for he too could thank God like Sir Roger de Coverley that he 'spelt like a gentleman and not like a pedant'—against killing 'the ould busshope' as 'a very cruel and abominable act'. This seemed unnecessarily squeamish to William Cecil, since 'the ould busshope' was a disgrace to the Church, with his host of bastards residing openly in the Bishop's Palace.

Throckmorton's most uncomfortable missions were to Mary Queen of Scots; first when she was all but a child in France, and he had to try to make her forgo the title and arms of Sovereign of England; and later when he had the still more unpleasant job of telling her, a widow at eighteen, that Elizabeth had refused her the ordinary formal courtesy of a passport of safe conduct on her voyage to Scotland. He did not tell her that Elizabeth had flown into a rage at even being asked for the safe conduct, but Mary had heard of it and with a flash of her own quick temper bade her courtiers draw back, as she did not choose to make a public scene as her elder cousin had done. Defiantly she told Throckmorton 'she was determined to adventure the matter, whatsoever came of it', and if she fell into Elizabeth's hands, 'then she may do her pleasure and make sacrifice of me'. In a sudden, baffling change of mood, the girl added low, as if to herself, 'Peradventure that casualty might be better for me than to live.'

He never forgot that extraordinary little scene: nor do we forget it; but half the time we forget that we owe it to Sir Nicholas' lively interest in persons, in contrast with Cecil's capacity to see them only as cyphers.

Sir Nicholas openly acknowledged Mary's fascination, exchanged pleasant letters with her, and did all he could to back the plan of a meeting between her and Elizabeth, which Mary passionately desired, and Elizabeth said she did, as the best hope of friendship and peace between them and their two countries. But when he was at last sent to Scotland it was with orders to forbid Mary's marriage to Darnley, and offer her Robin Dudley instead, hastily created Earl of Leicester to fit him for the honour. Throckmorton's hair must have 'stared' at this assignment, worse even than in France, where all took for granted that Leicester had for years been Elizabeth's lover and probably her husband.

And his second mission to Scotland made him again wish himself dead, for by then Darnley had been murdered, Mary

married to Bothwell, and the Scots Lords had risen against her
and held her prisoner. He tried to work for her safety, and in
accordance it seemed with Elizabeth's urgent wish; but could
not make head nor tail of all Elizabeth's contrary orders. In a
curiously moving sentence to find in an Ambassador's letter to
his Queen, he told her of Mary's agony of grief at being parted
from her husband, and how willingly 'she would leave her kingdom and dignity and live as a simple demoiselle with him. She
will never consent that he shall fare worse than herself.'

It did not soften Elizabeth's feelings for Mary; still less for
Throckmorton. William Cecil, too, had turned against him, and
must have shown the Queen his earlier letters from France about
the Dudley scandal and its injury to her prestige abroad, for she
knew all about them; and her angry displeasure, already often
aroused by his frankness, now flamed against him. In growing
desperation he came to back the plan to release Mary from her
English prison by marrying her to the Duke of Norfolk, as the
safest way to keep her under control and secure the Succession.
It began as a quite respectable scheme, but grew into a plot,
and then a rebellion. Throckmorton was not in it, but was
imprisoned for a time in Windsor Castle under suspicion. Soon
after his release he died, at fifty-six, of disappointment.

Now his daughter Bess was drawn towards her husband by
the very same qualities of rashness, and eagerness to trust friends
who were really foes, that had brought about the downfall of her
father. And Elizabeth had the chance to avenge on the daughter
the scandalized reports of the father on her own damaged
reputation. He had written of his Queen as a wanton; now his
daughter was very properly defamed as one. No wonder there
were special reasons for her harshness to Bess Throckmorton; the
only wonder is that one can so easily overlook it. As G. K.
Chesterton's Father Brown observed, the most hidden place is
under the light.

*   *   *

For Ralegh it looked like the end of his career, just as he was
reaching its summit. He had no idea how long he would be
imprisoned; perhaps for ever, as his rivals hoped. 'The Tower
will be his dwelling, where he may spend his endless days in
doubt,' one of them gloated; and added 'the Queen is most fiercely

incensed, and threateneth the most bitter punishment to both the offenders. Sir W. R. will lose all his places and preferments at Court, with the Queen's favour; such will be the end of his speedy rising, and now he must fall as low as he was high; at the which many will rejoice.'

Of course Ralegh could not plead for, nor even mention his bride: it would be the very way to make the Queen more implacable. The only chance for them both was for him to woo his Queen in letters to her and others, using the language of a forsaken lover, heartbroken by the loss of her presence. He did it. He overdid it. And his reputation has suffered from it ever since. Not that he cared about that. He knew from long experience what fulsome flatteries Elizabeth could swallow; and did not mind how ridiculous he made himself in feeding them to her. They were the current convention of speech at Court—only now he was urged to extremes by desperation. His language in any case was apt to run to extremes, being that of a poet writing prose in a frantic hurry.

So he flung off a bag of mixed metaphors to Robert Cecil, comparing himself with a 'fish cast on dry land, gasping for breath, with lame legs and lamer lungs', as though he were a coelacanth. The zoological comparison is odd, and highly undignified. Still worse were his famous, or infamous, descriptions of the Queen as 'riding like Alexander, hunting like Diana, walking like Venus, the gentle wind blowing her fair hair about her pure cheeks like a nymph', with the corollary that his 'heart was never broken till now', when deprived of these sights. Readers have rightly found it funny and shocking that a man should so write of a woman nearly twenty years older; but, again, the grotesque hyperbole is often quoted quite disconnected from the shocking reasons that urged it.

Essex was fifteen years younger than Ralegh, and nearly thirty-five years younger than the Queen; yet he could take to his bed after a quarrel with her, and write to complain how his 'sick body and troubled mind' were 'overcome with unkindness as before I was conquered by beauty. . . . Since I was first so happy as to know what love meant, I was never one day, nor one hour, free from hope and jealousy'; and later on would plead his 'spirits wasted with travail, care and grief, and heart torn in pieces with passion'. Yet the abject self-pity of such 'love letters' to a woman just old enough to be his grandmother, was not caused by his writing them 'in a dark prison, alone', as were Ralegh's flamboyant fantasies. Nor had Essex's wife been put in prison, away from him.

No appeals won Ralegh's release; nor did the bitter rage of his poem:

> 'Go Soul, the body's guest,
> Upon a thankless errand:'

attacking the falseness of all worldly powers, until it turns with a final thrust of contempt upon himself for 'blabbing' his complaint—to no purpose, since

> 'Stab at thee he that will,
> No stab the soul can kill.'

He alone won his release; through his country's need of him. This arose, as suddenly as by a miracle, to set him free.

CHAPTER NINE

‘ *The Especial Man* ’

SIR JOHN HAWKINS, OF RALEGH

THE Queen had often said she could not do without her Oracle. She now had it proved to her against her will. The very rivals who delighted in Ralegh's downfall found themselves obliged to urge her to forgive him, if only temporarily, yet sufficiently long to make use of him in the sudden emergency that had sprung up.

The fleet that he had got together by his own efforts and with his money, and himself led out to sea, himself laid down its strategic depositions, had won an overwhelming success and the richest prize ever seized in Elizabethan days. His Vice-Admiral Sir John Borough brilliantly carried out Ralegh's strategy, in Ralegh's own flagship the *Roebuck*, and won a desperate sea-fight of several hours with the huge Portuguese East Indian carracks off the Azores. Triumphant but bitter hearing that, for the prisoner in the Tower! And hardly less so for Frobisher who, again unlucky, was away with half the fleet watching the Spanish coast. The Portuguese carracks, weighed down with treasure, were bound for Lisbon; the largest of them was cut off from the rest by the Vice-Admiral, and captured; a towering sea-castle, seven decks high, glittering in coloured paint and gilding on the azure waves, and eight hundred men swarming all over the decks and the rigging of the gigantic painted sails, like little dark monkeys screaming and chattering, until at last they shrieked surrender. Enormous booty was piled up in the hold: ebony by the ton, no less than fifteen of them; diamonds big as walnuts for the King as a present from his Viceroy; crosses tall as young trees encrusted with jewels; and over five hundred tons of spices, the pepper alone worth £102,000. It took ten of the smaller English ships to carry the cargo to London, where it was valued at £500,000—and that was only what remained of it. For the success had proved all too literally overwhelming.

The huge carrack was towed into Dartmouth early in September, and the whole West Country ran mad with the lust for loot; and the sailors, who brought it in, nearly as mad with rage at hearing that their Admiral, the chief organizer of this their greatest triumph, was in prison—only for loving a wench too well! If this were the petticoat government's reward for service, they would help themselves to their own; and so they did. They mutinied against their officers, and joined in the orgy of plunder, together with all on shore who could get their hands on it, and these were by no means only the 'rascal multitude'. The Countess of Bath, wife of the Lord Lieutenant of Devon, wrote to the Judge of the Admiralty himself, frankly apologizing that she had had nothing 'by this rich carrack' to send his wife, since 'my Lord's house is far off, and so lighted of nothing'.

The common sailors did better than the Countess; one alone scooped three chains of gold and of pearls, and four pearls bigger than peas, and crystal forks and spoons set with gold and jewels. A corporal pouched a large bag of rubies; another fellow, one of diamonds; yet another had more than three hundred diamonds rattling loose in his pockets.

Robert Cecil wrote all this and more in dismayed horror to his father, Lord Burghley, when sent down to cope with the situation. He couldn't; though he searched every man 'which did smell of the prizes', put some in prison, and 'left an impression on the Mayor . . . but no more obstinate people did I ever meet'. It was the people, not the Mayor, who mattered, with their 'desperate ways', breaking loose all over the Devon ports with their spoils, and turning them into a frantic St Bartholomew's Fair. 'There never was such spoil!' exclaimed Cecil, a shade wistfully.

There was only one man who might possibly quell the riot. The Controller of the Navy, old Sir John Hawkins, insisted that Ralegh was 'the especial man' to do it, and even Robert Cecil, his friend, but more often his anxiously jealous rival, had to insist on his being sent down, under the private guard of a keeper, but with liberty to tackle the job that no one else could manage. So down Ralegh came again to Devon, hot on Cecil's heels, and swearing that if he met any of the plunderers coming away, 'if it be upon the wildest Heath, I mean to strip them as naked as ever they were born!'

But when he reached Dartmouth even plunder was forgotten, and even by the plunderers, in such thunderous rapture at the sight of him apparently at liberty, that Cecil was staggered by it. Not only, he wrote his father, Ralegh's own private 'poor servants to the number of one hundred and forty goodly men—but also all the mariners—came to him with such shouts of joy, as I never saw a man more troubled to quiet them in my life'. And some of the captains, he says, were in tears at meeting him again. He was uneasy at Ralegh's denying their congratulations by answering, 'No, I am still the Queen's poor captive,' for fear lest it 'diminish his credit, which I do vow to you before God is greater amongst the mariners than I thought for'.

He need not have feared. The credit or, rather, worship of the disgraced prisoner was so strong that he restored order even among the worst ruffians. 'He can toil terribly,' Robert Cecil admits, and rewards him with a pathetic sentence meant to influence the Queen, who was of course certain to see it, that when not busied, Ralegh's 'heart is broken; for he is very extreme pensive', and anxious to make amends for 'his brutish offence'.

Ralegh's own tone to Lord Burghley was nothing like so apologetic. There is a proud ring of challenge in his letter to the old Lord Treasurer, and through him therefore, to the Queen. He no longer begs his freedom and favour, but bargains for them. He had undertaken to rescue, chiefly for the Queen, the remainder of the treasure which his fleet had captured; and which would not have been jeopardized had he been there to prevent it. He was not going to be let loose for the job and then be returned to prison. 'My promise was not to buy my bondage, but my liberty.' As an equal, and no 'poor captive', he reminds the Lord Treasurer of 'the offer I made' of £80,000 to the Queen as her share of the booty; 'Fourscore thousand pounds is more than ever a man presented to Her Majesty as yet. If God have sent it for my ransom, I hope Her Majesty will accept it.'

Small wonder if there is a scornful flick in this offer of so huge a ransom, or bribe, to buy his pardon for having dared to want to marry after forty years, ten of them devoted to the emotional friendship of a woman twenty years his elder, whom he could never marry.

The Queen's shrewd intelligence must have noticed, and

possibly appreciated, its careless note of defiance as a change from fulsome compliments; which had certainly served his cause no better. Ralegh's 'offer' was in any case a mere flourish in her wary eyes. Elizabeth, alias Venus, Diana, Alexander and the rest, could, and did, take all she could get; and it amounted to a full half of the booty; although her investment entitled her only to one-tenth.

She had once told Mary Queen of Scots as reason for her meanness to her, 'When one is young one gives with both hands, but when old, only with the little finger.' Ralegh was the latest to make her feel old, when he turned for love to a far younger woman. So he was lucky to get even the sharply pared nail of her little finger.

The London merchants doubled the money they had invested in the enterprise. Ralegh had sunk his whole capital in it; had borrowed £11,000 for it at interest; and got nothing.

What hit him most was that, 'I took all the care and pains; carried the ships from hence to Falmouth and thence to the north cape of Spain; and they only sate still.'

It was a lesson he could never learn for himself. He had won his main objective, freedom from prison for himself and his wife to live at Sherborne. But he was banished from Court, so that though he still kept Durham House in the Strand, and some of his former appointments, yet the most influential of them, his Captaincy of the Guard, had to be handed over to a deputy. His enemies took their opportunity to thwart his work in the Stanneries, his colonizing in Ireland, and her exports to England. In compensation, his own land was growing in importance to him. He had to try and make ends meet at his new estate in Sherborne, with no extra money for it, and he spent most of his time there. It was a lovely place on the borders of Devon and Dorset, and he enjoyed planning improvements there, the building of a 'delicate lodge in the park, of brick, not big, but very convenient for the bigness', as a retreat for contemplation and writing. He planted great trees that his sons and grandsons would stroll under, down majestic avenues that he himself could not live to see full-grown. For his wife Bess it was indeed their happiest time, in spite of unjust treatment and dashed hopes. But they were safely away from London, and not only the Court, but from Durham House, which we are told she dreaded, no doubt for the sight of the ships sailing down river and out to sea, and her husband's eyes following them from the windows of his study in the little turret.

Here at Sherborne they were in his 'fortune's fold', a sheep-fold safely penned, where he sat and scribbled and discussed everything on earth or off it, with friends who were astronomers and mathematicians, philosophers, scientists and/or sorcerers, and capped verses with fellow-poets. The circle that he gathered round him at his home, or close by it at Cerne Abbas in Dorset, soon won for itself the ominous name of 'The School of Night'. Cerne Abbas has borne a reputation for witchcraft down to our own day, and had long before Ralegh's; probably ever since the vast outline of the Giant, a phallic god, was carved out of the chalky soil of the hillside for the worship of the older pagan religion. The yokels, and not only they, believed that the 'School of Night' followed that tradition, and enquired into dark and unholy mysteries. Its founder had been called 'Ralegh the Witch' because he had so suddenly bewitched the Queen and risen to power. Some thought the nickname applied literally to him and to his companions.

They were certainly a group to astonish any countryside. One was Thomas Hariot, whom Ralegh, as soon as he had come to Court, had employed as his scientific tutor. Hariot was then only twenty-one, but had since justified Ralegh's early recognition of his quality by winning a European reputation, and his discoveries were later to inspire Descartes himself in algebra and pure mathematics. These seemed impure to some. The sorcerer Dr Dee, another suspect friend of Ralegh's and visitor to Sherborne and Cerne Abbas, had been the first ever to give lectures on Euclid. They had caused a furore at the Sorbonne where the Parisian students, ragged slum-rats as they were, had swarmed up outside the walls of the packed lecture-hall to hear him through the windows. But they did him no credit with the many English who held that Euclid's 'pricks and lines' were symbols of magic. Ralegh's closest friend in the group was a Fellow of Balliol, Lawrence Keymis, who combined learning with a passion for seafaring and exploration, especially if it were with Ralegh. Another member was the enormously wealthy scholar, the Earl of Northumberland; he was collecting a vast library, believed to consist chiefly of forbidden knowledge; made sulphurous chemical experiments in pursuit of alchemy, and was known as the Wizard Earl.

Charges of atheism were brought against the coterie, and there was an abortive attempt to bring them to book in a rustic court; but it got no further than finding that one of them had remarked that you could spell God backwards and pray to Dog, and another (a cousin of Ralegh's) that he'd as soon hear a sermon from his horse as from a certain stupid cleric. Ralegh himself, less rudely, though more tellingly, had refuted another parson with, 'You reason not as a scholar.' His own heresy seems to have been directed only at Aristotle, whom he called 'obscure and intricate', and would never accept 'that God hath shut up all the light of learning within the lanthorn of Aristotle's brains'.

The County Court found it all rather beyond them and dismissed the charges. But public opinion took them up. A ballad called Ralegh 'mischievous Machiavel'; and the playwright William Shakespeare, to oblige his patron the Earl of Southampton and his friend Essex, made a skit on the circle in his popular comedy, 'Love's Labour Lost'. 'Black is the badge of Hell and School of Night,' he wrote, and the 'magnificent Armado' is most probably a caricature of Ralegh,

'. . . a refined traveller . . .
A man in all the world's new fashions planted.'

But the winning candidate for the black badge of Hell was undoubtedly Christopher Marlowe, the most remarkable of all Ralegh's strange company. A young man of low birth and towering ambition, he suffered bitterly from his sense of inferiority over the first, and from his cramped outlets for the second. For his double career as a secret political agent and a writer of popular back-yard plays could lead to no high advancement. So he was angry with most men, who returned his hate with interest. Kyd, who had shared a room with him, accused him of 'a cruel heart'; Richard Greene, of 'Diabolical Atheism', and 'horrible blasphemies'; Gabriel Harvey, of admiring 'nought but his wondrous self'. He kept the worst company, took pains to shock even them with his loud-mouthed talk against God and 'superstitious religion', and often fell foul of the law for brawling.

Yet Ralegh made friends with him, and listened with interest to his *Treatise on Atheism*, and made fun of his occasionally conventional verses, answering in lightly cynical parody his charming, artificial 'Come live with me and be my love'. And to Marlowe's false notion that reason is opposed to love, and the famous climax,' Whoever loved that loved not at first sight?' Ralegh replied more sternly that 'Conceit begotten by the eyes' is where 'reason makes his grave'. Astonishingly, the quarrelsome young man took no offence. The nobles complained of Ralegh's intolerant pride, but the shoemaker's son could recognize that he was no snob.

There is another and greater answer of Ralegh's, to those who accused them both of atheism, and also to Marlowe's Treatise on it. In his *Treatise of the Soul*, Ralegh wrote 'The mind in searching causes is never quiet till it come to God, and the will never is satisfied with any good till it comes to the immortal goodness.' Marlowe himself implicitly agrees with this in Faustus' anguished cry as he gazes in his last midnight hour on the Milky Way:

> 'See where Christ's blood streams in the firmament,
> One drop of blood will save me. Oh my Christ!'

And the despair of his Mephistopheles—later imitated, but unequalled by Milton's Satan—is the final expression of remorse:

> 'Think'st thou that I who saw the face of God,
> . . . . .
> Am not tormented with ten thousand hells? . . .'

In character, manners, and whole way of life, the splendid courtier and the 'intemperate' ruffian, with his sinister side-trade as a spy, were poles apart. In genius they were akin. It is Marlowe's magnificent poetry that has best described Ralegh's life:

> 'Our souls whose faculties can comprehend
> The wondrous architecture of the world,
> And measure every wandering planet's course,
> Still climbing after knowledge infinite,
> And always moving, as the restless spheres
> Will us to wear ourselves and never rest.'

The last two lines might be a summary of Lady Ralegh's anxious thoughts of her husband. Marlowe's murder at twenty-nine, apparently in a drunken quarrel over a game of backgammon, may well have been something of a relief to her. She had begun to be with child, over two years after she had been imprisoned for conceiving one—the longest labour ever recorded for a lady who was not an elephant. A son might provide an additional inducement to keep her husband quiet at home. It was a faint hope. For if her Walter 'sate still' it was, as Sir Robert Naunton observed, only to 'teach envy a new way of forgetfulness—but never to forget himself' and the ways he might return to power, 'as rams do, by going backward, with the greater strength'.

So he sat still, to still the fears of his rivals, while he revived his plans for his most outlandish adventure—to discover and prove true the dream that had haunted him since childhood, of a fairy city, built by giants, from gold and silver, on a lake with a thousand bridges in the depths of an as yet impenetrable jungle. But he would penetrate it.

He had reached the age and circumstances when most men of his time would have thought it sound to retire from public life, albeit in disappointment, and settle down with his new wife in the security of a charming home. Yet it was just then that he made plans to start all over again, as a boy might start on his earliest and wildest escapade.

CHAPTER TEN

'*Hold both Cares and Comforts in Contempt*'

'THE OCEAN'S LOVE TO CYNTHIA'

THE Queen's quick-silver 'Water' gave his friend Robert Cecil as much anxiety as hope. Cecil could never be quite sure if his own alliance with him were more of a liability than an asset; he totted it up at nights, and the answer always worked out different. Cecil had his own value with the Queen and well knew it, but knew also that she didn't really like him; no woman could who gave you the nickname of her 'Pygmy'. Cecil's chief reason for affection (if such it were) for Ralegh was that he never seemed to notice how much taller he was. Nor, for all the disturbing brilliance of his far too many parts, what a fool he sometimes was, compared with his pygmy friend. The smaller man could hug the flattering thought within his shrunken bosom, in the safe knowledge that it would never penetrate his friend's insouciance.

Ralegh was married, and far more happily than 'his brutish offence' to her had deserved, to such a kindly, sympathetic female intelligence that Cecil might actually have dared to woo her for himself, had he only plucked up his courage in time. He had hesitated to marry at all; and a morbidly pathetic letter of his has confessed how much this was due to his dread lest his deformity should make him repugnant to any pleasing young woman.

But with the new young Lady Ralegh, tall, fair and charming as she was, it was impossible for him to believe that she felt any of the usual feminine aversion for him; she was so naturally at her ease talking and laughing with him and writing him her fresh spontaneous letters, taking it for granted that he was an equally warm and affectionate friend to herself and her husband. She would have the sense to see their advantage in that, he perceived wryly; heaven alone knew how long they might have languished in the Tower but for Cecil's demand for Ralegh's part-release to stop the loot of the Great Carrack—but here his judicious mind had to admit also his own essential need of Ralegh as 'the especial man' to take over a job that had proved far beyond his own powers.

Together, the two of them could make the most powerful combination in England, himself as the administrator and political genius, Ralegh as the adventurer, colonizer and privateer; in all whose future hazards Robert Cecil now considered, after Ralegh's supreme success, he would be well advised to invest as large a sum as he possibly could—with all due safety for his main capital, which must of course remain untouched. And Bess Throckmorton, now Lady Ralegh, would be the delightful link to weld the union of himself and Ralegh. He had no doubt that his own would be the master-mind and supreme genius of this triumvirate.

Then suddenly one of the three broke loose from the coalition, without even any sense that there was one, or that he was the active part of it; and determined that he, Ralegh, after only three years of happy marriage and peaceful retreat in the country, should now, at forty-three years old, set out on such a venture as only an ignorant lad in his teens would welcome! So Cecil could exclaim in righteous indignation to 'their Bess', and in pity and anger on behalf of Ralegh's and Bess's adored first-born, Little Wat—an appallingly noisy, rumbustious brat, much bigger and stronger, though younger, than Cecil's own puny, strictly-mothered boy, Little Will. Yet the two babies would stick together even in their cradles, and Little Wat, who had learned long before speech to roar for whatever he wanted from his infatuated mother, roared as loud and effectively for whatever Little Will wanted too.

The baby Cecil was much at Sherborne, and even his father could not think it purely sycophancy on the part of Ralegh's wife. She could not bear to see a child sick or unhappy, and was determined to feed and pamper him into as good—or bad—a copy of her Wat (God help us!) as she could make him. Robert Cecil might dread that result, but was thankful for the rounder, rosier cheeks of his hitherto starveling-scarecrow child; he could feel something of indignation for himself that Ralegh should leave both the babies and his wife so soon after winning her. He entered into sympathetic alliance with Bess, who entreated him that 'for my sake you will rather draw Sur Watar towardes the

est, than heulp hyme forward toward the soonsett'; and reproaches 'Sur Watar', together with all public men, in such
quaintly poetic terms that they should not be obscured by her
even quainter spelling: 'Every month hath his flower and every
season his contentment, but you great counsellors are so full of
new counsels as are steady in nothing.' She adds a flagrant
flattery which her husband would scarcely have endorsed: 'I
know only your persuasions are of effect with him, and held as
oracles tied to them by Love; therefore I humbly beseech you
rather stay him than further him. By the which you shall bind
me for ever.'

The strange conspiracy was powerless in the face of Ralegh's
new emancipation. In winning happiness he had won something
even more precious, and that was his freedom. He had lived too
long and too soft at Court, for fourteen years now in the sunshine
of the Queen's favour, and had discovered it to be a chill and arid
light that repeatedly denied him the fruits he most desired, those
of a man's dangerous toil and endeavour. Always she had called
him back from seeking them, just as he was setting out on his
quest, by pleading, commanding, that she could not do without
him. Tied to the glittering strings of her farthingale he had grown
sick of his servitude long before he finally lost it for the love of his
Bess. She lived in his heart a long way away from his Queen, and
yet his love of both was true, and intermingled; as can be seen in
all his strange, tortured poetry of love.

The Ocean's Love to Cynthia, what we have of it—which is
relatively little—was written for parts of it to be shown to the
Queen; and that is perhaps why the only one that remains of its
twenty-five cantos was found at Hatfield House, among the
papers of Robert Cecil. What happened to the other twenty-four
cantos may be asked of Cecil's ambiguous shade. They seem,
from the opinions of those that saw them, to have been some
of the most original and extraordinary poetry of the age. Even
from the long but unfinished fragment that remains, with some
of its verses and lines left abruptly in the air, one can see that here
is the greatest poet in Donne's tragically austere vein before
Donne himself began to write. But it is like no other poem, even
by Donne.

The five hundred lines give no facts nor explanation, only his
state of mind, but with the sudden urgency of an exclamation.

'The verse scuds before the wind',[1] as in the terrible recurring passion of *The Lie*. The rush of its inspiration links its thoughts and images so closely that it is difficult to tear them apart for quotation, and this is the chief reason why it is so little known. Yet it can pack a lifetime of love and woe and rapture into a single line of monosyllables: 'She is gone, she is lost, she is found, she is ever fair.' It foreshadows his own fate, his voyagings 'clean out of sight, with forced wind', and 'The broken monuments of my great desires': even his last and greatest, though like all else, unfinished work, when in the evening of his day he would attempt to

> 'begin by such a parting light
> To write the story of all ages past,
> And end the same before the approaching night.'

Even this relic from the lost *Cynthia* was not discovered till the 1860's, less than a hundred years ago.

Only a few fragments remain of the 'broken monument' of his poetry. The chief comfort is that Ralegh himself could not have cared since he had been so careless. What he had written, he had written; all that mattered was what he would do next, and this time it would not be to write poetry, but to fulfil in action the new upsurge of life in him that made him a boy again.

[1] M. C. Bradbrook, 'The School of Night'.

CHAPTER ELEVEN

'Let us go on, we care not how far!'

RALEGH'S CREW, IN HIS
'DISCOVERIE OF GUIANA'

IN the first week of February, 1595, he set sail for Guiana: with five ships in all, and two trunk-loads of books in his cabin; with letters-patent from his Queen bestowing full authority on his expedition, while carefully omitting the customary adjectives 'trusty and well-beloved' from 'our servant Sir Walter Ralegh', just to remind him that his three-year-old marriage was still unforgiven, and would remain so until he had fulfilled his promised bribe to her of 'a better Indies than the King of Spain's'. With big money invested in his attempt by both the Cecils, father and son, paying anxious testimony to his enterprise; with the regretful memory of Bess's brave smiles, and of the enraged howls of little Wat at his leaving them, Ralegh watched the foggy wintry world recede behind him, and a strange, silent world roll up before him over the far horizon of the bright waters. The scene changed to one of flying fish leaping like small seraphs out of the foam of his ship's prow at dawn; of dolphins tumbling like laughing clowns in the clear sunlight that sparkled over the huge sea; of alien stars that rose each night in a newly appointed place, beckoning to him through the darkness towards lands unknown.

The Elizabethans' ships were as easily lost at sea as their poems upon land. Out of Ralegh's scant five, three disappeared on that uncannily bare sweep across the Atlantic, spanking along with the Trade Winds, before he had his first sight of a strange new continent. Even today in a modern steamship, it is fully eight days after leaving the Canaries before one sights the three towering forest-covered hills rising out of the tropic sea which made Columbus christen this new island after the Trinity.

Here was Trinidad, the landing-stage for Ralegh's first advance in person on his long dreamed of New World of America; guarded, it appeared, like the palace of Hampton Court, by heraldic stone monsters, for the fantastically carved shapes of pelicans still sit today immobile on the mooring-posts of Indian fishing-boats, as they did for centuries before Columbus came.

The Dragon's Mouth and the Serpent's Mouth are the two ominously named long channels for entry to the island; and deep in the maw of the Dragon's Mouth was the new Spanish settlement of San Joseph, now Port of Spain, under the Governor Antonio de Berreo. He had provided the immediate practical reason for Ralegh's haste, not merely to better his lost fortunes, but also to catch up in the fresh spurt of the race between England and Spain.

Berreo had begun a search for the golden city of El Dorado, whose fame had been so firmly believed and attested by the Indians that few Europeans thought of it as fabulous. It was believed to be far up in the mainland hidden among what *The Times*, in 1959, called 'the virtually unexplored jungles of the Amazon Basin and the Orinoco . . . and the still ill-defined frontiers of Columbia, Venezuela, Brazil and the Guineas. . . . The unknown reaches of the Orinoco are a glimpse of the beginning of human time.'

The Spaniard Berreo's initial attempt for the Golden City had been disastrously cut short; but he was still determined to find it. Ralegh was determined to find it first. He had sent out a reconnaisance party late in the previous year under his 'most honest and valiant' Captain, Jacob Whiddon. It had never reached the mainland, for some of them were hospitably invited ashore at Trinidad by Berreo, and then murdered in cold blood. As England and Spain were still openly at war, he doubtless felt his treachery a justifiable hint to the English that they were not welcome.

Ralegh at once followed his unlucky forerunners. Undeterred by the fact that he had now only one other ship to support his own, he made a surprise attack on San Joseph, and took Berreo prisoner; with the characteristically laconic comment, 'Which had I not done, I should have savoured very much of the Ass.'

But there was no ill feeling or unpleasantness between them. Ralegh treated his prisoner as an honoured guest and wrote charming compliments of him which show his extraordinary power of detachment, in view of Berreo's treatment of Captain Whiddon—and even more inhuman treatment of others, as

SERO, SED SERIO

Robert Cecil, 1st Earl of Salisbury, from a portrait at Hatfield.

By courtesy of the Most Hon. the Marquess of Salisbury

Ralegh quickly discovered. Yet he describes the suave and cultivated murderer that he had captured as 'a Gent, well descended . . . very valiant and liberal . . . of great assuredness and of a great heart'; and how he himself entertained him 'according to his estate and worth in all things I could, according to the small means I had'.

They had long and amicable talks as they feasted together on the luscious mangoes and glossy crimson and yellow globes of the juicy fruits that contain the treasured little kernel of the pistachio nut; and the nubbly, crusty little oysters, 'very salt and well-tasted', wrote Ralegh, who described their being plucked off the low-dangling mangrove branches at low tide—just as they are today—and so was accused later of telling Travellers' Tales—for whoever heard of oysters growing on trees?

Berreo told his travellers' tales of the green hell of jungle, monsters and savages along the Orinoco; and with warm, even passionate feeling, for 'he was stricken with great melancholy and sadness' as he begged his delightful host for his own sake not to risk his life in that horrible wilderness where he himself had so lamentably failed.

And Ralegh, with a tact equally friendly, refrained from assuring his guest that at least he would not assist his own failure by tying up five or six Indian chiefs together and leaving them to rot in a den underground. For this was one of the unpleasant discoveries he had made about his pleasant companion; and he had at once set free the wretched caciques whom he had found 'almost dead with famine and wasted with torments'. Berreo had burned many alive and had some torn to pieces by dogs, a livelier form of sport, depicted in early prints of the Spaniards in South America. He might have recognized his mistake, if not his crime, for his cruelty had caused the Indians on the mainland to revolt against him, force him to evacuate Guiana, and so leave it clear of Spanish rule for Ralegh to advance upon it.

Ralegh was quick to improve upon Berreo's methods; and even on those of Christopher Columbus ninety-six years before, the first European Discoverer of the island, who had won a reputation for 'sweetness and benignity' unparalleled by his later countrymen. But his business instincts had been a bit sharp for the natives, who still grumbled over their great-grandfathers' slow disillusionment after Columbus had struck a good bargain for himself by trading a large number of brass chamber-pots to them as an interesting novelty, whose value had quickly worn off as news, and left the recipients doubtful as to their use. They might indeed have earned their cost and keep as cooking-pots with their additional convenience of a handle, but their intended use as a 'convenience', in a world so warm and wide and indecent was, so Columbus tells us, 'but coldly met'. His sweetness and benignity to the natives also sounds rather cold and negative; for the chief instance given of it is that he refused to allow his crew, even when hungry, to kill and eat them.

Ralegh's appeal to the Indians was more positive and personal. He gathered all he could of the tribes together, and told them that he had been sent by his Cacique to set them free from the Spaniards, for he was 'the servant of a Queen who was the great Cacique of the North, and a virgin, who had more caciques under her than there were trees in the island'. The metaphor is the earliest instance of his quickness to understand the native mind. Already he saw how impossible it was for them to take in anything of actual numbers; time and space, as well as people, could not be measured, only suggested by some vivid pictorial image.

The wise old Chief Topiawari whom he met later on the Orinoco, and who became Ralegh's true friend, could only explain hard facts by such imagery, which Ralegh delighted to note down for their natural poetry: 'A land from so far off as the Sun slept (for such were his own words)', so he records in evident pleasure; and how the old man had told him there had once been a great nation in Guiana, 'so many of the ancient people as there were leaves in the wood upon all the trees'.

So Ralegh at once and instinctively entered into their minds, both in speech and action; for he excited their curiosity and then their sense of religious wonder by pulling out a fine gold chain that lay hidden under his collar, and showing to them, one after the other, the little jewelled miniature of his 'Great Cacique of the North'. In hushed awe they took the holy thing in their hands and gazed upon a magical face whiter than sea-foam, and hair of small gold twisted serpents, framed in transparent wings (and why should Ralegh explain that these were the modern feminine fashion in wigs and ruffs?). The portrait was plainly that of a goddess; and his new adoring allies fell on their knees

98

and would have worshipped her, had he not piously prevented them, so he wrote.

His speech to his own men takes a naturally poetic turn, for he made them swear on their knees a magnificent oath, 'by the Majesty of the living God' to show a perfect respect to all the native women, many of them 'very young and excellently favoured who came among us without deceit, stark naked'.

That oath they kept, though he admits it was sometimes 'very impatient work' to enforce it.

And 'for all his bloody pride', as they complained in London, there is no hint of class or colour snobbery in his own attitude to the Indians, no suggestion that he felt himself of a superior race. His chivalry to their women holds nothing of contempt for them, but of such admiration as, he is careful to emphasize, might equal that for any woman of his own race and class. One chieftain's wife, 'very pleasant' he says, might well compare with 'a Lady in England', and with a smile of amused courtesy at her recognition of her own charms he adds, 'knowing her own comeliness. Her hair was almost as long as herself, tied up again in prettie knots.'

The property of the Indians he insisted on being held as sacred as their persons. Not as much as one potato or 'pina' (the delicious new pineapple which he called 'the Princesse of all fruits') might be taken without due payment, on pain of death from himself. But as usual he scorns to take credit to himself for fine sentiments of humanitarianism. He prefers to rate his honesty and gentleness at their lowest value, as mere prudent foresight. Since he had been warned by the Spaniards' brutality, he therefore himself 'would not endanger the future hopes of so many millions'. The more 'advanced' and piously-spoken explorers of the nineteenth century could not look as far ahead.

The love and faith of these new savage guides Ralegh could trust as surely as those of his old companions, such as Lawrence Keymis, Fellow of Balliol, and Notary and Bursar to the College, who had abandoned his comfortably safe academic post to follow his friend and leader into an unknown wilderness, where his genius for mathematics and geography might be of help. The presence of an Oxford don must have been of reassurance to Ralegh when carried away by too much love of living—and *what* living, when you could bathe for four or five hours on end in clear blue water without getting chilled, and pick up coral white as ivory, fantastically carved by the strange insects within, and hear the plop of a coconut falling plump into the surf from the palm-trees which wade right out into it, and all you need to quench your thirst is to split one open with a *machete* and drink the fresh, sharp, un-matured milk out of the half-circle wooden shell of the nut.

He explored the coastline of Trinidad, cruising in and out of all the unknown creeks where wooded rocks cut straight down into at least sixty feet of swirling currents; a madly hazardous job to undertake in 'a bad galiota and small cock-boat', but well worth it to find out the best possible landing places. Also he noted what were the two best strategic points of defence on the island; and they remain by far the best even today.

He found, and worked, the famous Pitch Lake, an ugly muddy swamp in flat low-lying land, not nearly as picturesque as a peat-bog in Ireland, but the most precious possession to the country that owns it, especially at this day, which has discovered the uses of petroleum. Ralegh could of course know nothing of them, but at once discerned other valuable properties in that unending source of oil, bubbling up eternally from the centre of the earth. He made better use of it than did Columbus, who had also found it, but lost half his ships from the dreaded worm, 'Teredo Navalis'; whereas Ralegh 'made trial of it in trimming our ships' bottoms and found it most excellent good and melteth not with the sun as the pitch of Norway'. It would have amused his scientific mind to discover that even in this present mechanical age the 'Trinidad Lake Oil' still has to be worked by hand with barrows and spades, just as his men had worked it, since any heavy machinery would sink at once in it.

By then he was ready to start 'in one little barge and two wherries' added to the bad galiota and cock-boat, on his quest for El Dorado in the jungles of the mainland. It led him for five hundred miles up the huge and unknown maze of rivers that make up the Orinoco, where to follow the wrong one might be to get lost for ever; for 'all the earth doth not yield the like confluence of streams and branches . . . all so fair and large'—and, as he was to find so often—'no man can tell which to take . . . among these broken islands and drowned lands'.

His own book on 'The Discoverie of the Large, Rich, and

Bewtiful Empire of Guiana' remains the most vivid and exciting account of that legendary country. One may still get a glimpse of it by drifting through the flooded jungles in canoes, safely paddled by Indian guides through the dark tangle of huge trees that drip their long sinuous lianas like serpents into the water, and suddenly reveal the starry shape of an orchid among their branches. His book is about the best true adventure story ever written, in the freshness of its wonder, and sense of beauty and of terror. He and his men faced starvation at times, the fear of getting lost, of attacks by unknown savages, the dank wretchedness of getting drenched through in sudden torrential rains, sometimes ten times in a day, and unable to change their clothes. Yet far and away the chief impression left by the book is sheer joy, and not only his own. He still gives it to us today, as strongly and brilliantly as he did to his own followers, whom he was always able to cheer when they were down. Once when they had despaired of getting food, and then had the unexpected chance of a load of bread, their spirits rose to a pitch that equalled his, and all cried aloud: 'Let us go on, we care not how far!' He knew then the reward of adventure.

CHAPTER TWELVE

'She Sent her Memory'

'THE OCEAN'S LOVE TO CYNTHIA'

THEY had not found any indubitably precious stones, nor any solid gold, though many indications of it among the gravel and rocks they examined perfunctorily; for they had time neither to search nor test them thoroughly; time soon for nothing but to save their lives. It was maddeningly tantalizing, for at every step on the rocky higher ground which they had reached they could stoop and gouge out samples of ore with their daggers and knives and even their fingers, which were later attested by the experts in London to be definitely gold-bearing. Yet they could not stay to explore them further.

A power mightier than man now rose and forbade any advance, and certainly any scrabbling in the ground for an insensate metal. They had to let the dust run through their fingers, whether it contained gold or not; just as Ralegh has written in his 'Cynthia' of one who 'writes in the dust as one that could no more'.

Another Sir Walter, the two-centuries-later poet Scott, was inspired by his earlier namesake's prose to describe in 'Rokeby' the terrible force of nature that now all but overwhelmed Ralegh's little band, when the river rose in flood against them. For:

> 'Orinoco in his pride
> Rolls to the main no tribute tide;
> But 'gainst broad Ocean urges far
> A rival sea of roaring war.'

Ralegh's description of that rival sea is even more dramatic than Scott's long-later poem. 'Our hearts were cold to behold the great rage and increase of Orinoco', he wrote of the sudden upsurge of the flood-tide, of all the tributary streams that fed it, and the waterspouts of furious rain that swept upon them in storm after storm till they were as wet through upon the deck

as if they were in the river. They watched aghast as the floods
tore up great trees by the roots, and broke up the already broken
islands to hurl them downstream in the swirling muddy torrent
that continually threatened to swamp and submerge their fragile
little fleet of open boats. Yet they steered clear of all the heavy
trees and lumps of land, with drowning animals still clinging to
them, that were flung through the waves against them. The
raging rain swept away the vessels they put out to catch it, so
they had nothing to drink but the 'thick and troubled waters of
the river'. And every hour the river rose higher and 'overflowed
very fearfully'; so rapidly that 'those who were overshoes in the
water in the morning, found themselves over-shoulders in it
before the close of day'. 'The strange thunder of the waters' was
to haunt Ralegh all his life.

'Passions are likened best to floods and streams', he wrote; and
how well he knew it, who had watched a 'mighty river' rush
over the top of a mountain with such 'terrible noise and clamour
as if a thousand great bells were knocked against each other'.
He and his men saw, high up against the sky, huge waterfalls
leaping 'each as high over the other as a church tower', so that
they mistook the vast-splayed mist of spray 'at first for a smoke
rising over some great town'.

He was well nicknamed 'Sir Water', for the sound of it echoes
again and again in his poetry, and in the majestically rolling
rhythms of his greatest prose work.

Nothing more could now be done on the Orinoco but to try
to make their drenched and desperate way back to their two
ocean ships lying at anchor in Trinidad—'than which there was
never to us a more joyful sight'. But he was sad to say good-bye
to his Indian friends, and to 'leave Guiana to the Sun, whom
they worship'.

They implored him not to go. Who could help them now
against the cruel power of the Spaniards, who would surely
return when he had gone? But he reminded them they were now
his fellow-subjects, under the protection of the English Crown.
Of their own accord they had offered their land and people into
its safe keeping, and sworn allegiance for ever to him as representative of that Crown. They swore it again at his farewell; but
their vow of allegiance was to him personally, howsoever he
might explain it to them otherwise. They kept it, if not 'for ever',

for well over two centuries after he was dead; telling stories of him from one generation to another, still hoping and believing that he could not die; that he would come back and rescue them from their oppressors, and rule over them as their Cacique, their god, and their friend.

'Come back! Come back!' they cried, clinging to his hands and coat, and weeping; and he told them, truly, he was certain he would come back, as soon as next year he thought; and he counted the moons on his fingers to show them. Indeed it was his chief wish to come back and make Guiana a safe, prosperous and happy colony; to bring his wife and family there; and to develop the country, with himself in residence as its Governor.

But he was not to come back for over twenty years; and by then the case was altered.

* * *

All he could do about Guiana the next year was to send his representative, Laurence Keymis (who plainly preferred the job of explorer and gold-prospector to that of a Balliol don), to go out in his place in search of precious metals there, while he himself wrote his book about his own previous expedition. He had to do something, and quickly, to show that it had been worth while. 'The chase, not the quarry, makes the splendour of our days', was not the sort of argument to be advanced to either of his two Elizabeths; nor even to himself. It had been exhilarating to be an Elizabethan adventurer, to make friends with delightfully poetic old men ('savages' of greater courtesy than most courtiers) and with candid little naked girls 'without deceit', who rewarded his respectful kindness with innocent adoration. But it was not at all pleasant to come home to cold enquiries and incredulous reception of his answers.

'Where is the gold?' asked the Queen; and the Cecils, father and son, echoed her with murmurs about their investments, and what were the dividends?

We want results, they said. Nothing that did not glitter could be gold. A new Empire over a new continent—'a better Indies than the King of Spain's'—all this might lie ahead in the future, but what had he brought back in his pockets for the present? Some handfuls of dust that might, or might not, contain gold; a stone 'which I think is amethyst' (but an expert jeweller might not), and another, which 'if it be no diamond, yet is exceeding any diamond in beauty'.

What did they care about beauty? Ralegh had not produced solid value as a result of his enterprise; and nobody believed it could ever have that result. It was a short-sighted view, for both diamonds and gold were later found and mined very profitably in the regions he had begun to explore; and the petroleum, whose existence and use he had already half guessed at in the magical Pitch Lake of Trinidad, was to become one of the richest products in the world, and make vast fortunes. But that would not be for over two hundred years after his death, and long before then England had lost her chance of acquiring the richest of all regions for this new source of wealth. Ralegh of course had no glimmer of what that new source might ultimately bring; nor was wealth his chief interest in his new-discovered country, though he had got to make it seem so. What he longed to do, and there was only one way now to do it, was to convince his Queen, and all England, of the paradise they would throw away if they missed the opportunity that he had fought and struggled for, at great danger to his life, in opening up Guiana. There was only one thing that he could do, and that was to write a book about it, and tell them all. So he did.

'No country', he declared, 'yieldeth more pleasure to the Inhabitants . . . for common delights of hunting, hawking, fishing, fowling, than Guiana.' Also it was 'healthy'. True, his wife insisted that it had set up new rheumatic agues in him, but how expect otherwise after lying in burning sun, or wet through, at forty-three, without change of clothes, crowded with a hundred other men 'upon hard boards . . . so that never any prison in England could be more unsavoury and loathsome'? But that desperate voyage, in flood-tide, was no fair test of daily life in the country itself; and of its opportunities for happy living, for sport and commerce, for products of dyes and cotton and silk, or precious balsam-gums and spices such as pepper and ginger, to say nothing of sugar; and of new medicines that he had proved near-miraculous. And to crown all, 'Guiana is a country that hath yet her maidenhood . . . never entered by any army of strength, nor possessed by any Christian Prince'—and moreover 'so defensible' against any.

All this he handed on a plate to his Queen, with a magnificent peroration, trusting that 'the Lord of Lords will put it into her heart, which is Lady of Ladies, to possess it'. There is also a postscript which consigns his arguments 'to the consideration and judgment of the Indifferent Reader. W.R.'—a characteristic flourish as if to show his own indifference.

The readers, any that counted, remained indifferent; scoffed at his book as a pack of lies ('those yarns about oysters growing on trees!') or as a boy's adventure story—which it was, and of the best. It was reprinted and translated many times; but had its chief effect in the enlargement of men's minds, and the inspiration in them of curiosity and magnanimity, and of poetry. To this day we quote the passage made famous through his pleasure in watching the forest deer, as yet so unsuspicious of the unknown wild beast, man, that 'still as we rowed, the deer came down feeding by the water side, as if they had been used to a keeper's call'. The sudden tenderness in the description is due to the touch of homesickness that has crept in unawares, another echo from his 'Cynthia':

'To seek new worlds, for gold, for praise, for glory,
To try desire, to try love severed far.
When I was gone, she sent her memory,
More strong than were ten thousand ships of war.'

The emotion is intense though expressed, as so often then, in allegory, but none the less sincere. 'Cynthia' is never defined literally; she can be his Queen, or his wife, or 'she that dwells ten leagues beyond man's life', the spirit of beauty and desire that inspires his thoughts—'Yet will she be a woman for a fashion', and can send her memory to haunt his solitude.

*　　　*　　　*

His words, whether in prose or poetry, are unlikely to have touched the heart of his 'Lady of Ladies'. That heart was shrinking, withering under a new, cold touch. To her, his book was a prospectus, as indeed he so intended it. But she was fast growing indifferent to such unchancy chances. She was growing old, suddenly, and disillusioned; especially now by Essex, who had got more maids of honour into trouble, and was only prevented from marrying one because he had already done so.

It was with Essex as his comrade in arms that Ralegh had

now to go into action, in his most famous and triumphant exploit
at sea.

But Guiana was 'the dream and the business' that gave the
raison d'être to his life, and would crowd it, glorify it and ruin it.
Its adventure had lit his imagination since childhood; was the
project for which he had lived more than any other; and gave
him the essential drama that he needed to make him believe in
himself and his purpose. And he kept the dream until the end.

CHAPTER THIRTEEN

'*To be revenged for the* Revenge'

RALEGH

BUT the onslaught on Cadiz was his greatest victory. It put him without question at the head of all the great Elizabethan sea-commanders that still survived. He had urged the attack ever since 1587, when a major blow at the navies congregated at Cadiz, 'the maritime base of Spain', could so easily have prevented the long-threatened attack of the Armada in the following year. So he had stated, forcibly, and in concert with the long-tried advice of old Sir John Hawkins. What an easy and early victory could then have been won over Spain, so Ralegh wrote years later, 'if the Queen would have hearkened to reason'. But she had not done so. And now Hawkins was dead; so was Martin Frobisher, her latest white hope for the Navy, of the wounds he had got when storming the naval base on Brest water, set up by the Spaniards in renewed threat against England. Then news came that Drake had died at sea after his final failure to take Panama, 'the bottle-neck of Peru's treasure', and thus destroy the Empire of Spain and force her to make peace. For over twenty years his heart had been set on achieving this, and now it was broken. From that moment, wrote one of his officers, 'he never carried mirth nor joy in his face'.

So it was Ralegh and Essex, in spite of their notorious hostility, who were now called upon by the Government to enter into partnership; to advise and act together, for the protection of England's coasts against the fast recovering power of Spain. The Queen and her ministers had grown old and unenterprising, they 'did all things by halves', wrote Ralegh, 'and by petty invasions taught the Spaniard how to defend himself . . . which, till our attempts taught him, was hardly known to himself'. She was forced to hearken to reason at last, but only by the alarming roar of the new threat from Ireland, a roar very different from the banshee yells of savage bog-troopers who had been wont to rush out of the woods with flaming branches to fire a fort or town, and vanish again into the night.

This new threat to England was a highly 'civilized' campaign, a formal and pious alliance between Philip of Spain and the Great Earl of Tyrone, the Chief of the O'Neills in the North and the last of the Gaels to hold sovereign power. A magnificently cultivated and astute statesman, of great charm, his portrait in old age, long later in Rome, might easily be mistaken for the exquisitely moulded and reflective face of an Apostle; or else a philosopher of singularly gentle resignation. In less than five years he was, both as foe and friend, to bring Essex to his disgrace and death—unimaginable in this coming campaign, which would give a generous glory, even to the extinction of their private enmities, to both Essex and Ralegh. True, their partisans continued to make the most of those enmities. However earnestly and candidly the two great rivals wished to combine, there were a thousand jackals who wished to tear them apart by however mean a means.

Ralegh as Rear-Admiral had the bulk of the work in collecting the crews, and achieved it; though this was in the spring of the year 1596, following his expedition to Guiana, when he was fully occupied, one might have thought, with his book about it. In spite of his fame as a popular sea-captain, it was an exhausting and squalid job to get his crews together; as indeed it had been even during the imminent danger of invasion in '88. And this lack of patriotism in England's heroic age took a more positive form in the secret sales by the armament racketeers; for the Spanish galleons were largely armed with English weapons, sold and smuggled over to the enemy.

Ralegh wrote of the undignified ardours of his recruiting job in the amused, easy fashion that gives his letters so modern a tang, telling Robert Cecil 'as fast as we press men one day, they come away another, and say they will not serve'. He gives a humorous picture of himself riding at all the speed he could make through heavy rain and deep mud, 'hunting after runaway mariners and dragging in the mire from alehouse to alehouse'; and how he could get no paper in these country villages to write a report to the Generals, and could not now be doing so to Cecil 'but that the poursevant had this piece'—an intimate touch that clearly shows the great Lord Warden and 'Rear Admiral of her Majesty's

Spanish Fleet' sitting on a rough-hewn bench in a village tavern, his long riding-boots stretched out before him, mud-splashed to the thighs, while he scribbled on the only scrap of paper that he could get hold of. His difficulties gave a golden opportunity for Essex's sycophants, led chiefly by the two Bacon brothers, Francis and Anthony, to encourage complaints to him of Ralegh's 'slackness and stay by the way', due, so the Bacons hinted, not merely to sloth and negligence, but to pregnant design'—of what they did not say.

The pregnancy proved stillborn when Ralegh joined the other commanders at Plymouth with a bigger muster than was expected; and politely refused to be drawn into any dispute with Essex or anyone else. The coming campaign was far too important, as all could see by the extra amount of gold and silver lace on the officers, the richest ever worn on shipboard; also by the severity to deserters, for Essex had two of them hanged 'on a very fair pleasant green called the Ho'. After that encouragement to duty, the fleet set sail on June 1st, a Dutch squadron of twenty-four ships being added to the ninety-six English vessels of all sorts and sizes, divided into four squadrons, one of them under Ralegh.

In the first dawn light of June 20th, the few Spanish citizens of Cadiz who were then awake saw the dread spectacle of an enormous enemy fleet that had glided like a ghostly apparition upon them out of the northern seas, and now lay at anchor only a league away. 'The most beautiful armada that ever was seen!' declared the President of Cadiz, a true artist to show such aesthetic appreciation of the doom approaching his city. He had no idea if the armada were French, English or Dutch, or all three. He immediately sent for Medina Sidonia, who was ill at the time, but sat up writing demands for infantry and cavalry to be sent to defend the town, and had to leave the orange groves he had planted as Governor of Andalusia, and hurry up to Cadiz, along with other Spanish sea-captains from Seville.

Ralegh had had to lead his squadron along the coast to prevent any leakage of enemy ships either out of or into Cadiz harbour. He returned in a stormy sea to find a line of Spanish galleons of considerable strength drawn up at the entrance to the harbour, all ready to defend the town. He found far worse than that: English troops already trying to land, to storm the city, before any attack had been made on the galleons; and, worse again, in 'a great sea rolling in from the Outer Ocean', so that the English boats were capsizing on all sides in the rough water on the rocky coast, and many soldiers had already drowned. The long-boat of Sir Francis Vere's *Rainbow* (of the 'Fighting Veres') had been sunk, and the fifteen men in it lost in the waves, and all to no purpose.

In Ralegh's absence there had been a Council of War, and there it had been decided that as ships were more expensive than men it was better to land the troops (or drown them), so as to attack the enemy's city, before fighting off the fleet that defended it.

There was only one thing to be done, and on the instant. Ralegh swung himself into a cock-boat, disregarding all the protests against the risk of a small boat in a big sea, and had himself rowed to Essex's ship, the *Repulse*. Essex was hanging over the bulwarks, amazed to see this madman who shouted for a rope to be flung to him, and went on shouting as he climbed up it on to the deck, demanding to know what the Vice-Admiral Lord Thomas Howard was doing by landing their men on 'an iron coast', in a heavy sea and a high wind—when both these last were a godsend to the English fleet, to help them bear down in force upon the galleons lying packed together like herrings in the harbour, all handy and convenient for slaughter.

He took it for granted that Essex would agree, and had had nothing to do with so foolish a decision. Essex was in joint supreme command with Howard, but as Chief Commander of the land armaments, as Howard was of the sea. Sure enough, Ralegh tells us, 'the Earl excused himself and laid it to the Lord Admiral'. And what was better, 'all the commanders and gentlemen present besought me to dissuade the attempt . . . since the most part could not but perish in the sea . . . and if any arrived on shore, yet were they sure to have their boats cast on their heads; and that twenty men in so desperate a descent would have defeated them all. The Earl hereupon prayed me to persuade my Lord Admiral.'

So with Essex's backing to support him, Ralegh dropped over the ship's side again to be rowed to the *Ark Royal*, Howard's flagship, while Essex was left to stride up and down in an agony of impatience on the poop; and found to his surprise that it would after all be unfortunate if Ralegh got drowned, just when he had shown that he alone of the commanders knew how to bring victory to this great enterprise, instead of a senseless slaughter. Though Ralegh would probably tell the Lord Admiral all too plainly what a fool he had been (he had no prerogative to question the decisions of the Supreme Command) and perhaps get put under arrest for flagrant insubordination.

But Ralegh found the Lord Admiral badly flustered by the disasters his orders had already caused, and had no difficulty in getting him to revoke them. The landings were countermanded at once, and Ralegh was given a new order telling him immediately to engage the Spanish fleet in action; every one of whose ships had been left hitherto 'as idle as a painted ship, Upon a painted ocean'.

There was not a minute to be lost, for evening was drawing on, and darkness would have brought still further destruction, thanks to Howard's besotted refusal 'to enter with the fleet, till the town were first possessed . . . my Lord Admiral being careful of Her Majesty's ships', is Ralegh's ironic explanation. Within an hour Essex's nervous pacings up and down his deck were cut short by a shout from the watchman on the bows, and then from the ship's officers. Ralegh's little boat was seen bobbing up and down on its return journey; the tide was with it, half swamping it. He had no time to pay a second call on Essex, who had rushed to his ship's rails, shouting against the noise of wind and waves for one word of news. He got it, and in one word.

'*Entramos!*' shouted Ralegh in Spanish, as he steered past Essex for his own squadron, as drenched as a drowned rat, and brandishing his sea-draggled hat to show that he had prevailed; that the suicidal 'landing' of the troops had been called off, and the English ships would now enter the harbour. Essex answered with a cheer, cut a dance step upon the deck before all his officers, waved his jewelled cap, and flung it into the sea. At last, with the high waves rolling between them, the two men were at one.

The surviving troops and small boats, scattered, half foundered, were fetched back to their ships as best they could be. A day had been wasted, and some boats and a lot of lives; but that was the natural waste of war, so they had learned to say. Another council of war was held that evening in the swaying light of the ships'

lanterns; and a new line of attack decided upon, which was left
entirely to Ralegh; though it was not till ten o'clock that night
that he won permission to write out his order of attack for the
benefit of his supreme commanders. Not surprisingly, in view of
the disastrous start of the campaign, they proved accommodat-
ing, and had already followed his instructions to move the
English fleet up to the mouth of the harbour, to be ready to
attack at dawn. They even ceded to him the honour of leading
his own plan of attack himself, in his own ship—or so they said.
Lord Thomas Howard seemed not so sure; nor was Ralegh,
under the swaying shadows that the ships' lanterns cast up and
down on Lord Thomas' genial grin and enormous nose. He was
not going to be caught napping by any Howard.

'With the first peep of day therefore, I weighed anchor,' so he
wrote later, and set off at head of his squadron into the gaping
mouths of the seventeen Spanish galleons 'ranged under the wall
of Cadiz on which the sea beateth'. They stood at anchor, ready
'to flank our entrance', as Ralegh swung down upon them in the
forefront of the English fleet.

He led the van in his own *Warspite*, a name famous in naval
history down to our own day. The last ship to bear it was so
battered by bombs and mines that she earned Ralegh's own
reputation of being 'capricious . . . wilful ever afterward . . .
dogged and resilient'. Ralegh's, the original *Warspite*, was in
action at the first height of her country's sea-power; and her
captain, though only a secondary commander, realized that this
battle could prove 'the one home-thrust of the Elizabethan sea-
struggle'.[1] It was he who thrust home at the head of it, followed
by six other ships of fair name, the *Mary Rose* and *Lion*, the
Rainbow and *Nonpareil*, the *Dreadnought* and *Swiftsure*; thrust
straight into the narrow channel that entered the harbour of
Cadiz, under the very walls of the town and the shore batteries
of its forts. These opened fire on him; and the seventeen galleons
moved majestically against him behind their four Apostolic
leaders, the *St Philip*, *St Matthew*, *St Thomas*, *St Andrew*, drawn up
in line ahead at the narrowest point of the channel, and supported by a vast host of frigates, argosies 'very strong in artillery',
and flagships of the Admiral, Vice-Admiral and Rear-Admiral of
Nueva Espagna, as well as forty other great ships bound for

[1] Edward Thompson, *Sir Walter Ralegh*, p. 109.

Mexico. 'There was also a fort called the *Philip* which beat and commanded the harbour. There were also ordnance which lay all alongst the curtain upon the wall towards the sea. There were also divers other pieces of culverin, which also scoured the channel,' so Ralegh tells as if with an exultant whoop at totting up all these 'also's' ranged against him.

To his enemies' amazement, as he sailed into their massed fire, his only answer was 'to each piece of fire, a blare with a trumpet . . . disdaining to shoot one piece at any one or all of those esteemed dreadful monsters'. But then the galleys, 'mere wasps', which had fired on him from the shelter of the shore batteries, began to creep past him, hugging the shore as best they could for the protection of the galleons in the straits, and so offering him a broadside target. 'I bestowed a benediction amongst them', was his cheerful comment. He pulled up alongside 'the *St Philip*, the great and famous Admiral of Spain', that had brought his cousin Sir Richard Grenville to his death, for that was 'the mark I shot at . . . resolved to be revenged for the *Revenge*, or to second her with mine own life'. The general fleet action began with the furious crash of the galleons' superior fire-power; and Essex, to quote Ralegh's handsome tribute to him, 'being impatient to abide far off, hearing so great thunder of ordnance, thrust up through the fleet', and came on board the *Swiftsure*, close behind Ralegh. They had a fifteen minute consultation in Ralegh's skiff, and Essex urged on him the madness of his trying to attack the huge numbers on the *St Philip* until the fly-boats came up to help him board her. But the fly-boats had not come up, and might never succeed in doing so, choked as they were in the press of shipping in the channel.

For three hours Ralegh waited for them, battered by the enemy's broadsides, while his ships could only use their bow pieces, being in line abreast; and all the time 'the volleys of cannon and culverin came as thick as if it had been a skirmish of musketeers'. If he hung on any longer he would have no choice but 'to burn or sink' the *Warspite*. His only hope of saving her was to risk thrusting her near enough to the great galleon to board her towering decks, without the aid of any fly-boats. The Queen's fury if her ship were sunk or damaged would be worse than over any casualties, but he must take his chance of that. Essex had to agree with him. The shared danger and excitement had made sudden friends of them, and Essex swore 'he would second me in person, upon his honour'.

The Lord Admiral had a better idea—to be first, not second. During the quarter-hour of Ralegh's consultation with Essex, Howard tried to thrust his ship ahead of Ralegh's, to get the honour of first place against the galleons; and 'secretly fastened a rope on my ship's side towards him, to draw himself up equally with me, but . . . I caused it to be cut off, and so he fell back into his place', where, says Ralegh with wicked glee, he was in no danger. This struggle as of gallant schoolboys to be first in the fight was eagerly followed by Essex and Sir Francis Vere, till Ralegh made sure of his place in the vanguard by swinging his ship 'athwart the channel so long as I was sure none should outstart me again'; and then 'laid out a warp by the side of the *Philip* to shake hands with her'.

That mocking note of his was taken up by the pipers, who struck up a shrill, inhuman music, more cruel by far than the war-horse trumpeting of the clarions at the start of the battle. They teased and tweedled and wheedled a reckless devilry into the English sailors who were being piped over their ship's side, and on board the enemy's. Like rats the *St Philip*'s crew began to bolt from her on every side. They had run her aground, and fire had broken out. At the peal of a trumpet, the English cut the anchor ropes of all the four great Apostolic galleons; they began to heel over on the mudbank, and from the *St Philip* there came 'tumbling into the sea heaps of soldiers, so thick as if coals had been poured out of a sack . . . some drowned and some sticking in the mud. . . . The spectacle was very lamentable, for many drowned themselves; many, half burnt, leapt into the water; very many hanging by the ropes' ends by the ships sides, under the water even to the lips; many swimming with grievous wounds, stricken under water and put out of their pain; and withal so huge a fire and such tearing of ordnance in the great *Philip* and the rest, when the fire came to them as, if any man had a desire to see Hell itself, it was there most lively figured. Ourselves spared the lives of all, after the victory; but the Flemings, who did little or nothing in the fight, used merciless slaughter, till they were by myself, and afterward by my Lord Admiral, beaten off.'

Sir Richard Grenville's *Revenge* was thus revenged, as Ralegh had sworn; but his own account shows little enjoyment in it.

Horror and pity seem his strongest feelings at the 'very lamentable spectacle'; and it was his long-boats from the *Warspite* that
were the first to be rowed through the flames and blinding black
smoke from the kegs of powder exploding on the ruined galleons,
to try and rescue such Spaniards as were yet alive.

One of Essex's young gentleman volunteers, later to become
Dean of St Paul's, has also left a description of the scene, in verse,
but with less feeling, either poetic or humane, than Ralegh's
prose. His brisk summary—

'So all were lost which in the ship were found;
They in the sea being burnt, they in the burnt ship drowned',

is not a fair sample of John Donne's poetry.

'Hell was there most lively figured', to the victors as well as the
vanquished. Many English fainted, choked by the sulphurous
fumes of broiling smoke; many were killed or wounded by the
sharpshooters who kept up their hidden fire from such galleons
as were still unsunk. One of them took a chance shot at the
English leader and wounded him in the leg; the bullet had struck
up from the deck and interlaced the wound with splinters of
wood, so that Ralegh fell in agony and would have rolled into
the sea if his men had not caught hold of him in time.

He opened his eyes to see the Spanish Admiral before him,
offering his surrender; received it with all courtesy, and fainted
dead away.

'The one home-thrust of the Elizabethan sea-struggle' was
made—and won. And Ralegh, who more than any other had
won it, was lamed at the height of his victory, and would limp
to the end of his life.

CHAPTER FOURTEEN

'Those whom the gods wish to destroy, they first make mad'

JAMES DUPONT

FROM the moment of Ralegh's sea-victory, it was time for the land forces to take over, to storm and sack the already defeated town. Essex, as their official head, became the official hero of the whole campaign. It was Essex who sacked Cadiz, while Ralegh lay dangerously wounded in his cabin; Essex who secured huge ransoms from important prisoners, while Ralegh got no loot, except a Spanish Bishop's library, with which he helped to found the new Bodleian at the University of Oxford. Essex soon followed up Ralegh's gift with the beautiful 'Essex Cup', which he presented to the University of Cambridge.

At Cadiz it was Essex who got all the limelight, a reward he appreciated more than any other. There he was at the top, able to shower benefits on all and sundry—sixty-six knighthoods straight away, so that the title of a 'Knight of Cadiz' became a laughing-stock and a rude comic theme-song of the soldiers; for only five new knights had been created after the Armada. Cadiz marked in fact the moment from which Essex began to wobble unpredictably towards a passion for popularity and power that was dangerously lacking in balance. His jealousy of Ralegh once led him so far as to find out what Ralegh would be wearing in a certain tournament, and to dress all his own followers exactly the same, so as to divert attention from his rival—a singularly childish trick. He was still only just over thirty, and now as much the spoilt darling of the people as he had long been of the Queen. Women were infatuated with him, and the poets praised him as a national hero; Shakespeare, who was in the service of Essex's friend, the Earl of Southampton, went so far as to suggest comparisons between him and Henry V; and Spenser addressed him as

'Great England's glory,' . . .
'Fair branch of Honour, flower of Chivalry,' . . .
'Joy have thou of thy famous victory!' . . .

117

Joy he had, at first, but it made him lose his head. Even his most admiring friends had begun to notice this; for Anthony Standen, who had followed him faithfully to Cadiz, discounted the glory that he won there, in comparison with the true victor. He went out of his way to write as much to old William Cecil:

'Sir Walter Ralegh did, in my judgment, no man better, and his artillery had most effect. I never knew the gentleman until this time, and I am sorry for it, for there are in him excellent things besides his valour; and the observation' (i.e. consideration?) 'he hath in this voyage used with my Lord of Essex hath made me love him.' There is a world of understatement there regarding my Lord of Essex, from one who had long been his passionate partisan.

It was in the next joint campaign of his with Ralegh, the following year, 1597, that Essex showed his mental instability. He was this time Commander-in-Chief of both sea and land forces, and mismanaged the start of the expedition so that its first objective on the north coast of Spain had to be abandoned. It was then agreed to sail for the second, which was to capture the Spanish treasure ships on their return journey off the Azores. Sir Philip Magnus tells us simply that 'Essex's handling of the expedition seemed at that point to collapse. He hesitated, and issued no clear orders. . . . No final decision was taken.'

Ralegh joined him off Flores and dined on his flagship 'with great cordiality'. Whatever hopes he had of pulling Essex's wits together by friendly encouragement, and no doubt the now necessary flattery, were shattered by the discovery next day that Essex had suddenly taken it into his head to sail away with the remainder of the fleet, without any word to Ralegh of either warning or explanation—only an order that he left behind him telling Ralegh to follow him to the island of Fayal, and to join him there in an attack on the island's capital of Horta.

Ralegh obediently waited three days off Fayal with his squadron, but there was still no sign of Essex; only a disturbing view of the enemy hastily fortifying their port and entrenching it against the impending English attack. To delay any longer was plain madness, and might well lay him open to the charge of cowardice in hovering outside the port day after day as though he dare not assault it. Many officers indeed were afraid of his doing so; but their fear was of Essex's jealousy. 'I hearkened to them somewhat longer than was requisite', Ralegh explains, since 'they desired me to reserve the title of such an exploit for a greater person'.

But there comes a limit to such modest self-restraint when it goes on playing into the enemy's hands; he finally stormed the port and the capital of Horta, but told all his doubtful critics to stay behind, and 'took with me none but men assured'.

It was the only successful and decisive action of the whole campaign, and not as easy as Ralegh chose to make out, when asserting that 'it is more difficult to defend a coast than to invade it'. But his clothes were riddled with bullet holes after he had led the storming party himself, in spite of the limp that had hampered his leg since Cadiz.

The very next morning Essex's sails were sighted, and all those who had refrained from their share of the fighting, with Ralegh's generous permission, now hastened to tell Essex how nobly they had behaved in their regard for his honour; and how meanly Ralegh had acted, whose sole object had been to steal from Essex the glory of the attack.

Essex's injured vanity flared into megalomania. He summoned Ralegh to his flagship, accused him as 'a subordinate officer' of disobeying orders, declared he would have him court-martialled, and threatened to hang him. Ralegh pointed out that he was not a subordinate, but a principal commander, and had therefore to give orders in Essex's absence. Essex had told him it was his intention—or order—that they should attack Fayal; Essex had failed to turn up, and there was no way to find out what had happened to him. (Sunk at sea? Captured by the Spaniards? There were plenty of possibilities); and therefore Ralegh had carried out his order, after waiting for him long enough to endanger its success.

The easy-going Lord Thomas Howard managed at last to stop the quarrel by promising Ralegh that he would get Essex to drop his charges against him, if only Ralegh could bring himself to apologize. He admitted that there was nothing for Ralegh to apologize for, but declared that it was the only way to appease Essex's sense of injury. Ralegh's pride was certainly amenable to sense, for he gave the required apology without protest at its absurdity. On the two following evenings he dined with Essex and completely won him over to what seemed a real and warm friendship, Essex plainly expressing his delight in the other's company. But Ralegh had had his warning, and knew from then on that Essex, for all his charm and courtesy when he chose, held the seeds of insanity in his feverishly capricious mind.

These began to sprout in more and more reckless quarrels with the Queen. She was furious at the way he had bungled the voyage, of which he had insisted on being the Commander-in-Chief. He flung away from her to sulk in retirement; then two years later made a bid for power by going to Ireland as Lord Deputy to suppress the rebellion; but again showed hesitation and uncertainty in dealing with the rebels.

Then it was that the Great Earl of Tyrone proved his undoing. Essex, instead of fighting, negotiated with him (against orders from home) and made friends with him. The Queen's letters grew angrier and angrier. Essex had begun to intrigue with the Scots King James as her probable successor, and now encouraged him to make a bid for the English throne even before Elizabeth's death: a bid which Essex promised to support with all his power.

Suddenly he took fright. He did not know who might be working against him at home. Ralegh was back again in his old influential post as Captain of the Queen's Guard, and once more in her favour; and Robert Cecil was her new Secretary of State. Essex was certain they were both plotting against him. He wrote to the Queen, passionately, imploringly, 'from a mind delighting in sorrow'. He had to see her, he said; but she said 'No', and ordered him to stay in Ireland at his post.

In flat defiance of her command, he came headlong back to London. If he had lost the favour of an old cantankerous woman, he still had that of the crowd, and a strong backing of powerful friends. He would tell them and the Queen and everyone that Cecil and Ralegh were conspiring against his life, and that he had come back to defend it.

But in London he was arrested.

*   *   *

Essex was sound at least upon his backing by the crowd. The Queen arranged for his trial, but was torn in two; and not only by her private and peculiar sentiments towards this extraordinary relic of the old nobility, who combined the qualities of a Grand Young Man with those of a juvenile delinquent. She was shrewd enough to recognize his flattery to her for what it was worth, that of a young man on the make, to an old woman on the wane. She had no romantic ideals of knightly chivalry to lose in him, for she had lost them long ago. What she hated, and feared to lose, was her own popularity with her people. She dared not risk it in conflict with him at his trial. So she cancelled the trial, and set him free.

Before she did so, Robert Cecil, who wanted desperately to see Essex safely executed but dared not ask for it, consulted cautiously with Ralegh as to his opinion. Ralegh, with characteristic incaution, replied quite openly. And it is to be noted that his answer is carefully preserved among the Cecil archives; while there is no record of Cecil's questions, slid probably out of the corner of his mouth, and never put down in writing. That he *did* ask Ralegh's opinion is suggested by Ralegh's opening sentence, 'I am not wise enough to give you advice'. But he points out with true wisdom (though not in writing it to Cecil) that it was useless for Cecil to try to buy off Essex's malice; it 'will not evaporate by any of your mild courses, for he will ascribe the alteration to Her Majesty's pusillanimity, and not to your good nature'. Nothing could have been truer, as Ralegh had learned from bitter experience. Essex had quarrelled with everyone he could, but especially with those who had tried the hardest to yield to him what he wanted of them. All he really wanted was power; and the more he had of that, the more of an irrational and all but criminal lunatic he became—as Ralegh had learned three years ago at Fayal when he had had to apologize for guilt of which he was guiltless; and did so, cheerfully, because he had realized he was dealing with an irresponsible being.

But you cannot have an irresponsible being in a position of responsibility; and therefore, so he wrote in his downright, common-sense fashion, 'the less you make him, the less he shall be able to harm you and yours. And if Her Majesty's favour fail him, he will again decline to a common person.' It was not an 'absurd suggestion', for Essex had been one of the poorest of the nobles, and of no position or consequence, despite his rank, until Elizabeth's favour gave them to him.

This has been called 'an atrocious letter' of Ralegh's—'ruthless'—'Machiavellian'—and probably 'a plea for Essex's execution'. If it were, Ralegh was justified in making it; for there is no doubt that by this time Essex had become what Ralegh calls him, the 'canker' of the Queen's life and realm. But the letter is a plea, *not* for Essex's death, but for his deprival of office, and probably his banishment from Court. Anyone who had experience of Essex's pathological mental defects would have been a lunatic himself if he had advised putting him back into power.

*   *   *

Cecil, having got Ralegh to commit his opinions to paper, without committing himself did nothing, but left Essex to work his own ruin; which he soon did. He persuaded his friend and sister's lover, Charles Blount, now Lord Mountjoy and his successor in Ireland, to offer his army to King James of Scotland to bring him down south, and take the Crown by armed force from the Queen of England. In the meantime Essex worked to make the Londoners rise against the Queen and the Court. His friend the Earl of Southampton ordered his company of actors under William Shakespeare to perform their manager's play of 'Richard II' at the Globe Theatre; to show, so all thought, that Essex could as successfully copy Henry Bolingbroke in forcing his Sovereign to abdicate the throne.

Essex himself, more directly, openly declared that 'the fox' Ralegh was planning to assassinate him. When summoned before the Privy Council, Essex said he was too ill to come; as indeed he often was in crises, though none could say of what sickness: hysteria would seem to be the answer.

One of his most important fellow-conspirators was Ralegh's cousin, Sir Ferdinando Gorges, who came, with two others to protect him, to meet Ralegh, who came alone. They talked in a boat on the Thames, off Essex House. Ralegh had hoped to extricate his kinsman from the conspiracy, but Sir Ferdinando told him with glee that at least two thousand gentlemen were 'up' that day in London to fight for the Earl of Essex. One of them, Sir Christopher Blount, Essex's young stepfather, gave point to this statement by firing four shots at Ralegh from the river bank, but missed him. Ralegh coolly told Sir Ferdinando that there was a warrant out for his arrest, and returned to Whitehall.

Essex rode out at the head of his gentlemen through London, crying to the citizens that Ralegh had laid an ambush of muskets for him on the river; and calling on them to rise and protect himself and the Queen from such villains. They gaped in silence without any response, and his face grew 'ghast', the sweat pouring down it, and even his speech failed him; he could only shout incoherently, 'Say! Say! Sa! Sa!' as though he were mad, and so indeed he was for the moment.

The train-bands marched out against him; the heralds proclaimed him a traitor; Lud Gate was clanged to and locked against his retreat—but there was nowhere to retreat to, for Ralegh and Lord Thomas Howard and all the great captains then in London were surrounding Essex House with troops.

The bubble rebellion had been pricked in a few hours. Essex surrendered; and collapsed even more horribly. He accused everybody else of leading him into it; even his mother, and her young husband, Christopher Blount, who had been his most devoted friend; his adoring sister, and her faithful lover, Charles Blount, Lord Mountjoy. When he found he could not buy his life even with the sacrifice of those who had so eagerly loved and worked for him, he accused himself; and in agonized penitence admitted he was 'justly spewed out of the realm'. Before he made that 'good end', and during his orgy of incriminating those nearest and dearest to him, Lord Thomas Howard wrote to Mountjoy in incredulous disgust at 'this weakness and this unnaturalness' of Essex in exposing to everyone his sister's liaison with his friend.

Ralegh is supposed to have said in scorn of Essex's frantic bleatings that 'the great Boy was dying like a Calf'. The thrust, however cruel, strikes home at the root of the problem of dealing with Essex; that even now, in his middle-thirties (which meant middle-age to the Elizabethans), he was still an adolescent.

The all but incoherent fury of the 'Great Sir Edward Coke', the Attorney-General, all but muffed the prosecution, plain as it should have been, of the trial. It was Francis Bacon, whom Essex had done his best to befriend, at cost of the Queen's displeasure, who brought the charges neatly and firmly back to the point, and to the death sentence; and so struck the final blow at his 'friend'.

He was to do the same, seventeen years later, to another of his friends, Essex's greatest rival.

There were six executions, and Ralegh as Captain of the Guard had officially to attend them. Christopher Blount asked if he were there, and as he came up to him exclaimed, 'Sir Walter

Ralegh, I thank God that you are present! I had an infinite desire to speak with you'; and then begged his forgiveness, not only for trying to kill him when on the river, but for all their injurious slanders, that Ralegh had been trying to murder Essex. Blount now admitted these were purely lies, 'cast out, to colour other matters'.

They would indeed 'colour' Ralegh's reputation; darken and damage it; even to the future danger of his life.

Ralegh's answer was, 'I most willingly forgive you, and I beseech God to forgive you and to give you His divine comfort.'

When Essex came to die, Ralegh withdrew from his post on the scaffold, thinking that his defeated rival wished it. He went up into the Armoury in the Tower, where he stood alone at the window; and found that he was weeping.

He heard afterwards that just at the end Essex had asked for him, and wished to be reconciled with him; but by then Ralegh had left the scaffold, and it was too late.

Ralegh regretted that lost chance to the last hour of his life; and said so in that hour; and has been derided for saying it.

CHAPTER FIFTEEN

'Who Goes Home?'

B Y February 1601, Ralegh's chief rival had fallen, and he himself stood again at the top of the world. But it was not the same world. Once again he was first favourite with the Queen. But it was not the same Queen.

He was back in his old post as Captain of her Guard. She had made him Governor of Jersey, an honourable appointment with plenty of work attached, if one cared to do it, and Ralegh did; but docked of most of its profits. She gave him diplomatic missions and entrusted all foreign magnificos and great personages to his care. He was by far the most distinguished figure at Court, a fluent linguist ('except in English' said those who mocked at his persistent Devon brogue), and more tactful and gracious with foreigners than often with his own countrymen.

"I arrest you as my prisoner in the Queen's name!" he said, clapping the superb Duc de Sully, Henri IV's minister, on the back when he arrived in London, incognito as he thought; but so far from being annoyed, Sully embraced the genial Captain, 'telling him he should consider such an imprisonment the greatest honour'. The Queen followed it up with a deal of coquettish badinage with the two of them, demanding of Sully, "Do you break our fences thus, and pass on without coming to see me? I thought you bore me more affection."

Ralegh's diplomatic bonhomie entailed some exhausting work. He had to entertain single-handed the Duc de Biron, Constable of France, and his train of four hundred, while the Court was out of town. 'I sent to and fro and laboured like a mole,' he wrote in his friendly, intimate fashion to Robert Cecil very late one night, his only time to write; and of how he took them all to Westminster to see the Monuments, and to the Bear Garden, in the heat of a grilling September; and was even then, though it was now past midnight, dashing off at daybreak to order new clothes and harness in compliment to the French taste for 'all black and no bravery at all; so as I am providing me a plain black taffeta suit and black saddle, and leave all my other suits'. This extra-

vagant courtesy of going into mourning to match his guests was
an unlucky omen to them; and to Ralegh too, though he was not
to know it till after Biron, ten months later, was beheaded in
France. Biron's intrigues against his King had started before he
came to London, so he had some reason for the keen interest he
showed in one of the latest sights, that of Essex's head mouldering
on Temple Bar; and for his tactless questioning of the Queen on
the subject. On that occasion she certainly showed no coquetry.
Nor did she flinch from giving a straight answer.

Ralegh's friendship with Robert Cecil was also, as he thought,
at its height. Their shared danger from Essex had drawn them
close together in action and consultation. And Ralegh had given
proof of real affection in the warm sympathy of his letter after
Lady Cecil's death. 'You have lost a good and virtuous wife, and
myself an honourable friend and kinswoman.' With a characteristic simplicity, that is also sensitive, he showed his anxiety for
Cecil in his attempt to distract his thoughts from the bitterness of
brooding. 'The mind of man is that part of God which is in us,'
he wrote, and 'I believe that sorrows are dangerous companions.
. . . Sorrows draw not the dead to life, but the living to death.
Yours ever, beyond the power of words to utter.'

He was right to fear the effect of sorrow on that enigmatic
mind, probably the loneliest of the age. Cecil vowed never to
marry again, and kept this vow, either from lasting devotion, or
from his self-confessed fear of causing in women the same fastidi-
ous disillusion that shows in his own sad eyes and compressed
mouth. More than ever he lived only for politics, but with no
apparent pleasure in them. His son Will stayed more and more
at Sherborne, with the Raleghs taking full charge of his education
as well as his delicate health, and making him well and fat and
happy with country food and sport and bathing with his younger
and stronger playfellow, Wat. Cecil often stayed there too, and
when he could not do so, Ralegh wrote him careful and reassur-
ings reports of Will. 'His stomach, that was heretofore weak, is
altogether amended, and he doth now eat well and digest rightly.
I hope this air will agree exceedingly with him. He is also better
kept to his book.' And not even his wife could show more tenderness than did Ralegh in his reason for his letters: 'Because I know
that you can receive no pleasinger news from hence than to hear
of your beloved creature.'

Cecil's shrinking heart probably allowed him to receive only
the unpleasing news of how much he was in Ralegh's debt. 'He
worked with a cold fervour for the things of this world,' writes
C. V. Wedgwood, 'but he did not love the world at all . . . it
seemed to him no more than a painful, unrewarding purgatory.'

Ralegh loved the world, and his work in it. It was by no means
only ornamental. It was generally believed that he would be
given a peerage, but Cecil secretly prevented this. In the Commons Ralegh rose to his political zenith, and expected, as did
everyone else, that he would now at last be made a Privy Councillor. But this fell through as well as his predicted peerage: 'I am
left out till the Parliament, they tell me,' he remarked casually;
and then when Parliament met at the end of October 1601 he
was again baulked of the Council; though he still gave no sign of
chagrin. The chief obstacle was probably his opposition to the
Government's policy in home affairs.

Robert Cecil was Secretary of State as well as Leader of the
House of Commons, and made earnest efforts to regulate the
private lives of citizens into a neat and tidy pattern. His paternal
policy was one that has often since led to disaster. He tried to
enforce economy by law; it was 'most necessary' to insist on
coarser bread, and thinner beer, and fewer ale-houses, and
'opening hours' for them; they must be closed at least one day a
week (as in the modern 'Six Day Licence') and then, so he
argued, people would grow more food. Sheep-grazing was also
wrong, and must be replaced by crops of hemp and corn. A
religious warning was added to this in the Secretary's admonitory
fashion: 'The displeasure of Almighty God' had been shown by
many sheep dying on lands where corn used to be grown; though
as he added, 'in these last few wet years', their deaths might as
reasonably be blamed on the weather. Cecil's piety failed to
convince some of the M.P.s that men should be 'compelled by
penalties', as one complained, to grow the regulation amounts of
wheat and hemp, etc.

Francis Bacon's outstanding intellect came to Cecil's help with
heavily embroidered eloquence. This would be a 'law tending to
God's honour', for there was 'no conscience in destroying the
saviour of our life—bread, I mean', he added rather lamely,
probably because some M.P.s' faces looked blank. He wanted to
revive some old 'moth-eaten laws' (an unattractive term to

recommend them); quoted Ovid; added a puzzling aphorism which might have been uttered by Polonius; and assured the House that this bill was 'not drawn with a polite pen but with a polished heart, free from affection and affectation'.

That is more than can be said of his speeches. If they are any guide to his personality as an author, then he could not have written Shakespeare's plays.

By contrast with Bacon's incomprehensible rhetoric, Ralegh's forthright attack on the bill is startling. His pungent rejoinders made short work of the Government's high-flown theories. The practical knowledge he had gained as a child on his father's farm had shown him at first hand how absurd it was to try to legislate for land without experience of it. And there was something at stake more important to him even than the land—and that was individual liberty. 'I do not like this constraining of men to manure or use their ground at our wills; let every man use it to that which it is most fit for, and use his own discretion'. Let Parliament set corn and hemp at liberty, 'and leave every man free, which is the desire of a true Englishman'.

He won over the whole House. They shouted 'Away with the bill!' and persistently rejected it, though the Government pushed it twice to a division and defended it with a long, indignant speech from Sir James Croft, the Comptroller and Privy Councillor. There was nothing left but to pronounce its obsequy, which Bacon took it upon himself to do. He complained how unfitting it was 'for a House of gravity and wisdom, as this is, to bandy bills like balls'.

Ralegh, that 'liberal-minded independent',[1] also 'bandied like balls' the bills to enforce a right religion. There was one against the Sect of Brownists, whom he had agreed gravely were 'worthy to be rooted out of any commonwealth'. But just how, demanded the uncompromising realist, were they to set about rooting them out? ('I am sorry for it, I believe there be ten or twelve thousand of them in England') If by banishment, who was to pay their transport, and to where? And who was to maintain their wives and families? And did the House really know what exactly the Brownists were, even after a Committee had been locked in by Cecil to study a book of their Articles of Belief? They should be judged, Ralegh insisted, only by their acts, not by their opinions.

[1] J. E. Neale, *Elizabeth I and her Parliaments, 1584-1601*, p. 288.

Like his Queen, he would not admit to anyone the right to set up 'windows to peer into men's souls'.

His loathing of such spiritual tyranny helped to cut out the cruellest measures of repression. It was expressed again, in terms of sheer hard common sense, against the new bill to make church attendance compulsory, and the church-wardens act as informers to the J.P.s. With the brisk logic of mathematics, Ralegh pointed out that if there were only two offenders in each parish, their sum total, together with the church-wardens, would add four hundred and eighty persons to every quarter-sessions, and 'what great multitudes—what quarrelling and danger may happen, besides giving authority to a mean church-warden'.[1]

Church-wardens had already been mean enough to collect a shilling fine for non-attendance at church, and to keep fourpence of it; so Ralegh's supporters informed the House. And the J.P.s also came under fire as *'Basket Justices'*, who 'for half a dozen chickens would dispense with a dozen penal statutes'. Though one J.P. complained, 'I never had as much as a sheep's tail.'

Tolerance, or practical common sense, won the day, and the bill was lost, though only by one vote, and with violent controversy over that; for one of its supporters said the Speaker could vote, but Ralegh denied it, and so did the Speaker; and then another protested that an 'Aye' had been pulled back in his seat to prevent him from voting. Everyone was scandalized; and then Ralegh heedlessly caused the worst scandal of all. "Why! If it please you," said he coolly, "it is a small matter to pull a man down by the sleeve—I have done it myself oftentimes."

There was a shocked silence; then a storm of 'loud speech and stir', and a stern rebuke by the Senior Councillor, who wanted Ralegh called to the bar for his offence, and "I think he may be ashamed of it". Cecil scolded everyone impartially, more in sorrow than in anger, for the 'disorder' of this Parliament when "I had hoped . . . we should have ended modestly and at least with discretion". No man, he said, was worthy to be an M.P. "whose voice may be drawn forwards or backwards by the sleeve like a dog in a string".

Ralegh's lack of discretion was incorrigible. His off-hand candour was thought dangerously cynical; even when he showed

---

[1] For these figures, which *are as Ralegh gave them*, see Neale's *Elizabeth I and her Parliaments, 1584-1601*, pp. 404 and 405.

courtesy and consideration, his fellows were uneasily apt to suspect irony. It must have given satisfaction that it was put once
on record that 'Sir Walter Ralegh blushed'. This hit against 'the
gentleman with the bold face' was scored by a bishop, who
reviled Ralegh's Patent for cards as 'in the fore-rank of abuses'—
though in odd conjunction with another M.P.'s Monopoly of
salt—a rather greater necessity of life than cards.

In matters more vital it was Ralegh's voice more than any
that persistently championed the poor. He attacked with open
scorn the meanness of rich men who called it good policy to
squeeze the pockets of the poor and oppress their liberties. He
had defended the idle beggars wandering the country, to the
disgust of their rulers, who wished to have them shut up. As he
explained, they were mostly soldiers or sailors, broken in the
wars, who could get no other way to live. He had urged long
ago that the poor should not be taxed for the army subsidies,
but that the proportion assessed to them should be added to the
taxes of richer men. His sympathy even embraced the Queen's
need to keep up lavish appearances, for he realized how desperately pressed for money she was. In this Parliament of 1601
he spoke up in chivalrous praise of her example in contributing
all she could to the new defence forces against Spain; selling her
jewels and land, "sparing even out of her own purse and apparel
for our sakes". Yet many of her subjects, he reminded them
scathingly, owed her for heavy loans, still unpaid to her.

He championed the humble housewife as keenly as he did his
sovereign lady, and more dangerously for himself. Robert Cecil
spoke in patriotic praise of the news that "some poor people were
selling their pots and pans to pay the subsidy. . . . Neither pots
nor pans, nor dish nor spoon should be spared", he announced
unctuously. He was sure it would have an excellent effect on the
King of Spain when he heard "how willing we are to sell all in
defence of God's religion", etc. His listeners applauded this noble
sentiment. It has a hollow echo coming from a man who had
made a large fortune, as Master of the Wards, out of the sale of
their marriages—'a national scandal that cried aloud for reform'
—even louder than that of Monopolies; since the traffic in
human affections is baser than that in cards or tin.

His complacent eagerness to sacrifice the household goods of
poor folk was backed by Bacon. The poor *ought* to be taxed as

heavily as the rich: because, as he quoted in Latin, it was a right and 'sweet course to pull together in an equal yoke'.

This smug hypocrisy brought Ralegh to his feet. "Call you this an equal yoke, when a poor man pays as much as a rich? His estate may be no better than he is assessed at, while our estates are entered as £30 or £40 in the Queen's books—not the hundredth part of our wealth!" His outrageous frankness over this unfair advantage given to his own class, shocked his opponents. His final blow demolished them: "It is neither sweet nor equal."

Cecil at once gave in. Always anxious to placate Ralegh, he made the usual excuse that he had been "misinterpreted by the gentleman on my left"; hastened to withdraw the pots and pans, and did not really think anyone would have to sell them. Nor did anyone else think it, and so they all called out, thus emphasizing how false his special pleading had been. The acutely sensitive 'Monsieur de Bossu', as the French called the hunchback Secretary, was quick to see his mistake. But Ralegh, while exposing it so unmercifully before them all, was, as usual, hot only on his argument, and never saw the flinching little form of his friend.

Cecil went out of his way to profess Ralegh his friend. It was a truer description to call him 'the gentleman on my left', not because Ralegh so often took what might now be called the 'left' side in politics, but because 'left' implies 'sinister'. It was as a sinister danger that he thought of Ralegh, whose formidable personality might indeed thwart Cecil's growing influence with James of Scotland when he came, as he soon must, to be King of England.

He was already writing secretly to James that he must beware of the 'gaping crabs—Ralegh especially'—who in 'his light and sudden humours' would easily 'confess how contrary it is to his nature to be under your sovereignty', did not Cecil dissuade him, 'under pretext of care for his own well-being'. He warned James that if Ralegh spoke or wrote to him in generous praise of Cecil ('whereof sometimes he will be replete' when in a 'humour of kindness') then the King must understand that Cecil was taking care that Ralegh 'shall not think I reject his freedom or his affection'. But James could rest assured that this was only Cecil's stratagem to deceive Ralegh; and that Cecil could never, 'for private affection, support a person whom most religious men do hold anathema'.

The accusation that Ralegh was irreligious was the most damaging that could be made against him to the nervously superstitious Scots bigot, who feared even the 'heathenish' smoking of tobacco as an invention of the Devil. Having planted his most poisoned barb against Ralegh, Cecil eagerly contrasted his own religious devotion with that of his ungodly friend; by making his slanders of him, as 'I do profess, in the presence of Him that knoweth and searcheth all men's hearts'.

He boasted before God of his treachery; but took extraordinary precautions to hide it from men, 'Ralegh especially'. He urged on James that his letter was written under the sacred 'seal of confession'; and he sent it to him through secret agents all the way round by Dublin.

Ralegh had no suspicion of this. He was incapable of guessing that even his 'humour of kindness' was an insult to Cecil: and so also his person, as tall and vigorous and casual in bearing, as his friend's was cramped and timidly self-conscious. Cecil winced at Ralegh's nonchalance, his disregard of the conventions, his indifference as to what people thought of him; but most of all at the decisive realism and sardonic humour that instantly cut through any pretentious argument.

'In intellect and imagination Ralegh rose head and shoulders above Robert Cecil', writes Joel Hurstfield, although he is the historian most sympathetic to Cecil, and appreciative of him. Even Bacon's mind is diminished in comparison with Ralegh's, when revealed by their living words. With his fellow M.P.s, Bacon is shown as 'rather ineffective' in Professor Neale's great work on the Elizabethan Parliaments; 'a busybody', and 'officious as ever'. He seems to strain on tip-toe in his efforts to overtop the only other genius in the House to rival his; but 'his imagination was insufficient'. Lytton Strachey explains why. 'It was impossible for Francis Bacon to imagine that any good could ever come of being simple-minded.'

In that, Ralegh towered above Bacon, as above Robert Cecil; in sincerity and simplicity of vision, and of expression. These qualities are shown at their most moving in his letters. But his reports of sea-battles are among the best ever written, especially the 'Fight about the Azores', and the last fight of his cousin Sir Richard Grenville in the *Revenge*, where his prose has the magnificence of Tennyson's poem, without the melodrama. His prose was not, like Bacon's, a contrived work of art, apart from his everyday life. It was the natural expression of himself. The same living quality in it lights up his spontaneous words in Parliament; they drive straight to the heart of the matter, forestalling by two centuries the command to 'Clear your mind of cant'.

'Leave every man free.' The freedom that he urged, as the right of the humblest of men, was within eighteen months to be denied to one of the greatest, himself. The tyranny and treachery that he fought would crush not only Ralegh, but continue to crawl into the policies of public men. At the end of each Parliament the question is called: 'Who Goes Home?' Of all the voices that spoke in his last Parliament, where 'the long-winded lies are long forgot', it is Ralegh's that sounds the clearest, and goes home to us today.

CHAPTER SIXTEEN
'Yet Her Majesty Rose and Danced'

AGE can be an asset in rulers. Queen Victoria's belated popularity grew with every year she added to her reign. Her death, like Elizabeth's, came just after the death of her century, and like hers marked the passing of an age of triumph. The homely affection and respect she earned was utterly different in kind from the half-pagan worship of Elizabeth, who was the last Queen to win such idolatry; and left such memories and hopes that in the following century many thousands of Englishmen went abroad to fight for King James' daughter, the 'Winter Queen' of Bohemia, and wished to bring her back to England as a second Queen Elizabeth.

But the shining reigns of the two old Queens both set in clouds; Victoria's in those of the Boer War, and Elizabeth's in the public discontent and personal grief that she suffered after Essex's death. She knew her glory diminished by it. So, often, was she herself. 'More than a man, and sometimes less than a woman', she now earned the final part of that judgment of Cecil's, by swearing at her Court ladies, stamping and cuffing them in sudden bursts of rage as uncontrollable as her father's. 'Nothing pleased her', they said. Once she admitted it; and often showed it in fits of melancholy when she would sit drooping, brooding, noticing nothing around her, and already with that strange trick of putting her finger to her mouth, possibly only to feel an aching tooth, but it looked as though she were holding back some terrible secret. So she was. She must soon die, and without ever having lived as the shy, sly, smiling faces of her ladies showed what they meant by living. She had loved Tom Seymour when too young; Essex when too old. And both had had their splendid heads cut from their necks because of her; the second, by her command. Even so had her father loved and killed her mother.

Between Seymour and Essex she had known many other loves, and especially that of Leicester, so steady it was almost that of a husband, except that he had had other wives. He had been cast in something of the same mould as Seymour and Essex; but with nothing like their fire and fury. Ralegh had been cast in it fifteen years before Essex, and would live for seventeen years longer, the most absolute as well as the last of the Elizabethans. Now Essex had broken the mould.

All thought Ralegh was now again first favourite; but it was too late for Elizabeth to take a fresh favourite, still less a former one. Ralegh had survived Essex but not, as people believed, supplanted him. That game had been played out, with more bitterness to Elizabeth than is realized, for she had proved more lastingly unforgiving of Ralegh's marriage than of any other. It was not merely his marrying that she could not bear, but his steadfast devotion to his wife. His family life was almost unique in that Court in his constant friendship both with wife and son. Since his marriage he had written dazzling letters and queer sombre poems of his love for the Queen who was his Goddess, his Muse and inspiration; but she could never enter within that family circle, nor have the power to move him that she had with her other favourites, however much married and mistressed.

Harshly outspoken and abrupt as Ralegh often was, without apparently realizing it, yet he was aloof, withdrawn; and for all his passionately written words the Queen felt him imperturbable, and therefore probably insincere. By now she thought she knew what such ecstasies amounted to, for Essex, her last love, had shown her. 'I find that all my Lord Essex's protestations of affection amount only to his hope that I shall restore to him his monopoly of sweet wines.' It could only be for such profit that men would now woo her. She had known that she was old; only now did she know that all men knew it. 'Her conditions are as crooked as her carcase'; Essex's cruel words are believed to have signed his death warrant; it is as likely that they signed her own. At the least, they consigned her to old age. She had always had one shoulder a trifle higher than the other, but she held herself so straight (in these latter years so rigid) that she thought she could defy anyone to notice it. But someone had noticed it, and the one that mattered to her more than all others. Her carcase was as crooked as her conditions; for her, that was the important way round for the phrase. And she had a new nightmare, that she saw her naked body, surrounded by flames, 'marvellously lean and fearful'.

She could still look amazingly young, even in the eyes of unfriendly ambassadors, when at a little distance; but it had to be at a distance. She could still ride ten miles in a day, walk for hours in the gardens, hunt, even six months before her death, and dance country dances which are extremely active. But all this she was keeping up for outward show. She could no longer keep up the strain of private personal relations. She was too old for a tale too often told.

'That witty fellow my godson,' as she called Sir John Harington, who had once been her 'Boy Jack' and later amused her with his improper verses, found her at a bad moment 'quite disfavoured and unattired'. She had not cared enough to change her dress for the young man, nor to 'take any pleasant food or drink'.

> 'Care no more to clothe or eat,
> To thee the reed is as the oak.'

Those hawk's lids slid over her eyes at the sight of smart Sir John, nervously trying to cheer her with some more of his 'fooleries'.

'When thou dost feel creeping Time at thy gate,' she began, and then, 'I am past my relish for such matters.'

And for life itself. Her relish for that had gone, because her people had tired of her. Their love had been hers far longer than that of any man. 'I keep the good will of all my husbands—my good people,' she had once boasted to Harington's wife, 'in merry sort'. What were husbands or lovers in comparison with her people? Essex had done far worse than deprive her of her last love for a man. He had cut the thread of her whole life, for he had cut her off from her people. Their love, and hers for them, had saved her when, after condemning the Queen of Scots to death, she herself had suffered a death of the spirit. Only her country's danger from the Armada could then arouse her and bring her back to life.

Now she was fifteen years older, and there was no such trumpet call to life, and no dear accustomed Robin Dudley by her side to help; nor long-devoted old Burghley, for whose death she still often wept. This time she would have to rouse herself, alone, to win back her people; and did, before she died.

'A Lady whom Time hath Surprised.'
Portrait of Queen Elizabeth attributed to
Mark Gheeraerts the Elder.

By kind permission of Lord Methuen

But before then she had to watch a ghost usurp her crown. Essex, alive, had been the glittering idol of the people. Dead, he became its martyred saint. ('My martyr,' mumbled King James in the North.) They applauded the sermons preached against Essex as a traitor, and which thanked God for the Queen's deliverance; but they muttered that of course the preachers, since the Queen was Governess of their Church, had to toe the line. And all the time songs were springing up, no one knew by whom, with more power than any sermon, for their words rhymed and were sung to a tune, and so were remembered, and could no more be forbidden than the grass from growing. Such lamentable ballads as that of 'Essex's Last Good Night'—

> 'Our jewel is from us gone
> The valiant knight of chivalry'—

echoed on through the reign, even at Court.

> 'Sweet England's pride is gone,
>   Welladay! Welladay!
> Brave honour graced him still,
>   Gallantly, gallantly.
> He ne'er did deed of ill,
>   Well it is known.
> But Envy, that foul fiend
>   Whose malice ne'er did end
> Hath brought true virtue's friend
>   Unto his thrall.'

The foul fiend was not left anonymous. Other verses shouted out in the taverns to the comfortable accompaniment of clinking cans, specified two of his names very clearly.

> 'Little Cecil trips up and down
> He rules both Court and Crown
>
> He swore he saved the Town
> Is it not likely!'

> . . . . .

> 'Ralegh doth time bestride
> He sits 'twixt wind and tide,
> Yet uphill he cannot ride,
> For all his bloody pride.'

The real charge against Ralegh was that he had always been Essex's opponent, and had now come out on top. The crowd was sure that he must have helped towards his rival's downfall. 'When jacks go up, heads go down,' said the Earl of Oxford as he watched the Queen playing on the virginals with Ralegh standing beside her.

But it was the Queen who went furthest down. Her people had adored her and been managed and bullied by her too long, and it would be a refreshing change to have a King again at last, and a young man, or fairly young, for James of Scotland was of the same age as Essex. So it became all the more important for her to keep up a brave show before the Scots ambassadors, and she was angry when there was only a small attendance of the Court at her country palace of Nonsuch. In revenge, on her next Progress she mockingly told all the old lords to stay behind, and took only the young and active ones with her; but then they were avenged in their turn, for she was so tired after walking all over the Sidneys' fine house at Penshurst that she called for a stick as she went upstairs. But she smiled at the ladies who danced before her at the trumpet call of cornets in the gallery, and she ate two morsels of rich comfit cake and drank a small cordial, and admired her hostess' purple skirt fringed with gold, and her host's collar of needlework and 'underbody of silver and loops'—whatever that may have been. And she looked at the portrait of young Sir Philip Sidney lying under a tree like a shepherd, to compose a pastoral poem, and at his sword and perhaps even at his shaving mirror, as so many thousand later visitors were to do; but never sighed aloud that the most 'perfect gentle knight' in Christendom was no longer at his home to welcome her.

Yet she went to the Herbert wedding in a spangled shrine like that of a holy image, held high above the heads of the crowd by twelve of her most famous mariners. She came down to earth and was 'wooed' to lead the masquers' dance by Mrs Mary Fitton, whose enormous sleeves spiked upward like the fins of a pre-historic lizard, with a jewel crowning every point. 'Who are you?' asked the Queen, and her masked wooer never answered as she might, 'I am the Dark Lady of Master Shakespeare's Sonnets'; her bold eyes peered in a shrewd smile through their slits as she replied, 'Affection'.

' "Affection!" said the Queen. "Affection is false!" Yet her Majesty rose and danced.'

* * *

The Court was growing cold and sophisticated, bored by all these childish shows of grandeur. Their Queen of Love and Beauty was turning into a Pantomime Fairy and superannuated. She had grown sick of it herself, but it was too late to change the rôle.

She shut her eyes deliberately to the fact that some of her most trusted friends had intrigued, and even been ready to fight, against her. 'Her faithful Mountjoy', who had once fought a duel for her sake with Essex, and then become his ally even in treason, had been forced unwillingly to take Essex's place as Lord Deputy in Ireland. He was making good in the field; but it must have cost his Queen a severe effort to coax him on the old laughing, chaffing ground she had always managed so well. Her quips at him as 'Mistress Kitchenmaid', when he complained of his 'scullion's' job in clearing up the mess in Ireland, could not have been easy to make to the man who had so lately been prepared to lead an army against her. Yet she wrote him long, intimate and cheering letters in her own hand, with inspiring messages to his army that 'every hundred of them will beat a thousand . . . I bless them all. And putting you in the first place I end, scribbling in haste, your loving Sovereign, E.R.'

She could still win her soldiers to her, even their formerly mutinous commander; but not the nation at large. She spoke frankly of their changed feeling for her, though not to any close friend. There was none such now. But she had always had the gift of casual intimacy, and it was easier to make fleeting contacts with someone she might not see again, a visiting ambassador, or an old antiquary. Glancing through the Records in the Tower with their new Keeper, William Lambarde, she paused at some of Richard II's reign, and remembered how Essex's followers had commanded the performance of that new play of Shakespeare's, so as to show to the people the deposing of a monarch. It had since been banned in the theatre but, said she, 'This tragedy has been played forty times in open streets and houses. . . . *I* am Richard II. Know ye not that?'

Lambarde murmured sympathetically that Essex had been 'a

most unkind gentleman—the most adored creature that ever your Majesty made'. She shrugged that off with, 'He that forgets God will also forget his benefactors.' It was not of Essex's ingratitude she had spoken, but that of the people in the streets. Her thin hands flicked over the pages of the records; and little comfort was there in them since Richard's day, with two more kings deposed and murdered, and a third killed in battle by his subjects, and peasant armies twice over-running London, before the first Tudor monarch could at last enforce peace on his countrymen. They were supposed to be longing for it, but took strange ways to show it; raised rebellions for first one Pretender and then another, and called in the foreign armies of Scotland and Burgundy to help them. The English themselves had a proverb (was it a boast?) that 'the vice of the French is lechery, that of the English, treachery'. Europe had declared orderly government impossible in such a country. The struggle to impose, and maintain it, had changed her grandfather from a reckless good-humoured adventurer, fond of fighting in tournaments, of gaiety and fine shows, into a tight-lipped wary miser, sometimes merciless. He had made the first Pretender a favourite servant, but hanged the second, and executed the White Rose Earl of Warwick (who never 'pretended' at all) merely as a precautionary measure. For Henry VII had learned that it was not power that corrupted, but insecurity. And his granddaughter knew it when she had once flared out on the difficulty of ruling 'these English wild beasts'.

She did not do so now to Lambarde. She turned back to earlier records, hoping, she said lightly, to be a scholar in her old age, and at least she would not have to start by mastering the Greek alphabet as an old philosopher had done just before his death. Some great name in chivalry caught her eye, and she said: 'In those days force and arms did prevail; but now the wit of the fox is everywhere on foot, so as hardly a faithful or virtuous man may be found.'

Then she dismissed him with, 'Farewell, good and honest Lambarde.' He died a fortnight later and she never saw him again.

* * *

Elizabeth knew that the foxes and their messengers were footing it fast between England and Scotland; 'Little Cecil tripped

up and down' in order to 'rule both Court and Crown' in both
Kingdoms. There was little that her secret agents could tell her
without her knowing it already; 'Tush, Brown, do I not know!'
she would interrupt one of them, to his amazement. It was plain
by now that James would have to be her successor, though she
refused to name him as such, and so 'wrap her shroud around
her'. Her servants did not wait for that; they were hastening to
pay court to the next monarch, as they had done to herself when
her sister Mary Tudor had lain dying. There had been hardly
anyone to stay by her bedside—a memory that had increasingly
grown in dread for Elizabeth. She sometimes showed hysterical
fears 'now that the dangers are all over', as she had never done
when they were present. The creak of a board or rustle of a
curtain could send her into such paroxysms that she would
snatch up a sword and thrust it through the arras at some
imagined assassin, then fall back weary and indifferent. Exhaustion from all she had gone through in her long life, from love,
rage, terror, disillusionment and despair, would sometimes clog
her mind so that she could only sit weeping and alone, calling
low, or in shrill cries, on Essex's name.

She had earned the right to be tired. She had achieved more
than any had believed possible for a woman monarch. Before her,
indeed, no one had believed that a 'weak woman', without a
husband, could be a monarch at all. Yet she had all a woman's
nervous weaknesses, had been often ill (and was believed sometimes to be at the point of death) since her adolescence, and in
most cases the origin had been hysteria. Outrageous tragedies
had attacked her nature and her health as well as her fortunes,
ever since her father had beheaded her mother before she was
three years old, and had cast herself down from her proud
position as his petted favourite to that of a neglected bastard. Her
first lover had been executed because of her when she was fifteen;
she had demanded a public proclamation against the 'shameful
slander' that she was with child by him; was kept in close custody
and spied upon for years in her early youth; then for weeks in the
Tower in the same rooms as her mother's, above Traitor's Gate,
in daily fear of the same hideous public death. And secret
assassination had threatened her always, before and after coming
to the throne, which few believed she could keep for six months.
Yet she had kept it nearly forty-five years, and brought her

country from its bankrupt, helpless dependency as a province of Spain to a triumphant awareness of itself as a strong and splendid nation.

To achieve this she had had to commit what she had felt to be criminal, and cover it with what she knew to be false; to deny herself many natural pleasures, and play the part of a virgin goddess, combine sexual coquetry with statecraft, and find her brief release in hoydenish tricks, loud mannish oaths, a slap or a box on the ear.

Now her emotions were strained to breaking point by her order that Essex should be beheaded. Heads struck from their ragged bleeding necks had haunted her memory from early childhood, when her mother's had begun the ghastly sequence of those beloved by their slayer, even as that of Essex had been loved and caressed by her long fingers, stroking and trying to tame his ruddy, unruly hair. It was safer not to remember too much.

Harington, who had helped Essex 'deal' with Tyrone, was dismayed by her sudden lapse into vagueness on the matter. He tells that she exclaimed, ' "Oh now it mindeth me that you was one who saw this man elsewhere," and here she dropped a tear and smote her bosom.'

'This man' was her great enemy Tyrone, and 'elsewhere' was Ireland, the road to Englishmen's ruin, to Essex's scaffold; but even that road had, for the moment, grown dim to her.

Then of a sudden her seemingly moribund body would be galvanized into life and spring up to be 'set upon jollity', to dance, hunt, romp and joke with old courtiers till they felt themselves as young again even as herself, to wear hair 'of a colour never made by nature', and summer clothes of white and silver taffeta in ice-cold weather, so that Robert Cecil's ponderous elder brother begged him to warn her that 'there is no contentment to a young mind in an old body'. She could still prove that wrong; not merely to the Court but to the vast nameless troublesome family of her people. For she was given a last chance to woo them again to her, and her mind was still young enough to seize it; to understand their wrongs and set them right, to tell them her love and to win back theirs, in her last public speech, of so great a spirit that not even her speech to them before the Armada could equal it.

It was danger from Spain that once again roused her to life, and gave her her supreme moment. Yet another, and the last, Spanish Armada had set out to conquer England, this time through Ireland, and had actually landed an army of 4,000 at Kinsale to join the Irish rebels under Tyrone, to whom the Pope had already sent substantial aid, and also a phoenix feather and the blessings of all Catholic Europe. All this had been directly encouraged by Essex's treachery; so his partisan Mountjoy had small reason to complain of 'the mess' he had helped create. That his Queen chose to ignore his share in it showed at least as much heroism as his efforts to clear it up. Like her father, and unlike most women, she could show 'the nonchalance that is the best part of policy'.

Money was as much needed as heroism, and had to be raised instantly. Elizabeth sold more of her lands, some of her jewels, tried to cajole loans from her Dutch and French allies, whom she had helped to defend against Spain. But Holland was niggardly, and Henri IV of France had already taught her that 'If there be any sin in the world against the Holy Ghost, it is ingratitude.' Her help had made him strong enough to throw her over, and to make a separate peace with their joint enemy; so he gave her 'fair words galore', but not as much money as to his mistresses.

There was nothing for it but to do the thing she most dreaded, and call yet another Parliament.

CHAPTER SEVENTEEN

'With Your Loves'

QUEEN ELIZABETH

EVERYBODY must have thought that this Parliament would be Elizabeth's last; nobody could have guessed that it would give her back 'the glory of her Crown'. The most mutinous that ever she had been driven to hold (for all her Parliaments were forced on her by some immediate necessity), it threatened her, for the first time, with a serious political attack on the Crown. This was not caused by the need to raise money. There was no trouble over the army estimates; the danger from Spain and Ireland was too acute for that, and larger subsidies were voted than ever before. But a new angry spirit was in the air, expressed in openly grudging words and in muttered challenge of the Queen's authority: even of unfriendliness to her person. Before, when she had passed through 'her faithful Commons' to open Parliament, they had all cried with a will 'God save your Majesty!' This time only a few were heard to say it.

She stood rigidly before them, her thin body weighed down by her massive robes, her face shrunk to a wizened point, white round the fixed staring eyes. For a moment the image wavered and seemed about to fall. Some gentlemen rushed forward to give a supporting hand. She forced herself to recover her balance; both of her body and her mind. She guessed at once what lay behind the resentful discontent in the House. It was nothing less than a direct challenge to her royal prerogative; and therefore to her whole constitutional power. It sought to deprive her of her right to pay indirect salaries to her chief servants through indirect taxes levied on certain articles. These Monopolies or Patents had arisen from the desperate state of the Queen's finances, and from her need to meet public expenses out of her own private purse. The ugliest was the traffic in forced marriages among the orphaned Wards of the nobility, who must either marry as their Master of the Wards directed, or else buy their freedom to marry as they wished, with cruelly crippling fines. The most unfair was the false assessment of great estates at a mere fraction of their true value: this was where Ralegh, though himself a rich man, fell foul of other rich M.P.s by his attack on the lie.

Such abuses sound more abominable than the raised prices on certain goods caused by the Monopolies, but the latters' nuisance value was more general, for they touched more people's pockets more obviously. And the number of them had grown continuously. The Queen's right to grant them had already been questioned and had raised a storm in the previous Parliament; and she had weathered it. But the wind of it was now rising to gale force, and throughout the country.

There was an unseemly uproar in the House when a member indignantly read out a list of Monopolies in household goods that stretched from salt and starch to brandy and blubber oil, and even to a patent for drying pilchards. "Is not bread there too?" shouted a derisive back-bencher, and another roared in answer, "It *will* be, by next Parliament!"

Cecil expostulated and grew strident. The other men thought him too big for his boots, because he felt too small for them; he scolded them as 'more fit for a grammar school than a Parliament'; but they only jeered at their truculent schoolmaster and 'cried and coughed him down'.

Ralegh alone secured 'a great silence', though a sullen one, by his hot defence of the tin Monopoly. An elder statesman asked reprovingly for freedom of speech for all. They got it. Councillors who tried to control the fury could not even make themselves heard; M.P.s stamped like cart-horses, 'hemmed and hawked' and spat. Cecil's grammar school seems too polite a comparison. He had survived seven stormy Parliaments but complained, 'never yet did I see the House in so great confusion'. The noise of it spread out into the streets where the crowds bellowed out their tavern songs against those who

'Seek taxes in the tin,
Peel the poor to their skin.'

More frighteningly, they shouted in organized demand for 'the overthrow of these Monopolies'.

Neither the roar of 'these English wild beasts', nor the brawls in Parliament, could daunt the frail old woman who had so recently tottered before her hostile Members. She instantly perceived that by now the country was backing Parliament; that Parliament was fast growing in power, and would strike at the throne itself if she did not at once prevent the danger of a division in the House.

Her father had himself invented these divisions; his 'royal stomach' would not digest the M.P.s' impudence in twice throwing out a bill he was pushing; so he had gone down to the House in person and commanded all those who desired his and his kingdom's welfare to stand on one side of the House; all opponents to it to stand on the other. It had simplified the debate beautifully; but this new weapon that had proved so useful for himself could now be turned against his daughter.

She was long-sighted enough to foresee what could happen to the Crown and the country if there were a division in the House on the Royal Prerogative. Two reigns hence her successor's son, Charles I, was to use it to insist that the whole country should help pay for its Navy, instead of leaving the entire cost of its upkeep to only five seaports. This extraordinary anomaly had outlasted even the Armada; but Charles I's attempt to remedy the abuse with a general tax on the nation for Ship Money, and to enforce it by his prerogative, was to pull down his throne, and himself to his death as a traitor; while his opponent John Hampden has been revered as a patriot to this day in a public monument for refusing to pay a small tax, unsanctified by Parliament, towards the Navy that guarded his country's shores. The acknowledged fact that English boys and girls on those shores were being kidnapped by Turkish pirates for their slave markets did not count beside the principle that only Parliament should by now control all taxes.

Elizabeth saw that England was learning to put principles above Princes. Righteous indignation, in this increasingly Puritan age, could from the highest motives drag England into Civil War. She forestalled it for forty years. She accepted the warning of the future, and ignored false encouragement from the past; forgot the example of her tyrannical father, and remembered instead that of her prudent grandfather who 'could not endure to see Trade sick'. So she coaxed her Secretary into giving the House her message to them, with no more lecturing, but in mild conciliation. Cecil was at his best in such a rôle; he radiated playful charm as he repeated her words. Tender and humorously homely, they told the House that as their Queen had always held their good 'most dear, so the last day of her life should witness it'. A Royal Proclamation would be issued within three days to examine all Monopolies, and to abolish many of them at once. So from this very moment they should now 'eat meat more savourly' with salt freed from its Patent and therefore 'good cheap'. 'Cold stomachs' should have their Aquavita or brandy, and 'weak stomachs their vinegar. Train oil shall go the same way: oil of Blubber shall march in equal rank; Brushes and Bottles endure the like judgment.'

The Commons turned from bilious rage to rapturous gratitude; they begged to go and express it to her in person in her chamber at Whitehall, and their only quarrel now was who should be chosen to go, for they shouted, "All! All! All!" There they knelt before her and addressed her in religious fervour: "Prostrate at your feet we present our most loyal and thankful hearts and the last spirit in our nostrils to be poured out, to be breathed up, for your safety."

So she seized her last chance to win back their love and, through them, that of her people. She had despaired of it, almost ceased to desire it, in the exhaustion that could make her only wish never to feel anything again. But now, surmounting both lethargy and anger, she rose to it. Her numbed emotions came to life in words more warm and simple than any she had found before. The ageing voice rang out in a song of praise to God who had made her "a Queen over so thankful a people". He had given her more "than any treasure, for that we know how to prize; but love and thanks I count inestimable". He had raised her high. "Yet this I count the glory of my Crown, that I have reigned with your loves."

Then, telling them to rise from their knees for their comfort, she said how exceeding grateful she was to them for their true information of the abuses of the Monopolies, and so for her chance to set about their remedy. There was a pause while she summoned the will to speak of her hidden sadder self, without breaking down.

"To be a King and wear a crown is a thing more glorious to them that see it than it is pleasant to them that bear it. The cares and troubles of a crown" were pills gilded over, but "indeed are bitter and unpleasant to take . . . I should be willing to resign the place I hold, and glad to be freed of the glory with the labours; for it is not my desire to live, nor to reign, longer than my life and reign shall be for your good. And though you have had, and may have, many mightier and wiser princes sitting in this seat, yet you never had, nor shall have, any to love you better."

They were her last words to her people, and, as though she knew it, she asked them all present to come and kiss her hand in farewell. This, her 'Golden speech', came to be treasured more even than her call to arms across the open fields of Tilbury against the invaders from Spain.

CHAPTER EIGHTEEN

'A Lady whom Time hath Surprised'

RALEGH

A LITTLE over a year later Ralegh, with a black plume on his helmet and black band on his arm, marched as Captain of the Guard beside the coffin of the Queen. It was the last service he could give to his 'Lady whom Time hath surprised'.

Some thought he said that in irony, since she was old, and had fought death standing in silent agony some days before she died. His thought of her was not so literal. In his verse it was

> 'a durable fire,
> In the mind ever burning,
> Never sick, never old, never dead,
> From itself never turning.'

Nor can the love in his poems to her be taken literally, as in his letters to the other Elizabeth, his wife; but the deep intensity of his feeling in them show it to be true. Their grave monosyllables peal out like 'the strange thunder of the waters' that he had heard on 'Orinoco in his pride'.

> 'When I was gone, she sent her memory,
> More strong than were ten thousand ships of war.'

Now it was she who had gone; and still she sent her memory to him, who had been left behind. He was bereft at last of his Queen and Goddess Cynthia, whose moon had drawn the tides of his 'Ocean's' motive power. And in her he had lost his intimate and passionate friend of the past twenty years. She had been an exciting companion; an exacting mistress; fickle, cruel, capricious, and abominably jealous. But she had also been so bewitched by him as to give him great power and riches; so admiring of him as to listen to him as her Oracle; so possessively fond of him as to keep him at her side away from the voyages that he had longed to undertake.

'She gave, she took, she wounded, she appeased.' No one else could so sum up in a single line of verse what Elizabeth had been to her lovers.

They had laughed together at her pompous advisers and her foolish wooers; at his travellers' tales of oysters on trees and a lake of ever-bubbling pitch, that proved true in centuries to come; at his new-fangled long pipes and 'lips splendid with smoke', and the earrings gleaming in his piratical black beard. They had flaunted their pride against each other like peacocks fanning out their gorgeous tails; had enjoyed their duellos of dangerous wit that made fighting an artistic pleasure, and their repartees an impromptu comedy.

She had loved his young rival Essex, but had not heeded his slanders of Ralegh. He had loved his wife Elizabeth, and she had treated them both atrociously for it; but had shown finally that she could not do without him. She could never forgive him his wife; but she pretended to forget.

Most valued of all her gifts, she had given him employment, that word so beloved of the Elizabethans. She could have given him far more of the kind he most desired, if only she had allowed him to go himself to carry out his exploring and colonizing plans instead of chaining him to her side. In that she had been his evil genius, holding him back from what should have been his greatest triumphs, both in his lifetime and in the future histories that failed, like his contemporaries, to recognize his true qualities; for they still repeat the contemporary view of him as a showy courtier, an expensive luxury, splendid but sinister, above all too versatile to make good in his many far-reaching schemes.

But, without her, what opportunity would he have had to launch his schemes at all? 'She gave, she took'—she gave him his chance, and took it away from him. But without her he would not have been able to start the English Empire of the future beyond the Western Seas. The Empire that she withheld from him would be none the less of his making.

They had worked well as a pair in harness. They would have worked still better had he not insisted on a wife and home; these had fulfilled his manhood and given him his deepest happiness; but weakened his chief friendship. Now he had lost that friend, the greatest in power as well as in affection and quality. There could be none else to give employment for his 'Eliza-consecrated sword'. 'Golden Eliza' was gone; 'She is gone, she is lost'; never again could the line end on the triumphant cry—'She is found, she is ever fair!'

Her funeral procession marched on with him to the tolling of the bell; it tolled for him as for her, for the passing of the age that they had made their own. But he did not hear its warning note, though it had echoed long before in the slow sad march of his own verse:

> 'She hath left me here all alone,
> All alone as unknown,
> Who sometime did me lead, with her self,
> And me loved as her own.'

Now indeed he was 'all alone as unknown', but still he himself did not know it.

The Scots King James, now riding down on his triumphal progress to take over his new kingdom of England, was an unknown quantity.

But Cecil, Ralegh's close friend, had managed to make friends with James. He had engineered James' peaceful succession to the English throne in so adroit a fashion that the new King was bound to be grateful to him, and Ralegh was sure that Cecil, at the least, would stand by him.

'At the least'—but he had never spoken to, or of, Cecil as 'little', as the Queen had done, even in her dying hours. When he had told her she must go to bed, she had rebuked him with, "Little man, is 'must' a word to use to princes?" Now she was dead, the new reign would be that of little men; but Ralegh did not foresee it.

Within two months little Cecil would be made a baron, a viscount, and the Earl of Salisbury. Within four, he would have helped to turn Ralegh out of his Captaincy of the Guard and tenancy of Durham House, and would be among the judges to charge him with high treason. But Ralegh as yet knew nothing of this; only that Cecil was very busy with his arrangements for the new reign; and hoped that he would help him too to find work among them.

Cecil was still his partner in privateering expeditions, and taking shares in them (though more privately than Ralegh realized); he would no doubt wish to try to further them with the new King. A 'young King', fifteen years younger than Ralegh, cramped and thwarted till now by poverty and anxiety among his quarrelsome nobles who had always bullied him, surely he would, in his new freedom, leap at the chance to expand the power and glory of his new kingdom through its greatest surviving adventurer?

But the man in his middle thirties, now slowly proceeding towards this confident adventurer—that man had never been young. Security had always been the chief aim of his life, and now at last he felt himself within reach of it. A proposition to seize the West Indies away from Spain was the very thing to send him sky-high in an indignant fluster of nerves.

And this was just what Ralegh was already intending to write to James, in the fond belief that he could persuade him to an enterprise so helpful to England's future, and the one in which Ralegh's sword would be most useful. Once again he saw only the project in his mind, and not the person to whom it would be addressed.

He also was one whom Time had surprised. At fifty-one, he was still 'the hasty child of vigour and hope'. To the end of his days he would 'keep the bird in his bosom'; it was soaring even now towards new heights. None of what he was yet again hoping and planning would come true; but the vision of his sanguine, incautious and eager mind would remain,

> 'Never sick, never old, never dead,
> From itself never turning.'

The unluckiest of the great Elizabethans was in some ways the happiest. The years that lay ahead for him were to be the finest in his life, and make his name deathless.

James I of England and VI of Scotland. By an unknown artist.

BOOK 2

RALEGH AND JAMES

"And like a Star you must Fall,
  when the Firmament is Shaked"

RALEGH'S JUDGES

CHAPTER NINETEEN

A Wind out of the North

'There came a wind out of the North,
A sharp wind and a snell.
A dead sleep it came over me,
And from my horse I fell.'

SCOTS BALLAD OF
'TAM LIN'

THE turn of a century is apt to bring a change of air. Virginia Woolf has observed how the crisp clear climate of the eighteenth century became damp and dim all through the nineteenth. Trees and ruins dripped with mosses and wet ivy; the shut windows were draped with curtains, so were chimney pieces and piano legs. 'Women must weep', they were told, and did. Wrapped and muffled, the nineteenth century shuffled sadly out in the death-throes of the Boer War, followed by the funeral procession of a very old Queen, who had been swathed in widow's weeds for more than half her reign.

All at once the curtains were pulled back, and the twentieth century's glare of electricity and sunshine gilded all that 'summer afternoon of the Edwardian Age'; even the butlers went out of doors, to bear silver tea-trays on to the lawn, where even the bees hummed the national chorus of 'genial monarch', 'No War-ar', and the buzzing boom, 'Biarritz'.

But neither of these turns of the century changed the climate so drastically as when, at the start of the 1600's, the long Elizabethan day had faded, and the wind changed with what was, literally, a vengeance. For it blew from the North, from England's age-old enemy, Scotland; in dead contrary from the course that it had taken since the beginning of history. Always England had invaded Scotland and tried to put an English king on the Scots throne. And always the Scots monarchs, who had been Stuarts for the last two centuries, had fought back and threatened England.

But when James VI of Scotland became the likely heir to

155

Elizabeth of England, it was plain that his succession would be the best way to free the two uneven halves of a small island from their eternal civil war, and unite them into one country. Robert Cecil's far-sighted vision worked for it as profitable for the future of the nation, as well as for himself.

King James' eyes had always goggled hungrily towards the English throne, eager to sacrifice his mother and his honour to secure it; and indignant that, having done so, he had to wait another sixteen years for Elizabeth to die. Did she mean to thwart him, he demanded plaintively, by 'lasting as long as the sun and moon'? Even more than England's wealth and power he craved her security. 'Saint George surely rides upon a towardly riding horse,' he had written enviously, 'where I am daily bursten in daunting a wild unruly colt.'

The daggers of Rizzio's murderers had flashed before his mother's eyes and threatened her womb, shortly before his birth; it was said that was why he always flinched from the sight of bare steel. 'A scabbard without a sword', was the Spaniards' nickname for him. From his infancy he had been kept from his mother, and brought up by a brutal tutor, George Buchanan, whom he dreaded; though later, as a scholar himself, he admired Buchanan's famous Latin scholarship, and also no doubt his infamous story of the 'Detection of Mary Stuart', since its gross, often fatuous lies absolved him from any obligation to try to champion his mother.

He grew up estranged from women, and must have felt their distaste for him, since he neither washed nor changed his clothes —an increasingly protective armour of quilted bolsters—till they were ragged; rolled his eyes nervously at everyone, lolled out a tongue too large for his mouth, and ate and drank in a 'very uncomely' way; coughed and fidgeted all the time, 'his hands always busy where they should not have been', and could not sit still, nor walk, or rather waddle, on his weak legs without hanging on the arm of one of his elegant youths. These were his only emotional consolations since boyhood, when his first kind and beautiful favourite had been torn from him by those 'wild unruly colts' the Scots nobles.

James went in hourly fear of them. They were always trying to kidnap or indeed kill him, as they had tried, often successfully, with his forbears. It is to the credit of his dogged cunning that he finally got the whip-hand over them, though his methods were not always creditable—nor credible. His dubious accusations destroyed powerful nobles and put their wealth into his pocket. The young Earl of Gowrie's corpse was propped up in court to be convicted of conspiracy and witchcraft, *after* it had been stabbed to death by the King's servants. 'Ah weel,' as the old lady said two hundred years later to Sir Walter Scott, 'it is a great comfort that at the Day of Judgement we'll a' ken the truth about the Gowrie Conspiracy.' Few kenned it then, but most said that James had been unco' canny.

Suddenly in his middle twenties he made a violent effort to break away from his canny, craven self, and prove himself a man. He was betrothed to a beautiful princess, Anne of Denmark; the wintry storms prevented her sailing at once for Scotland, for it was an old seaman's law that no ship should take the Northern seas between St Jude's Day and Candlemas. Yet James insisted on sailing himself to fetch his bride; he would not, he said, be thought 'an irresolute ass wha could do nothing of himself'. There was a ghastly aftermath to the gallant adventure. He heard that another Wizard Earl, Lord Bothwell, had all but wrecked the royal bridal fleet by despatching two hundred witches from the tiny church on North Berwick shore; they went to sea in several sieves, but floated comfortably, 'stayed with flagons', to call up an ill wind to drown the King. James attended all the subsequent trials from a hiding-place behind the Courtroom chimney, and heard endless confessions and sentences of burning to death.

But not of the Earl of Bothwell, the son of Mary Stuart's bastard half-brother Johnnie, since legitimatized, and of her husband Bothwell's young sister Jean, who had worn a knitted dress and squirrel coat till they fell to pieces, because they had been given her by her sister-in-law Mary of Scots. Her son, the present Bothwell, had also carried loyalty into his clothes, for he had appeared at the Scots Court in black armour when his aunt Queen Mary was executed by the English, and told the King, who was wearing the discreet purple robes he had put on for his mother, that his best suit of mourning would be a coat of mail at the head of an invading army. He was far too dangerous and too close to the throne to be charged, or convicted. But he was widely believed to be the Master chosen by the Witches' Coven to impersonate the Devil, and give them his orders. He had also

before now made open attacks on James in his own palace, and
had once caught him with his breeches down in actual fact, so
that James had had to escape by the back stairs, clutching them
to his person. Even danger lacked dignity with James.

So did romance. He braved the wintry North Sea storms for an
unknown bride; and brought back a silly good-natured girl who
laughed at him, and was friendly, too friendly at times, with his
pretty young men; but did not object to his being so; encouraged
them in fact with pet names like 'her kind Dog' and orders to
'lug her sow (i.e. James) by the ear' when his manners, as so
often, became too unpleasant.

These reports caused misgiving among the dignified Elizabethan gentry. Witch-burnings *en masse* were not yet popular
with the English, as they were to become under a Puritan régime.
It was an ill wind that blew towards them this miasma of unnatural mysteries and foggy charges of conspiracy. And it blew
from the wrong quarter. To unite the two kingdoms under the
rule of one sovereign had always been the English hope—but it
should be under an English King of Scotland, certainly not a
Scots King of England. His nobles would now be uppermost, and
no longer the 'beggarly Scots', as they complained the English
had called them. James reassured them in a pawky joke that
carried a shrewd nip of the new raw air from the North: 'Content
yourselves, for I will shortly make the English as beggarly as you.'

This uncouth, uncivilized, yet cunning and learned monster
out of a Northern fairy-tale, was now to be King of England.
His accession has for so long proved the natural solution for
uniting the two countries, that it is difficult now to see how far
from inevitable it appeared three hundred and fifty years ago.
James' claim to the Succession was by no means the only one, nor
entirely obvious. He had actually decided to accept Essex's
invitation to come and fight for it while Elizabeth was still alive,
and in eager response had sent his commissioners scurrying down
to London—only to find that the Queen, so far from losing her
mastery, as Essex had written, had promptly beheaded him as a
traitor. Equally promptly, James had recoiled in horror from the
impious idea of taking arms against the ageing Queen. His commissioners, badly disconcerted, had been on the point of return
when Robert Cecil had summoned them privately to his house
and given them other messages for their King. Essex's foolhardy

plan of fighting for him had failed before it started. Robert Cecil was now the man to negotiate with James for his inheritance, but in the strictest secrecy. From that moment all was prepared peacefully for James, who was thankful to have exchanged 'my martyr' Essex for 'my little beagle', as he now called his greatest statesman.

The dying Queen had been beyond the power of speech when urged to acknowledge King James VI of Scotland as her successor, but had at last lifted her hand in a gesture of assent. So now he had only to travel South to take over his new Kingdom. And by good luck, his new book on the rights and duties of a king, *Basilikon Doron*, was on sale in London only a few days after the Queen's death, and instantly proved a huge success. He did not hurry South. He had no wish to reach London in time for Elizabeth's funeral; it wouldn't look well, so he said with thoughtful delicacy, to have to pay respects to the lady, alive or dead, who had executed his mother. Besides, his slow journey was far too pleasurable to be cut short. He was fêted everywhere, given more to eat and drink than even he could conveniently take, and encouraged to talk his head off, instead of facing the stupid Scots lords' yawns and barely concealed jeers at his 'gift of the gab'. He was given grand sport in hunting, the thing he loved best in the world. For the strange creature had his own persistent power of enjoyment, as well as of survival. Nor was it enjoyment merely of slovenly sensuality. In a world of frightening shadows, he could still have the taste, and make the time—between all the books he read and wrote, and all the learned, though often silly lectures he loved to gabble out—to sit all day in his heavily padded breeches on a horse to follow the red deer over the hill. It was an easy form of sport, but at least it brought fresh air to his nostrils, and a sight of the open sky. He was in such good humour that he made a host of new knights, so many that when people asked of one: 'Is he a Gent?' the answer frequently was: 'No, only a Knight'.

There were two flies that stuck in all this rich ointment. One was when he ordered a pickpocket to be hanged straight away without trial. The prudish English were too dainty for 'Jedburgh Justice', which hanged Border robbers out of hand. They muttered tiresome objections about their Common Law, and Sir John Harington, that privileged wag, proclaimed loudly: 'If the new King hangs a man before he is tried, will he then try a man before he has offended?'

The jest proved all too true a prophecy.

*   *   *

There was a darker cloud on the King's horizon, for it rose from the ruling passion of his life—fear. There were both negative and positive reasons for his fear of Sir Walter Ralegh. As to the negative, Ralegh had been almost alone among the important English dignitaries to make no attempt to get in touch with James and assure him of his support; while the others, in the two years before Elizabeth's death, had been out-pacing each other in the race for what they themselves called 'preferment to be got by Footmanship'. It seemed sinister to James that the most influential leader of the Court, the Captain of the Queen's Guard, had not even started. It may have been only because Ralegh, as oddly simple in some ways as he was bafflingly complex in others, did not think of the Queen as dead until she was so. If so, it was 'incredibly foolish' of him, his biographers have agreed, and another instance of how unworldly this man of the world could be; one who could hunt fortune, but take no care to keep it.

The positive reasons were far more deadly. James feared Ralegh chiefly because Robert Cecil had told him to do so. Ever since Cecil had got in touch with him, he had warned him that Ralegh was the greatest potential menace to his throne of any man in England; that he had no wish for James' accession, and had continually spoken against it to Cecil's own brother-in-law, Lord Cobham, a witty but incautiously talkative weathercock of a creature, towards whom Cecil felt no more family loyalty than was the usual cold custom in most Elizabethan families. Nor did he feel any towards his friend and his friend's wife, Lady Ralegh, who wrote him the most enchanting warm letters that any woman of the age (except the Queen herself) had written to any man who was merely a friend. Cecil reserved his loyalty only for his King. So he encouraged Cobham's chatter and Ralegh's sardonic comments, merely, he assured James, to discover how necessary it was to put him on his guard against them; especially against Ralegh, who was 'insolent, extremely heated' and dangerously 'able to sway all men's courses'. And at the same time Cecil told how cunningly he was putting the two off their guard, by writing to Cobham as his 'loving relative', and to Ralegh as his 'faithful friend', and showing 'extraordinary care for his well-being'.

What he did *not* tell the King was how cleverly he lulled any possible suspicion of his treachery by continuing as Ralegh's grateful (and secret) partner in Ralegh's privateering expeditions at sea, of which James highly disapproved. So Cecil showed his trust in his faithful friend by writing to him, 'I will be contented to be half-victualler . . . but I pray you conceal our adventure, or at least my name'; that is, he was content to take half profits, if Ralegh took all risks.

Cecil's careful abuse of his friend was backed by letters even more venomous from Lord Henry Howard (a cousin of the Lord Admiral), whose envious hatred of most men exploded in near frenzy against Ralegh and his friends Cobham and the Wizard Earl of Northumberland. Yet a third Wizard Earl, and down in England this time, was too much for James. Lord Henry alarmed him badly by his sworn assurances that this Southron warlock and his associates, Cobham and above all Ralegh, were James' 'sworn enemies, who would rather see him buried than crowned. . . . Hell did never show up such a diabolical triplicity, that denies the Trinity, of wicked plotters hatching treason from cockatrice eggs that are daily and nightly sitten upon.' Cecil's calmly beautiful eyes did not blink at such ravings. He had got James' measure by now; whatever he sponsored or said himself in the way of cockatrice eggs or 'gaping crabs' was swallowed by the King, who solemnly answered: 'We are exceeding far inamorat of them.' For he now entirely trusted his little beagle's nose to ferret out secret dangers; and did not see that the dangers Cecil feared most were for himself.

James had always been susceptible to a handsome and splendid type of man; it would be disastrous if Cecil's new-won favour with him should be outshone by the most magnificent of Elizabeth's courtiers, who might well come to command the King as he had done the Queen. The dead Essex had declared that it was his fear of Ralegh's influence over the Queen that had prompted his rebellion and his wooing of James to a premature advance into England; that he had never wanted to attack the Queen, only 'that knave Ralegh', as he had done literally when his men fired at Ralegh on the river. So it was easy to make James believe that his noble ally's martyrdom had been due to Ralegh's sinister influence.

It was also easy to play on the anxious royal bigot's fears of a man whom Cecil declared to be anathema to religious folk. Though not proved to be an atheist himself, Ralegh had openly been friends with some notorious atheists; and had encouraged all men, even Papists and criminals condemned to death, to speak their opinions freely to him. 'The badge of Hell' was to be seen clearly in 'the world's new fashions planted' by him, especially the tobacco grown on his estates, and the pipe-smoking that he had made the rage at Court. Only the hellish powers of 'that great Lucifer', as Henry Howard called him, could have enabled Ralegh within ten years to impose on the elegant English Court 'so vile and stinking a custom—loathsome to the eye, hateful to the nose, harmful to the brain, dangerous to the lungs', and also effeminate, leading to 'mollicies and delicacy' corrupting courage and tending to drink, the 'root of all sins'.

Yet the frankness of James' wife and his often disdainful favourites ('I kiss your dirty hands', wrote one of them to him) must have told the royal author of this diatribe that his sodden old clothes and unwashed person stank worse than a smoker's pipe; that he was effeminate, a coward, and drank 'exactly like a fish'. Ralegh was the precise opposite of these things. It did not help their meeting.

*   *   *

It was a duel between them from the first, though Ralegh, quick as he was to fight off a physical attack, failed to recognize how deadly. He had taken James by surprise, for the latter did not wish to be approached by 'unauthorized persons' on his journey South. But Ralegh, accustomed to privilege, regarded himself as an exception. Somebody (could it have been his wife?) must have pointed out his obvious error in having paid far too scant attention to the coming Sovereign, who had nearly reached London before Ralegh joined his fellow-courtiers in welcoming his accession.

So Ralegh at last rode a short way North, and met 'a sharp wind and a snell'.

"Rawly, Rawly," said the new King, 'in most crabbed and choleric manner' "and rawly ha'e I heard of thee, mon." It was the sort of plebian pawky snub that a grocer might deal out to one of his prentice lads; but Ralegh did not flinch under it. He had heard that the King delighted to test his new English grandees by such methods.

The test went further. James referred to the fact that he might have had to fight for his throne. Ralegh burst out with 'Would to God you had! Then Your Majesty would have known your friends from your foes.'

That was a clash with a vengeance, and one that would be 'never forgotten nor forgiven' until finally repaid by death. Ralegh had once again snapped his fingers at fortune, and so let it slide through them. It seems he could not bother to be careful with this gross buffoon, nor to hide how sickened he was by the scheming and intriguing under the polite surface of the Court. He did not know how his reputation had been poisoned to James; and by his intimate friend, Robert Cecil. He had never cared what people said; if to his face, he knew how to meet it, and 'if behind my back, then my tail is good enough to answer them'.

And he had no notion that his superb looks and bearing were an affront to the shabby, shambling monarch who by now adored manly beauty only in his juniors, whom he could pet and pretend to in a cosy fashion as their 'sweet Dad'. Ralegh had no right to be so handsome, upright and alert when fifteen years older than his king. And no subject had a right to carry such a wealth of fine clothes on his back unless the King had put it there. He was an expensive luxury, which James would certainly not keep up. This tall, scornful magnifico had been the showpiece at the splendid Elizabethan Court, chosen above others of far higher rank to impress and entertain great foreign potentates; it would be better sport to pull him down than to shoot a stag of ten. 'The Awe and Ascendancy over other men' that was noted and long remembered in Ralegh, at once aroused James' resentful hostility. Ralegh is said to have looked 'too straight' at people. The King must have shuffled and fidgeted worse than usual under his direct gaze. Cecil had no need to fear any rivalry to himself, with whom James felt comfortably at home as with another uncouth and uncomely oddity.

Ralegh did not consider how James might be seeing him. His own eyes, for all their apparent keenness, could hardly have seen James at all. He went on taking him for a normal, youngish man, coming down to double his small kingdom; and never saw that he was at heart far more of a frightened old woman than the late Queen in her seventieth year. His meeting with him 'failed to take root', as Cecil wrote with satisfaction. Ralegh, aware of the failure, though not of the reasons, thought to remedy it by his plan to seize the West Indies from Spain and present them to his King. His letter stating this tempting proposal convinced James that the man was not only a warlock but a warmonger.

Peace with Spain (to be considered the chief continental power for a long time yet) was the desire of James' heart; the greatest obstacle to it was this reckless old pirate, the last one still alive to shake his fist at Spain, and, with wanton blindness, at James' craving for peace with her. Though for long Ralegh could

'Time bestride, And sit twixt wind and tide',

now the tide had turned, and was running fast against him; the wind had changed, and blew in his face a thin haar of treachery from his friends, and a sharp sleet of hate from his enemies.

Everyone watched and waited to see what he would do to reclaim his place, as one blow after another was aimed at him. First, the Captaincy of the Guard was taken from him and given to a Scot. Ralegh prepared a protest, but before he could launch it the Bishop of Durham weighed in with a demand for the return of Durham House on the river. It had been granted by royal decree to Ralegh as his London house, full twenty years ago, and he had spent several thousand pounds on repairing and improving it; but now at the end of May 1603, only two months after the Queen's death, he was ordered to clear everything out within seventeen days. Again Ralegh protested. The Bishop, he perceived dryly, 'did not lack good friends'. Only this very spring Ralegh had provisioned it for forty persons and twenty horse, and now 'to cast out all my hay and oats into the streets at an hour's notice, and to remove my family and stuff in fourteen days after, is such a severe expulsion' as is 'very strange; the poorest artificer in London hath a quarter's warning given him by his landlord'.

His enemies chuckled. The great Ralegh was now less than the poorest Cockney workman. What then would he do? He would surely busy himself on a bigger scale than the removal of his innumerable books and bales of dried tobacco from Durham

House? He had vast acres in England to which he could retreat, and summon to his side his kinsmen, 'at least a hundred gentlemen of Devon' alone, and friends. Many thousand mariners and miners down in the West Country had already proved themselves, against the approval even of the Queen, let alone of this new upstart Scot, as willing to follow him to the end.

For that matter, he could sail over in a night to his still vaster Irish estates, raise an army of kerns and, in the all but impregnable fortress that he had made of Lismore Castle, defy the Lord Deputy, as the Lord Deputy had always feared he would do; and from there negotiate with the offers that he was supposed to be receiving from Spain.

Yet he did neither of these things. He did nothing; which is fair evidence in itself that he knew himself guiltless of any plots against the new Government. But he never guessed how guilty he was of the arrogant belief in his power to outface danger. He ignored all warnings; failed to recognize his foes; and refused to see that now

> 'Uphill he cannot ride,
> For all his bloody pride.'

He still rode uphill; outfaced the mocking stares of the Court; listened to the brightly wavering talk of Cecil's brother-in-law, Cobham, who suggested that an English Republic might be better than a blood-sucking swarm of Scots under a Sodomite king. Even James' little cousin 'Arbell' Stuart might be better as another queen, since she had an equal hereditary right to the throne, and a better legal one, being an English subject holding English land, where James was wholly alien. Arabella seemed colourless, and her only idea of politics to escape from the tutelage of her aunt, the shrewish grey mare, Bess of Hardwick. Ralegh had shown what he could do with a Queen as magnificent as the Virago of Tilbury; he would have a still freer hand with this bread-and-butter miss. Countries under queens were often better governed, since under them it was the men who ruled. What treason was it to break with this unnatural though peaceful conquest by the alien king of England's age-old enemies, and of his unnatural Scots favourites, all agog to filch the government from the English?

Ralegh may well have listened, and agreed that James Stuart

was an unpleasant substitute for the late Queen, who had loathed the thought of him on her throne.

But if he meant to do anything about it, why then did he do nothing? Because his imperial vision was both long-sighted and unselfish. He had made it his life's work, and had devoted a huge fortune to England's future in the American colonies; he must have seen that no future could be secure for her while she continued to have Scotland as an enemy at her back; that the countries would be best united under one throne, whoever sat on it.

This seems the most likely answer to the question why Ralegh made no attempt to revolt. But it doesn't explain why he made none to escape. Those whom the gods destroy they first make mad, and the name of the madness is *hubris*: a pride that defies gods as well as men. He seemed unconscious of it, and of his danger.

> 'A dead sleep it came over him,
> And from his horse he fell.'

He went to Court as usual; early in July he wrote to his wife, reassuring her that Cecil was still his eager though secret partner in his privateering joint-stock ventures, and still therefore his staunch friend. Ten days later he went to Windsor to attend the King out hunting. He was waiting on the terrace in the heavy sunshine while the horses stamped and tossed their heads against the stinging flies, when Cecil came out to him and asked him to come into the Castle and attend on the Privy Council. 'They have some questions to ask you.' Ralegh went inside. Within a week he was in the Tower.

CHAPTER TWENTY

Say to the Court it Glows

'Say to the Court it glows
And shines like rotten wood.

If Church and Court reply,
Then give them both the lie.'

I T was assumed Ralegh must be guilty of plotting against the
King, because the King had given him every provocation to
do so. He had been insulted, deprived of one post and privilege
after another, and now the one he most treasured, the Warden-
ship of the Stanneries in Devon and Cornwall, was the latest
though not the last to go. So he must be feeling unfriendly to the
present Government; it was even brought forward later in proof
of his treason that he was discontented 'in conspectu omnium'.
As a man might indeed be discontented, whose careless self-
confidence, the conquering habit of a lifetime of fifty years, was
suddenly shattered by the discovery that his new Sovereign was
determined to ruin him.

It was now too late for him to do anything about it. He was
locked up in the Tower while his judges collected all the reports
and gossip they could against him; while his supposed confederate,
Lord Cobham, accused him of everything that would blacken
him and possibly clear himself; then, 'troubled by conscience',
took it all back; then, in a fresh attempt to shift the guilt on to
Ralegh's shoulders, accused him all over again.

Ralegh knew at last how insanely foolish he had been in
listening to Cobham's hare-brained chatter of possible schemes
to improve their discontented condition. He had in fact for some
time begun to weary of this excitable character, but had thought
it prudent to know just what were the 'eggs in moonshine' that
were hatching, or more probably going addled, in that uncertain
brain. Ralegh's ideas of prudence were such as to make devils
weep, for he had no thought of using this knowledge to inform
against Cobham before Cobham could inform against him.

Instead, he had let himself get engaged in the coils, and realized too late that the King, already determined to ruin him, would now stop at nothing to destroy him. James' English servants-at-law would be equally determined to show their loyalty and eagerness to please their new monarch by bringing in the verdict that he wished. Judges had been dismissed their office, and jurymen fined and even imprisoned, for acquitting a prisoner against the Royal will, as Ralegh's father-in-law had found under Mary Tudor, and again under Elizabeth, though she had prudently retracted, being far more chary of meddling with the law than this new King had already shown himself, in ordering a man to be hanged before he was tried. Now, as Harington had foretold, he was ordering a man to be tried before he had offended. It would be a short stage from that to an equally inconsequent verdict of 'Guilty', before it was proved.

Suicide seemed the best way out, not merely for himself, but for his wife and son, since they would then retain what was left of his estates and property, instead of forfeiting them to the Crown if, as seemed certain, he were condemned as a traitor. So that there was a practical reason for suicide, as well as an emotional. He had just discovered that Cecil had tricked Cobham into accusing him, by telling Cobham that Ralegh had accused him; and that Cecil would bear testimony against Ralegh as one of the judges at his trial. Even Ralegh must have had some perception of Cecil's tortuous character; but had never thought he would act against himself. Cecil had given many proofs of his friendship—mainly, it is true, by accepting those of Ralegh's; in paying long visits to Ralegh's home and sending his invalid son there; entering into a profitable partnership which he trusted Ralegh to keep secret; and encouraging those delightfully intimate easy letters scribbled by Ralegh after midnight for the sheer pleasure of sharing his amusement with him. There were also the letters in Lady Ralegh's erratic spelling, to comfort Cecil with her motherly reassurance about his motherless son; and to seek his, with trustful confidence in his advice, about her husband. So that Ralegh, for all his sudden horrid stabs of doubt in Cecil lately, had believed that the little man was in the last resort his friend. Now he knew that he was not.

There are fashions in emotion. The one paramount in the Elizabethan age was love between the sexes, preferably unfulfilled. Family love rated very low in the scale; and so did family loyalty. An heir could easily overlook the fact that his father had been executed—so long as he himself retained the title and the lands pertaining thereto. Parents were often strangers to their children. But Ralegh had made close friends of his wife and son; and he had believed more than most men of his time in friendship. He and his family and friends had always stood by each other. As an untried young adventurer, to the great danger of his own advancement, he had spoken up furiously, aggressively, for his half-brother Humphrey Gilbert, as the best man to clear up the troubles in Ireland. Just so, he had known, Humphrey would have spoken for him. Humphrey had been the first to teach him what friendship meant; and though he had lain under the Atlantic waves this quarter-century past, he was still a living friend in Ralegh's mind.

Now, suddenly, as a man just past fifty, he suffered the shock of finding that friendship did not count to others as to himself. Yet in the prophetic glass of his poetry he had foreseen it years before:

> 'Tell fortune of her blindness;
> Tell nature of decay;
> Tell *friendship of unkindness*;
> *Tell justice of delay*;
> And if they will reply,
> Then give them all the lie.'

But it was too late to do so. He was helpless in prison; and his friend Cecil, who could have given them all the lie, was outside, safe and secure, so long as he did not embroil himself as a friend of the hated prisoner. Ralegh had sent his

> 'Soul, the body's guest,
> Upon a thankless errand.'

And now learned only that

> 'Stab at thee he that will,
> No stab the soul can kill.'

So he tried to kill himself, by stabbing a dagger into his breast; found, like many would-be suicides, that it took longer than he thought; long enough, for him to realize that the agony it would give his wife would outweigh any material gain to her. It was better that he should face his accusers and prove, to her at any rate, and possibly to a more clear-minded future, that he had behaved honourably. His critics, later as well as contemporary, wrote down his attempt at suicide as 'a theatrical gesture'. That made no odds to him. His soul resumed its thankless errand, in answer to his command:

> 'Go, since I needs must die,
> And give the world the lie.'

If the world did not take the lie, either then or later, that had nothing to do with him. So he pulled himself together to endure the ordeal of a trial that was planned from the start, as he well knew, to go against him. The adventurer, opportunist, careerist, cavalier-of-fortune or what you will, had had every chance to break away from England, and prove himself in one or other of these rôles that might at least have brought him safety. He had taken none of them. So now he must stand alone to face a charge that demanded he should be hanged, drawn and quartered, and dismembered, before he was dead.

The Plague was raging in London, so by November it was decided to transfer his trial to Winchester. The cold damp of his stone cell by the riverside had set up a rheumatic ague in Ralegh. His journey to Winchester gave promise of a quicker death than from the Law, or even Plague. The mob in London and the suburbs outside rose like a furious sea to surge round his coach, throw mud, stones and tobacco pipes. They yelled their threats to drag him out and tear him limb from limb, to avenge the death of their idol Essex, who 'ne'er did deed of ill'. Cecil's terrified secretary was in the same coach, and wrote that their fury was such that 'it was hob or nob if he would escape alive through such multitudes of unruly people'—which, however, he 'neglected and scorned'.

'Dogs do always bark at those they know not,' Ralegh observed coolly. But it showed him that his duel with Essex was not finished. He had triumphed two and a half years ago; now once again it was Essex's turn. His ghost was pursuing him to his trial, and would work against him there.

CHAPTER TWENTY-ONE

'For I, my Lords, Embody the Law'

W. S. GILBERT

RALEGH'S most dangerous antagonist now awaited him in Winchester. This was his chief prosecutor, the Attorney-General, Sir Edward Coke.

Coke's career shows his character. It is reputed one of the most extraordinary contradictions in history; yet from another point of view it can be seen as remarkably consistent. From his earliest youth he worked so hard and 'scorned delights' that he was already buying land even before he was called, unusually early, to the Bar, and quickly won fame with the important 'Shelley case' in real property, in which his decision still remains the last legal word on the matter.[1] Thereafter he rose rapidly from one legal office to another, always investing his earnings in land and making it pay: a list of fifteen new manors in his minute handwriting is only a sideline among them. He had no brothers to challenge his supremacy, but eight sisters, all younger than himself, to foster it. He married them all off extremely well; found a rich heiress, nobly born, for himself, and took the precaution to cast an eye behind him as well as before, for the heraldic glory of his family. His crest was a 'Turkey Cock Proper', which seems to have stung him as being too near home, for he changed it to an 'Ostrich Argent', and his coat of arms to 'Three Eagles Displayed'. He added a Latin anagram which advised his future heirs to

'Learn virtue and righteous toil from me,
Learn fortune from others',

a curiously ostrich point of view, if he were really blind to the fact that his purchases of land amounted to well over £100,000.

'The Great Sir Edward Coke' bears an oddly dual reputation. In his position as Attorney-General, and in his later one as Lord Chief Justice, he is said to have shown 'two different minds, almost two different people'. Even his handwriting could be both

[1] C. W. James, *Chief Justice Coke*.

171

excellent and execrable. Historians have called this supposedly complex creature 'the most brutal' and the 'most offensive of Attorney-Generals,' which G. M. Trevelyan enlarged to 'one of the most disagreeable figures in our history'. But he had been agreeable to the Privy Councillors in directing debates in Parliament the way they wanted. And Members of Parliament had made complaints in Elizabeth's reign of his pocketing a bill confirming Magna Carta's guarantee of 'liberty of the subject' and taking it to Court 'to please the Queen', and 'what became of it after, he' (Coke) 'best knoweth!'[1]

Of his conduct of Ralegh's trial it has been stated that 'not even under Judge Jeffries was the law ever more openly bent beneath the Royal Prerogative'.[2] Judge Jeffries, a sick man enflamed by pain and drink to bestial rage, has remained a legend of horror to this day. But then his victims were nearly all ignorant yokels, poor hedgerow sparrows, and it is easier to feel sympathy for them than for the nobler prey which Coke, though in the full flush of his health and success, destroyed with such gusto. Appropriately to his new coat of arms, he flew at eagles.

There is something pleasing to many in the sight of a great man dragged down; it gives a comforting belief in the justice of fate, if not of law. 'He hath brought down the mighty from their seats' is a consolation to those who could never be mighty. It was so to many who saw Sir Walter Ralegh brought down; and has been so to many since. Coke had the support of public opinion as well as of the King, and never realized that his own behaviour might soon change that opinion. In any case, it was the King who mattered to him.

'A word from the King mates him,' Francis Bacon wrote of him. Coke, who had been at such pains to 'please the Queen', was yet more eager to please the new King, on whose favour depended all chance of future success. But James was to turn public opinion, and Coke's, against himself by his insistence on his Divine Right. So it was that the abuse of the Royal Prerogative, which had been a minor menace under the last of the Tudor sovereigns, swelled into a major one under the first of the Stuarts. It produced its oddest result in turning Coke into an apparently

[1] James Morice, the Puritan, 1593. Quoted in F. Thompson's *Short History of Parliament, 1295-1642.*
[2] E. Edwards, *Sir Walter Ralegh,* 1868.

different person. The 'most disagreeable figure in our history' then became 'our greatest lawyer', 'the most admired and venerated of Judges', and one of 'the stoutest defenders of the rights of the people against the arbitrary King'.

But this change of front did not arise from any change of heart or character. It arose simply from a change of job. His life-long rival in love and law, Francis Bacon, adroitly got him kicked upstairs to the far less profitable post of Chief Justice, and answered his reproaches with a neat jibe at his swollen profits as Attorney-General: 'You must needs grow in height as well as width, my lord Coke, lest you become a Monster!' Bacon certainly owed Coke one, if not two, bad turns, for having first snatched the Attorneyship from his anxious grasp, and then the heiress, Lady Hatton. Coke, to whom all was then fair in love and law, rushed to propose to her within five weeks of the death of his devoted 'First and Best Wife' and mother of his ten children. This indecent haste was because he knew Bacon was wooing her, and in desperate need of her money. Coke, though enormously rich, thought two heiresses better than one, cut out Bacon, and lived unhappily ever after. Bacon was avenged by the life-long squabbles and scandals that Coke suffered from his Second and Worst Wife. And Bacon's other revenge in pushing his doubly successful rival into the Judgeship was greater than he could guess; for by then Coke's self-confidence, nourished ever since infancy, had swelled in proportion to his gains in land, money, and above all power, so that he was emboldened to fly at higher game than captive eagles, even at the King. Both as Judge and as an influential leader of the House of Commons, he discovered the inconvenience to himself, as well as to others, of the King's Prerogative, especially when it made a claim to taxes on imports and exports, etc.

So he then reversed completely the policy of his whole former lifetime. Instead of 'bending the Law' beneath the demands of the Prerogative, he attacked the demands. Instead of pocketing and suppressing a bill to confirm Magna Carta's guarantee of the liberty of the subject, he set himself 'with irresistible logic', as Dr C. V. Wedgwood has shown, to interpret Magna Carta as a flat contradiction of the current legal ruling 'Rex is Lex', or the King's Will is Law. It was therefore a contradiction also of his own former practice of the Law. In still more flagrant contradiction, he gave the lie to his former self. 'Magna Carta is such a fellow that he will have no Sovereign.' That was racy; what follows, magnificent: 'Every oppression against law, by colour of an *usurped authority*, is a kind of destruction . . . and it is the worst oppression that is done by *colour of justice.*' [1]

Did he then never see his former self, nor ask what colour justice had worn at Ralegh's trial? The answer is that with regard to himself he was all his life colour-blind, his head deep in the sand of his own 'virtue and righteous toil'. His certainty of himself made him blind even to the consequences to himself. His courage had grown with his conceit, for his persistent opposition to the King landed him in the Tower for a few weeks, and he was even threatened with the appalling prospect of being transferred to a post in Ireland. The voyage alone would kill him, he protested, as he had never been on the sea.

Hence the astonishing about-turn of opinion, which has turned Coke into a near-hero for opposing James, whom he had formerly obeyed so subserviently. Yet he really remained entirely consistent all through his very long life. His actions, both earlier as Attorney-General and later as Judge, were inspired by the same unalterable conviction, that whatsoever he decided was right.

'For I, my Lords, Embody the Law.'

His conceit was not only of omniscience, but a moral arrogance not unknown in other judges, of belief in himself as sole arbiter of right and wrong. His true view of Justice in Ralegh's trial was that of the King in Beaumont and Fletcher's *Valentinian*:

'Justice will never hear you! I am Justice.'

*   *   *

The Law did not then presume a prisoner to be innocent until proved guilty. Roman Law had done so, but the Common Law considered his innocence only a 'privilege of proof'—a very different matter. The conduct of the Law had in fact deteriorated even in the past hundred and fifty years, from the mediaeval idea of it as a power of its own, above rulers as well as subjects. There

[1] C. V. Wedgwood, *The King's Peace*, pp. 430-1, quoting Coke's Commentary on Magna Carta in his *Second Part of the Institutes of the Laws of England*. (The italics are mine.—M. I.)

had been an attempt to reform it under Edward VI by forbidding the sale of legal appointments, but this still went on in secret. Coke was paid two thousand angels for securing someone a judicial office, and King James became the biggest salesman of all, taking bribes up to £17,000 each for different legal appointments. He gave the game away by referring bitterly to the only man who refused to pay up as 'the Judge that would give no money'. As Judge Jeffries said eighty years later, and he should know, 'Most of the Judges were rogues.' They were no longer an independent order of state, with ideals of their responsibilities on the Bench, as they had been even in 1450. By 1603 they had degenerated, as the late King's Remembrancer[1] has told us, into 'the King's servants. They might be dismissed at any moment. They were there to do his bidding, just as much as the King's butler or steward. . . . Their chief concern was to take care of the royal prerogative. . . . The personal wishes of the King dominated.'

So that those writers who say Ralegh's trial was in order, and a fair one according to the formula of the time; that the Judges were all 'honest men' or they wouldn't have been Judges; that Cecil was one of them and Ralegh's friend; and that therefore their verdict of 'Guilty' must have been at least somewhere near the truth, are not facing the facts. Ralegh was presumed guilty from the start. The charge against him had to be justified by law, and that was what the lawyers were there for; not to seek out justice, but to prove their own justification.

That was the formula, but this instance of it is the most unbearable. To quote the highest legal opinion, it was 'a trial marked from first to last by injustice and crime, clothed—scantily—in judicial forms; not an act done hastily in excitement, but deliberately carried out in cold blood. It is criminal procedure seen at its worst.' And the King's Remembrancer adds, 'You may have visited an old prison and its loathsome dungeons and instruments of torture. The feeling inspired by such a visit is much the same as that excited by reading the proceedings in this case.'

---

[1] King's Remembrancer and Senior Master of Supreme Court of Judicature, Sir John Macdonnell, K.C.B., *Historical Trials.*

CHAPTER TWENTY-TWO

'The Happiest Day that ever he Spent'

CARLETON ON RALEGH AT HIS TRIAL

RALEGH was brought from his prison cell into the Court Room that had been set up in the great stone hall of Wolvesey Castle at Winchester. In the low-lying town, sunk in the valley, the autumn mists coiled white, for it was past mid-November, and the icy barred cell in which he had spent the previous night had increased his ague, so that his first concern was to keep his hands from shaking, as if from fear. There was good reason for fear. He had learned on arrival that six out of seven conspirators had already been condemned to death, a cheerless conclusion to a journey in which his guards had had to fight the mob howling for his blood. Erect as ever, his aching joints made him move more stiffly, and therefore proudly, and he seemed taller because thin to emaciation, his cheeks sunken from illness in the Tower, the bones showing clearly in the immensely high dome of his forehead.

His intent and wary eyes watched the blur of faces around the crowded hall, many of them there since daybreak, some waiting outside since the day before for the doors to open. The Lady Arabella or 'Arbell' Stuart herself was there, up in the minstrels' gallery by the side of old Lord Nottingham. Her rather vacant, pink and white face was as childish now in her late twenties as when Ralegh had once met her at dinner about sixteen years before. 'I never liked her,' he said of the little ninny. Ironically, her passion for masquerade was to give her the rank of a queen at last, but by mistake, for after her death the portrait at Hampton Court of her in fancy dress was believed until just lately to be one of Queen Elizabeth.

Ralegh saw that a friendly neighbour of his had been removed from among the jury overnight, and his worst enemy appointed as an extra judge. Yet he declined to question them, which would have been useless, and merely answered courteously he 'thought them all honest and Christian men', as casual a touch as Hamlet's careless question before his fencing match: 'These foils have all a length?'

Yet on the special Commission of Judges appointed by James was Lord Henry Howard, who had always openly hated him, and as Ralegh had begun to know, though nothing like as clearly as we do now, had made it his chief business for the past two years to poison the King's mind against him. With him was Robert Cecil, who had egged Lord Henry on to do this, while distilling his own poison in subtler and more discreet wording. The two together had laid all the groundwork for Ralegh's prosecution well before James came to the throne.

At the head of the 'honest and Christian men' was Chief Justice Popham to pronounce judgment, huge as a barrel and grossly ugly, who had continued to share profits with highwaymen even when a barrister; then made amends for his 'wild youth' by 'persecuting poor pretty wenches out of all pity and mercy'— so wrote that respectable citizen Mr John Chamberlain, himself such a stickler for propriety that he wished the Reverend John Donne 'would give over versifying' when appointed Dean of St Paul's. Popham and his fellow Chief Justice, Anderson, had shown unusual brutality in religious trials, with the saintly Edmund Campion as their noblest victim. Yet another judge, Sir John Stanhope, had ordered a clergyman, though not a Catholic, to be tortured. The Counsel, Serjeant Hele, who was to open the indictment, was notorious as an usurer and brawler; and his speech would be followed for the Crown by the Attorney-General Sir Edward Coke.

Ralegh had observed the stocky, dapper, consequential figure of his chief prosecutor, bulky in his robes, both in Parliament and at Essex's trial; his bushy but well-trimmed beard and moustaches shone with the same high polish as did his eyes, hard and glossy as chestnuts, fixed in an inimical bull-like stare, even in his official portrait. It had become a glare of fury at first sight of the prisoner. Ralegh had met that look in many faces of 'envy, hatred malice and all uncharitableness', and had smiled in scorn at it. Now as its prospective victim he recognized how deadly it could be to him. Coke hated him, not for anything Coke believed, or did not believe, that he had done; but for himself, with the instinctive hate that conceit bears to pride.

The trial was from the start a duel between these two single antagonists, of about the same age and, in their different spheres, of almost equal eminence. But their weapons were not equal. Ralegh used a rapier; his prosecutor a bludgeon. In attack Coke hit out savagely and wildly and often wide of the mark. His almost incoherent abuse of Essex had so confused the case that it had needed Bacon to restore it from 'so many digressions' and skilfully damn both Coke as a muddler, and the prisoner, Bacon's friend and benefactor, as a traitor. But Coke's bludgeon had all the weight of the law behind it, and was wielded by the most doggedly successful lawyer of his day; while Ralegh had never studied law, and paid for his ignorance with the loss of much of his property.

Coke could barely wait for Hele to finish reading the charge, the main point of which was that Ralegh had conspired with Cobham to 'deprive the King of his Government and advance the Lady Arabella to the throne, raise up Sedition, alter religion and bring in the Roman Superstition, and to procure foreign' (i.e. Spanish) 'enemies to invade the Kingdom'.

Ralegh pleaded 'Not Guilty'. He was not allowed to call or question any witnesses, and must conduct his own defence—when or if Coke would allow him to do so, for he at once interrupted him with a long-winded pedantic lecture on all the various phases of treason, and then with a panegyric on the 'sweetness and innocence' of King James. Ralegh tried to get him back to the point, and at that their duel started in earnest, Coke's heavy weapon flailing out in a transport of rage.

"Thou art the greatest Lucifer that ever lived. Nay, I will prove all. Thou art a monster. Thou hast an English face but a Spanish heart. . . . I *'thou'* thee, thou traitor!"

The familiar 'thou' as to a servant was by way of an insult, and the 'Spanish heart', to a man who had fought Spain all his life, a palpable absurdity; but Coke was trying to provoke Ralegh into a passion and so discredit him. He plunged into a long description of an earlier and quite different plot by some Roman Catholic priests, which had nothing whatever to do with the case. This time Ralegh managed to break through and remind the jury: "I pray you, Gentlemen, remember that I am not charged with this plot."

Even Coke had to agree that he was not so charged; but found a picturesque excuse for dragging it in. All these treasons, 'like

Samson's foxes were joined together at the tails, though their heads were severed'. This 'irresistible logic' sounded rather weak as an example of his pet maxim: 'Reason is the life of the law . . . and law is the perfection of reason.' So he broke it off and suddenly swung round again on Ralegh, with the question: "To whom, Sir Walter, did you bear malice? To the royal children?"

It failed to throw the prisoner off his balance, for he merely reminded Coke that he was still talking of the wrong plot; and so, "I pray you, Mr Attorney, to whom or what end do you speak all this? . . . What is the treason of the priests to me?"

His voice, always low (as Sir Edward Hoby had complained in Parliament) and now weakened by long anxiety and illness, exasperated Coke into what reads like a series of frenzied shouts: "I will prove you to be the most notorious traitor that ever came to the bar. . . . Go to, I will lay thee upon thy back for the confidentest traitor that ever came at a bar. . . . Thou art the most vile and execrable traitor that ever lived."

The prisoner at last made himself heard between the explosions. "You speak indiscreetly, barbarously and uncivilly."

Coke gasped out: "I want words sufficient to express thy viperous treasons."

Ralegh replied: "I think you want words indeed, for you have spoken one thing half a dozen times."

The thrust drew blood, for there were smiles and titters in Court. Coke struck wildly back again; and again far wide of the mark.

"Thou art an odious fellow, thy name is hateful to all England for thy pride!" It might well be true, but was scarcely a capital charge. And Ralegh's answer brought the charge home to Coke himself.

"It will go near to prove a measuring match between you and me, Mr Attorney."

It was a very palpable hit. Coke's blundering weapon had been knocked clean out of his hand. There was now open laughter in Court against Mr Attorney, though not uproarious, for nobody knew who might be listening. The spectators saw, and some have recorded, how Ralegh warmed to the pleasure of the fight; his bearing no longer rigid but at ease, his eyes now as bright as they were watchful, and even, at times, amused. The crowd too was warming in astonished admiration; here was a game-cock indeed to give such sport, or rather, since the odds were too unequal for a cockfight, and Judges in Bacon's damagingly truthful phrase were 'Lions under the Throne', here was a lean, lithe greyhound who could fly at the Lions' throats and worry them shrewdly.

They had indeed had a worrying time all these past weeks of examining evidence, trying to collect enough to bring on the Trial at all. The French Ambassador, the Count of Beaumont, said openly how he had written home that 'the Council find it difficult to sustain Ralegh's prosecution', since Lord Cobham had 'denied what it is alleged that he charged against Sir Walter', adding cynically that nevertheless 'their power to put him to the death, despite his innocency, he well knows'. It was uphill work for such lawyers as believed in what Coke called 'the gladsome light of jurisprudence'. They knew that Cobham had confessed to his Vicar that 'Ralegh had done him no hurt, but he had done Ralegh a great deal'; that he had written to the Lieutenant of the Tower telling him his remorse for having wrongly charged Ralegh: 'God is my witness, it doth trouble my conscience.'

It did not trouble the conscience of the new Lieutenant, Sir George Harvey (hastily substituted for the former Lieutenant, who had been dismissed for liking and admiring Ralegh). Harvey had agreed with the Judges that what mattered most was that the State should not be troubled, nor, above all, King James. So Sir George thought it 'convenient' to suppress his letter from Cobham. But his son had already made friends with Ralegh in prison, and young Harvey told him of his father's treachery in concealing Cobham's remorseful confession, and offered to convey a letter asking Cobham to repeat it, but this time direct to Ralegh. This landed the youth in jail—through Cobham's talebearing, not Ralegh's, who never disclosed his part in the game. A game it was, for young Harvey, being a good shot, and free to walk outside the prison walls, bowled an apple clean through Cobham's upper window—and inside the apple was Ralegh's letter. The end of the game may be told now: how Sir George clapped his 'unworthy son' into prison, and waited a good month after all the trials and convictions were over before asking for his release. Sir George then produced "the enclosed letters written unto me by the Lord Cobham, whereby he hath, under his own hand, manifested the great desire he had to justify Sir

Walter Ralegh, which course was by me then stopped, as was fit".

It would be interesting to know what young Harvey said to his father when at last set free, too late to give any evidence at Ralegh's trial. All that Ralegh admitted at his trial was that he had sent Cobham a letter in an apple, by 'some poor fellow'; and the Prosecution made the most of this shockingly deceitful connivance with a fellow prisoner. Ralegh in answer made the modest understatement, "It was not ill of me to beg him to say the truth."

Sir Edward Coke furiously denied both his right to ask for the truth, and the truth itself. He could give no proof of what he said, but he shouted at Ralegh exactly how, why, and when he had led Cobham into rebellion. "Now you must have money. Aremberg" (the Spanish Ambassador) "was no sooner in England than thou incitest Cobham to go and deal with him for money . . . to raise Rebellion in the kingdom."

Ralegh: "Let me answer for myself."

Coke: "Thou shalt not."

Ralegh: "It concerneth my life . . ."

But Coke interrupted: "All that he did was by thy instigation, thou viper! I will prove thee the rankest traitor in all England."

Ralegh: "No, Mr Attorney, I am no traitor. Whether I live or die, I shall stand as true a subject as any the King hath. You may call me a traitor at your pleasure, yet it becomes not a man of quality and virtue to do so. But I take comfort that it is all you can do, for I do not yet hear that you charge me with any treason."

The dignity of his answer plainly had its effect on the Court, for Chief Justice Popham hastily intervened to remind them that "Mr Attorney speaks out of zeal of his duty for the King, and Sir Walter Ralegh for his life. Be patient on both sides."

Coke showed his patience by further abuse, and then asked eagerly: "Have I angered you?"

"I am in no case to be angry," was the quiet answer.

Coke's speeches have been condemned by our Supreme Court of Judicature as 'unsurpassed in a court of Justice for downright ruffianism—unequalled even in the French Revolutionary Trials at their worst'.[1] The same legal authority supports Ralegh's

[1] Sir John Macdonell, K.C.B., Senior Master of the Supreme Court of Judicature. *Op. Cit.*

appeal to the laws passed by Edward VI, which said: 'No man shall be condemned of treason unless he be accused by two lawful accusers'; and that they 'must be brought in person before the party accused'.

Ralegh pressed hard for this. "If you proceed to condemn me by bare inferences without an oath, without a subscription, without witnesses, upon a paper accusation, then you try me by the Spanish Inquisition."

'He was unjust to the Spanish Inquisition,' says Sir John Macdonell, 'its procedure would have been more regular.'

Ralegh demanded as his right to have at least his single adverse witness in Court.

"My lords, I claim to have my accuser brought here face to face to speak. I beseech you, my lords, let Cobham be sent for.... If my accuser were dead or abroad it were something; but he liveth, and is in this very house."

It was true. Cobham was imprisoned just underneath the Court Room. Yet the Judges refused to have him, their one and only witness, brought into Court to face the man he accused; and they could give no reason for their refusal. For the reason was all too plain. They had had the greatest difficulty at first in extorting Cobham's 'confession' against Ralegh; and even then he had for a long time refused to sign it. Popham had at last induced him to do so by telling him that Ralegh had persistently betrayed and blackened *him*. This lie worked Cobham up into one of his famous rages, so by then it was an easy matter to thrust the pen into his hand while he was shouting "That wretch! That traitor Ralegh!" and get him to sign.

Once the former friends came face to face, Ralegh would soon show that he had been no traitor to Cobham, and that Cobham had been tricked into his confession, which he would retract all over again. The Judges dared not face the truth—as Ralegh boldly pointed out. *If* Cobham really believed that Ralegh had given him 'wicked counsel' and 'been the cause of all his miseries', then he would certainly repeat it here in Court to avenge his wrongs by proving Ralegh guilty. By refusing to admit him, the Judges showed that they themselves did not believe in his charges.

Ralegh pressed it home passionately that there was nothing against him in this case but Cobham's accusations—which

Cobham had forsworn. "Let me speak for my life. It can be no hurt for him to be brought. . . . If you grant me not this favour, then I am strangely used."

He swung round upon Popham and Anderson: "Campion was not denied to have his accusers face to face."

It was a deadly thrust, for Popham and Anderson were the Judges who had consigned the Jesuit priest to his hideous martyr-dom nearly twenty years ago; and few had believed even then that Campion had been a traitor. It stirred too an uneasy recol-lection in the Court that Popham and Anderson had ordered Campion to be racked and tortured for weeks, even before his trial, in the hope of extorting confessions of his guilt.

Yet they had both, with the other Judges, just been protesting their indignant denials when Ralegh complained that they had threatened to rack his friend and servant Kemys (who had been kept in prison eighteen weeks) to make him produce evidence against his master.

There had been a shocked outcry.

"Kemys was never at the rack."

"No such rigour was ever used."

"We protest, before God, there was no such matter—to our knowledge."

You would have thought they had never heard of anything so illegal as torture being used in England. But Ralegh stood his ground and insisted: "Was not the Keeper of the Rack sent for; and Kemys threatened with it?"

He forced the truth out of them at last: Kemys had been *shown* the rack, and "we told him he deserved it; but we did not threaten him with it".

The whole audience could see through so thin an evasion; and the other commissioners hastily withdrew the hems of their garments: "It was more than we knew!" they exclaimed in pious disapproval.

But the audience could see through that too. And now Ralegh had reminded them that his chief Judges, who had just denied in horror that they had even threatened the rack, were the very same as those who had tortured Campion nearly to death with it. Yet even 'Campion was not denied to have his accusers face to face'.

They could give no reason for denying it to Ralegh, so they

ruled against it on a point of law; saying that the Edward VI statutes had been repealed by Philip and Mary. This has been quoted again and again in history, as if the new ruling had become an indisputable point of law. But it had not. The Court of Judicature has decided that 'the repeal, if there was a repeal, was only by implication; and, what is little to Coke's credit, in his *Institutes of the Laws of England* he expressly states that the statutes of Edward VI were *not* repealed'.[1]

Coke's immense and superb work on the 'Institutes', our legal Bible to this day, as Lord Birkett calls it, shows he had a greater knowledge of the law than any man. But he could deny the truth even of his own work when it suited him. If you embody the law, you can dress it as it suits you. What he wrote for fame and posterity, to prove himself the wisest lawyer in England, was one thing. What he chose to practise in a Court of Law, so as to win his case, was another.

He denied Ralegh's request to hear and answer the questions separately, as his memory, never good, had weakened with his illness in prison; but Coke objected that if the evidence were broken up it would spoil 'its grace and vigour'. His vigour indeed was almost that of an actor 'hamming' his part, as in fact he probably was, for he was pretty certainly playing to a more important audience than any that was visible.

The King was staying near by, and was known to have a great liking for a secret 'lug', or ear, where he could listen to legal proceedings. The hiding place where he is believed to have lurked in the Winchester Court Room is shown to this day. Coke's persistent rage came naturally enough in face of Ralegh's unbreakable calm, but his ranting would also impress the King with his zeal in his service. His digressions in fulsome praise of James—and even of Essex—were also directed at this invisible royal audience, who would hear of them even if not at the moment listening to them. Coke had bullied Essex to his death as the flagrant traitor he had proved himself; but knowing James' friendly sentiment for him he now praised him, and roared at Ralegh that he was "a damnable atheist", whereas Essex had "died the child of God, and God honoured him at his death". So James would hear 'his martyr' praised for his religion, in contrast to 'that Great Lucifer'.

[1] 3 Inst. 24-7.

"Spider of hell!" was another example of Coke's 'grace and vigour'; and he went on to compare Ralegh with beasts of prey—wolves and bears that press close upon a dying man, for "Thou, Ralegh, wast by when Essex died."

This was the old slander, the only one that had the power to hurt Ralegh to the quick all his life, that he had stood near to Essex on the scaffold, and gloated over his death. The truth has already been told, that it was his duty to be present as Captain of the Guard and, in spite of it, he had withdrawn to the Armoury where in solitude he had shed tears. And then heard later that Essex had asked in those last moments where he was, and wished for a reconciliation. So regret was added to the bitterness of that ancient lie of his triumphing over his fallen rival, which Coke now shouted out again in Court.

The wild-goose chases in search of any possible evidence flew far afield; they pursued even a crumb of gossip about a humble English pilot who had heard an unknown Portugee say in Lisbon that 'the English King's throat would be cut by Don Ralegh and Don Cobham'. Needless to say, the nameless Portugee could not be produced; and the pilot, the only so-called witness ever to be brought into this Court, was a poor sailor who could evidently be paid to say whatever he was told—even, presumably, that he understood Portuguese. Ralegh scornfully dismissed this "saying of some wild Jesuit or beggarly priest—what infer you from that?"

"That your treason hath wings," was Coke's 'perfection of reason'.

Farce went still further in the 'evidence' of a book written twenty-six years earlier against James' title to the throne, which Cobham had said he had taken off Ralegh's table, without asking him for it, and that Ralegh had said 'was foolishly written'. Yet it was now advanced as a proof of treason that Ralegh had possessed it. Where had he got it?

"From a certain Councillor's Library."

"Which Councillor?"

"Why, from my Lord Treasurer Burghley."

This was awkward for Burghley's son, Robert Cecil. He sprang up in a flutter of embarrassed explanation and excuse, arguing angrily that it was right for his father to have had the book, but wrong for Ralegh. There was a long chase of this new wild goose,

which proved just as much against the Cecils as against Ralegh—
that is to say, nothing at all.

Like many tensely strung persons, Ralegh could forget the
sickness and dismay he had suffered all these weeks in the
excited enjoyment of winning round after round with his quick
and forceful logic or quiet mockery. An acute eye-witness, Sir
Dudley Carleton, observed how gallant and even gay he looked;
and wrote that he answered all his enemies 'with that temper,
wit, learning, courage, and judgment that, save it went with the
hazard of his life, it was the happiest day that ever he spent'. It is
the best tribute to his heroic quality as a fighter.

Carleton's letter added that if he had not been given an ill
name, 'and an ill name is half hanged, then in the opinion of all
men he had been acquitted. In one word, never was a man so
hated and so popular in so short a time.'

The height of his popularity came with his speech in his
defence, one of the magnificent speeches in history. It was been
justly compared with Milton's prose at its clearest and most
passionate. But Ralegh's was spoken on the spur of the moment
by a lone man fighting for his life, with no knowledge beforehand
of what charges would be sprung on him. These had been
prepared for months before by his judges and prosecutors,
who sprung one surprise attack after another, many of them
quite off the point, and aimed only at knocking him off his
guard.

Some historians have belittled his defence as being only for
himself, in that 'he stood for no great cause'. But fairness, and
liberty for the truth to prevail, are a great cause. He stood for his
own ringing cry in Parliament: "Leave every man free, which is
the desire of a true Englishman!" He fought for all Englishmen
down to this day in forcing the ideal of justice back into the
degenerate formulas of the law. He spoke, too, for the glory of the
past Elizabethan age to which he himself, the last of the great
sailors, belonged more truly than any man still living; an age that
had won freedom from the fear of Spain, and had made England
a great nation. She should be greater than ever "now that
we have the kingdom of Scotland united—Ireland quieted—
Denmark assured—the Low Countries our nearest neighbour.
And instead of a Lady whom Time hath surprised, we have now
an active King who would be present at his own businesses. For

me, at this time, to make myself a Robin Hood, a Wat Tyler, or a Jack Cade—I was not so mad!"

The poetry of his phrase for the old Queen, a legend in life and after, has become famous; but how often is it remembered that this phrase was surprised out of a man who was fighting a desperate battle for his life? The courage that can spontaneously express itself in poetry at such a moment is rare indeed. And it was in a strain of poetry that he proudly gave the lie to the senseless charge that he had 'a Spanish heart', for Ralegh's poetry was never divorced from life and action, but was his natural expression of it. He told of the long fight against Spain that had lasted all his lifetime; of his part in it, and of its triumphant conclusion in Spain's present "weakness, his poorness, his humbleness. Six times we had repulsed his forces, thrice in Ireland, thrice at sea— once upon our coast, and twice upon his own. Thrice had I served against him myself at sea—wherein for my country's sake I had expended of my own property forty thousand marks. I knew that where aforetime he was wont to have forty great sail at the least in his ports, now he hath not past six or seven. . . . I knew that of twenty-five millions which he had from his Indies, he had scarce any left."

With precise reasoning and quiet irony he pointed out how iodotic it would have been for him to conspire with an enemy whom all his life he had helped to weaken and impoverish; and equally idiotic that the enemy should wish to pay him, and the flimsy Cobham, vast sums without "some assurance for his money! The Queen of England lent not her money to the States without she had Flushing, Brill and other towns for it. Nay, her own subjects, the merchants of London, did not lend her money without they had her lands in pawn for it! And to show I am not 'Spanish'—as you term me—at this very time I had writ a treatise to the King's Majesty of the present state of Spain, and reasons against the Peace!"

He had indeed, and many there must have known what an indignant flutter it had caused in James, so that he had almost accused Ralegh of treason then and there for daring to write projects against Spain. Even the King could hardly have it both ways. It is to be hoped that he was listening, though the magnificence of the whole speech would almost certainly have had no effect on him. But it had on most of the audience. One man there,

Roger Ashton, had the pluck to tell the King that 'Never man spoke so well in the time past, nor would in the time to come.' Another, Lord Hay, who as a Scot was deeply prejudiced against Ralegh, believing him to be against the Scottish succession, told James that 'whereas he would at first have gone a hundred miles to see him hanged, he would now have gone a thousand to save his life'.

Ralegh had won his triumph. 'The best-hated man in England' had suddenly become the best loved. It even began to look as though the jury might be so carried away by the turn in his favour as to run the risk of fines or imprisonment by bringing in a verdict of Not Guilty. Which would be very awkward for the Judges, who would then certainly be dismissed from office for failing to direct the jury as required. The awful warning of Sir Nicolas Throckmorton was in all their minds. The justice that the law had so imprudently given him, must now be paid for by his son-in-law. Whatever Coke might write later on Lex versus Rex, he had now got to make Rex triumph over Lex. So he bellowed in renewed attack, and shook his clenched fist in the long, shadowed face of the prisoner, whose low voice had held this vast crowd in so deep a hush.

Coke's newly aroused anger was goaded further by the sudden, amazing disloyalty of his best colleague. Robert Cecil, who had done more than anyone to engineer this trial, was showing himself more and more uneasy as it progressed. At its beginning, he had sworn to God that he had loved Ralegh "and had a great conflict in himself" to see him "fallen from the State", thus assuming, though one of his Judges, that he was guilty, before any evidence had been given. But he twice reproved Coke, the first time mildly, when he was shouting Ralegh down, and Cecil interposed: "Be not so impatient, good Master Attorney. Give him leave to speak." At which, so the reporter in Court wrote, 'Mr. Attorney sat down in a chafe, and would speak no more until the Commissioners urged and entreated him.' He had to be coaxed out of his 'apoplectic silence'[1] into his scolding 'direction of the jury'.

But he had enough restraint to withhold his trump card to the end. This was yet another letter from Cobham, written since he had been brought to Winchester. In it he took back his former

[1] C. V. Wedgwood, *The King's Peace*, p. 136, on 'Coke under Charles I'.

retractions and accused Ralegh all over again; with the added indictment that Ralegh had bargained with the Spanish Ambassador, Aremberg, for a yearly pension 'to tell what was intended by England against Spain'.

At which, the reporter wrote, 'Sir Walter Ralegh stood much amazed'—and no wonder. Hearing yet another about-turn from Cobham, after all he had solemnly sworn to the contrary, was like listening to the random ravings of a madman, as indeed they probably were.

But Coke was sane enough to prove himself an astute lawyer by holding back this only plausible piece of evidence to the end of the trial, when judges and jury were sick and tired of it, knowing that it could only have one end, if they were to consider their own safety. So no wonder it was reported that 'Cobham's confession seemed to give great satisfaction'. The evidence had 'stood very doubtful', but now it seemed clear that Coke had won.

"Now, Ralegh," he said triumphantly, "if thou hast the grace, humble thyself to the King and confess thy treasons."

Mr Attorney was irked by a few pettifogging questions from the Judges, but it was quickly decided that Cobham's letter was entirely spontaneous; he had not been offered any promises or threats to produce it.

"I dare say not," said Ralegh, as coolly as ever, in spite of his shock. "But my Lord Cobham received a letter from his wife, that there was no way to save his life but to accuse me." Already 'he seemed to gather his spirits again' as he then told them what had suggested this astonishing new lie. It was that 'Cobham had offered him eight thousand crowns for the furtherance of the peace between England and Spain' (the very cause that James himself most desired) and that he, Ralegh, had brushed it aside with the flippant remark, " 'When I see the money I will make you an answer', for I had thought it one of his ordinary idle conceits and therefore made no account of it."

To those who knew Cobham this was reasonable enough. Irresponsible and touchy, it was 'his fashion to utter things easily', while his nervous speed to take offence, and his 'bitter railings' were notorious. His passions had 'such violence that his best friends could never temper them'. Nobody would want the bother of arousing them by a direct denial of his tall talk, if they could avoid them by a casually evasive answer, such as Ralegh was all too likely to give with a wave of his silver-mounted pipe, blowing away Cobham's boasting offers of 'great sums of money' in a puff of smoke.

But it gave Popham a chance for one of his gravely moral rebukes. "I perceive that you are not as clear a man as you have protested all this while, for you should have discovered this matter to the King." So he should, if he had wished to act as a shabby informer and ruin Cobham, as Cobham had ruined him; but Ralegh had "hoped to turn Cobham away from such courses", and thought he had done so.

Cobham's brother Lord Brooke had said under examination by the Council that the two of them had hoped to secure Ralegh's help and complicity in their vague plottings; and had failed to do so. This evidence was never produced in Court, nor allowed in Ralegh's favour. But it worked heavily against Brooke, who paid with his head for failing to back up his brother's accusations.

Ralegh too had held back his trump card to the end, and realized now too late that Coke had already over-trumped it with his brand-new confession from Cobham. But he produced it bravely; put his hand into the breast of his doublet and held up a sheet of paper. "Here now, I pray you," he said, "what Cobham hath written to *me*." He handed it to the Clerk to read aloud, but once again Coke tried to suppress the evidence. 'Mr Attorney would not have this letter read,' wrote the reporter. 'And upon Lord Cecil's advising him to hear it, he said "My Lord Cecil, mar not a good cause." '

This was too much even for that Court. Hissing broke out, first in a few whispers, then all round the Court.

It was too much also for Cecil. "Mr Attorney," he exclaimed, "you are more peremptory than honest. You must not come here to show me what to do."

Cecil had already tried to support Ralegh's claim to hear Cobham's charges from him face to face in Court, and had been over-ruled. Even Cobham's letters of accusation were never produced in Court, nor seen by the jury; only quoted as hearsay. Cecil insisted that Ralegh should at the least be allowed to show his own piece of evidence. Coke, who thought he had just won, was actually reduced again to silence in his fury at this meddling little man. Ralegh was quick to ask Cecil himself to read Cobham's letter aloud, since he knew his brother-in-law's handwriting well, and could tell there had been no forgery. He pointed out that, unlike the letter Coke had quoted (which was not under oath), it was a confession written under the most solemn oath a Christian man could make, when in danger of death. Cecil then read aloud what Cobham had written to Ralegh.

"I protest upon my soul and before God and his angels, I never had conference with you in any treason, nor was ever moved by you to the things I heretofore accused you of. And for anything I know, you are as innocent and as clear from any treasons against the King as is any subject living. . . . And so God deal with me and have mercy on my soul, as this is true."

*   *   *

It made no odds, of course. Coke's 'good cause' had been a bit marred; he had been openly hissed in Court, and rebuked twice over by one of the judges; and the prisoner had frequently made him look a fool—but in this, Coke's ostrich quality came to his aid, for he could not believe such a thing possible. Had not the great Lord Mountjoy himself, the only successful Commander-in-Chief in Ireland, declared that he would fly the country rather than come under the flail of Coke's tongue? And never had it flailed as furiously as in this trial. Yet even his egoism must have perceived, however indignantly, that in public opinion the prisoner had won the case.

Before the trial, nearly everybody had believed Ralegh guilty; after it, practically no one did. If they played for safety, they murmured that it was all very incomprehensible, 'a dark kind of treason, and the veil is still on it'. If they spoke out frankly, they agreed with Sir John Harington, who said that Sir Walter 'seemeth wondrously fitted, both by art and nature, to serve the State. . . . I doubt the dice be fairly thrown, if his life be the losing stake.'

No one who saw or read the reports of the trial had any doubt but that the dice were loaded. Coke summed up for the jury the reason for the final condemnation in a word: "The King's safety and your clearing cannot agree"; i.e. Ralegh was thought by the King to be potentially dangerous, and therefore could not be cleared of the charges, in case he might commit them hereafter.

The Sovereign's safety, at the beginning of a new dynasty, when there must be no disturbances in the State, was the one thing that really mattered.

The jury took the 'direction', brought in the required verdict 'Guilty of Treason', and Popham put on the black cap and pronounced judgment, both in this life and the next; for he warned Ralegh that as an atheist "you shall find eternity in Hell Fire!" He then delivered a long 'unbridled tirade', as a great lawyer has called it, against the condemned man's private faults, his 'heathenish and blasphemous opinions' and his 'covetousness like a canker'. He 'grieved' and 'marvelled' at, and thereby derided, the fall of 'a man of your quality' . . . 'of your wit', and one who had 'always been taken for a wise man'.

Suddenly a bright after-thought interrupted this irrelevant sermon. "And now it comes into my mind why you might not have your accuser brought face to face!" Whatever came into his mind then made little odds, for he was putting the black cap on his head. But he gave the other judges an awkward moment, for the reason he told was more or less the true one—that Cobham was sure to take back all his accusations yet again. They must have agreed with Bacon that 'a much talking judge was like an ill-tuned cymbal'. His final comment added a singular judgment on the trial itself: "I never saw the like Trial, and hope I shall never see the like again." Many there echoed his comment, though not as he had intended it.

He then gave the sentence: "You shall be drawn upon a hurdle through the open streets to the place of execution, there to be hanged and cut down alive, and your body shall be opened, your heart and bowels plucked out, and your privy members cut off and thrown into the fire before your eyes; then your head to be stricken off from your body, and your body divided into four quarters, to be disposed of at the King's pleasure. And God have mercy upon your soul!"

Ralegh remained standing, 'with admirable erection', as Sir Thomas Overbury observed. He 'hoped the jury might never have to answer for their verdict'. Some of them went on their knees to ask pardon from him. He went up to a few of the Judges to ask them quietly to do what they could to give him an honourable death instead of the hideous dismemberment. They said they would do this. Cecil was in tears. Ralegh followed the

Sir Edward Coke, aged 41.
Attorney General to Queen Elizabeth and
James I; later Lord Chief Justice.
By kind permission of the Earl of Leicester

Sir Francis Bacon, Lord Chancellor,
Baron Verulam and Viscount St Albans.
After Paul Van Somer.
By permission of the Trustees of the National Portrait Gallery

High Sheriff back to his prison cell, and the great hall slowly emptied amid a buzz of angry murmurs.

One spectator wrote that 'Cobham's accusation', as the main evidence, 'was no more to be weighed than the barking of a dog'; another, that there had been 'no proof at all. . . . I would not for much have been of the jury to have found him guilty.'

Coke had left before the verdict, and is said to have been astonished by it. 'Surely thou art mistaken. For I myself accused him but of misprision of treason' (i.e. the knowledge of treason and its concealment). If so, he had failed entirely to make this clear at the trial; but as his fury had so frequently made him incoherent, it may possibly have been his intention. The 'story' is contemporary, and is therefore considered unreliable by those historians who believe nothing that was told at the time. Another so-called story, though it was confidently quoted by his contemporaries as a well-known fact, is that one of the Judges, Sir Francis Gaudy, said on his death-bed that 'never before had the justice of England been so depraved and injured as in this Trial'.

And long later Ralegh's younger son, Carew, observed with the dry sardonic detachment that was so like his father's: 'I would fain know what it was that ever Cobham accused Ralegh of; for never I could. Likewise whether ever any man was condemned by a single witness, and he not present either.'

CHAPTER TWENTY-THREE

'Hammers Working in his Head'

SIR DUDLEY CARLETON, OF RALEGH

A YEAR later, four of Ralegh's Judges were secretly allotted
pensions by the new Spanish Ambassador, in return for
any information they might supply to Spain, again of
course in secret. Lord Henry Howard's and Lord Robert Cecil's
services as spies were rated at £1,000 a year each; and the
following year Cecil saw to it that his annual bribe was raised to
£1,500, since his supreme position as James' chief minister
should put the highest price on his espionage. Then, as Lord
Salisbury of Hatfield, he raised his price again, and continually
demanded payment in large sums for each piece of information
given. The Spanish Ambassador, sick of being so persistently
pestered, noted that he was 'a venal traitor, ready to sell his soul
for money'. There was nothing new in this except that the price
had gone up. Sir John Hawkins, the first and oldest of the great
Elizabethan sea-captains, had received Spanish pay for some
years before the Armada, without doing anything for it; and had
shared the swag and the joke with his Queen, to Philip's fury.
Cecil was probably equally ready to double-cross his pensioners.

But the fact remains that he, with three other highly-paid spies,
had condemned Ralegh to death for merely listening to talk of
the offers that they so greedily consolidated.

*　　　*　　　*

Ralegh was told that the warrant for his execution had been
dated for December 13th, nearly four weeks hence, postponed
until after all the others. He had wished for this, in hopes that
Cobham at point of death might yet again retract and clear his
former friend. But the King had postponed it in hopes of just the
contrary. The sudden violent turn of public opinion in Ralegh's
favour had alarmed the councillors; they advised James to wait
and see if he could get some confirmation of Ralegh's guilt from
the other prisoners on the scaffold. He could buy such confirma-

tion with promises of pardon. Ralegh had nothing to offer; and there was nothing he could do but live out such a lifetime in the next twenty-four days as can only be lived under sentence of death. A dead reaction had fallen on him after the tense drama of his trial. He had had no real hope of its outcome. 'I plainly perceive', he wrote to his wife, 'that my death was determined upon from the first day.' Yet so superbly had he played his part that there had been a desperate exhilaration in his lone fight, in the pride and panache with which he had stood up to one blow after another, and parried them with a thrust of sharp sense, of glancing wit, or grave rebuke. He had made rings round his opponents, stripped them of their pretences, and exposed their naked intention to destroy him. He had won over a thousand enemies to show themselves his friends, and had known it in the deep hush that filled the judgment hall as they hung on every word of his great speech that told them of the glories of the Armada, and the other victories that had freed Englishmen from half a century of the Spanish Terror. They were free of it now, so could forget it; but he, whom Spain called the Old Pirate, was condemned to die for having a 'Spanish heart'. The jury's hostile verdict was plainly not echoed by the country.

As his Queen had done shortly before she died, so Ralegh knew that he had won over to him the hearts of the people, even those that had so lately shown their hatred of him. He has been accused of being a great actor (and so has Elizabeth), but not of playing to the gallery, as she so frequently did; but he had never courted the favour of the crowd like his rival Essex, and this was the chief cause of his unpopularity. Now in a few hours he alone had changed all that, and found himself, both in the Court Room and in the echoes from the outside world, to be the most admired and loved of Englishmen.

But the scene was played out, the audience had all gone, he was back in his cold cell, with only his racing thoughts for company, and no arguments to answer, no adversary to fight. His high-strung nerves had given him in action the tense calm of excitement, but after it was over he fell into the agonizing dullness of solitude and sick despair, where death seems the only release. He could hardly bear to wait the three and a half weeks for it; and it is a measure of his sickness that he brooded even over Judge Popham's final harangue against him after his conviction, impertinent in every sense, since it was beside the point to smear his 'gloating malevolence' over what extra faults he could think of in a man already dead by law. When normal, Ralegh would only despise an old man who thus kicked at a dead one. But now to his tormented mind, Popham had the last word against him for ever, and there was no longer any chance for him to wipe it out. 'Oh God! I cannot live to think how I am derided,' he broke out in a letter to his wife, 'the scorns, the cruel words of lawyers, the infamous taunts and despites, to be made a wonder and a spectacle! Oh death, destroy the memory of these and lay me up in dark forgetfulness.'

So raw and sensitive was the reverse side of his pride. 'And now, I pray, let me be layd by, and never thought of '—that dying wish of Webster's Cardinal is an echo of Ralegh's utter disillusionment in himself. Pride had failed him; his noble bearing and brilliance of speech, the piercing logic of his arguments and demands for a true hearing, all had failed to save him. There was only one way to do so—throw pride to the winds and plead; but not for justice, nor even for common sense; the law had denied him these. Mercy alone, personal and capricious, at the whim of an alien king, was the only thing to which he could now appeal. So he wrote to Cecil and other Lords Commissioners, and though he began by a brief and incisive exposure of the false and feeble 'evidence' used to condemn him, he admitted that it was no use to argue, since the law had gone against him, and his only hope now was in 'the mercy of my Sovereign'. He begged them to intercede for it.

He has been severely criticized for this, and even his most understanding biographer, Edward Thompson, has regretted 'he was not a man of such moral greatness' as to tell his judges, like Socrates, "We go our ways, I to death, and you to life. Which is better, God only knows."

If Ralegh had been married to Socrates' scold, Xantippe, he might have shared his indifference to his fate. But his dear Bess and their son, little Wat, were now always in his mind, torturing him with remorse at having failed the two beings he loved best in the world. He had planned and worked to make them glorious, rich and at ease, with great estates to carry on their name; 'But God hath prevented all my determinations.' His execution would ruin them utterly; 'most sorry I am, as God

knoweth, that being thus surprised with death, I can leave you no
better estate. . . . To what friend to direct thee I know not, for
all mine have left me in the true time of trial.'

His worst dread was that his death would kill all happiness in
Bess. His pride was not worth such a price. Eleven years ago he
had thrown it away to make his peace with the Queen, who had
clapped them both into the Tower for daring to love and marry.
His pleas of adoration to an old woman have been constantly
quoted in ridicule of him, though he had been pleading not only
for himself, but for his new young wife, utterly helpless except for
him; and so she was again now.

Elizabeth's jealous cruelty could have been predicted. With
James it was impossible to predict anything. Caprice in him
touched inhuman depths, as of an occasionally half-crazy delinquent. So indeed he had remained, for all his learning and
cleverness, and with plenty of the correct excuses for being
one. He was to give one of his worst examples of this capricious
'humour' presently. In the meantime the trials had gone on and
the executions started with those in the priests' plot. They 'led the
dance', and because they refused to admit their guilt were 'most
miserably tortured', so wrote an eye-witness, 'to the great discontent of the people, who now think matters were not so heinous
as were made show of'.

Then after a week's agonizing pause, Cobham's brother Lord
Brooke went to the scaffold. There were rumoured hopes of last-
minute reprieves; but he had lost all chance of one, since he had
confessed the truth, that he and Cobham had tried, but failed, to
get any help in their plots from Ralegh. Brooke was let off the
priests' penalties of castration and disembowelling while alive;
yet was so ungrateful as to be 'resolute' and even jocular, asking
the executioner to show him the proper procedure as he 'was
never beheaded before'. His bleeding head was held up to the
crowd by the executioner who shouted the correct formula, 'God
save King James!' But only the sheriff's voice echoed it out of all
that vast multitude.

Cobham's trial came nine days after Ralegh's; and 'never was
there so base and abject a spirit', agreed those two leading gossip-
correspondents of the day, Sir Dudley Carleton and John
Chamberlain, comparing it unfavourably with Ralegh's. Cobham
not only confirmed his accusations of Ralegh, but managed to

implicate young Harvey, 'whom Ralegh', he said, 'had corrupted to carry intelligence between them'. So the 'poor fellow' of Ralegh's white lie was now betrayed as the son of the Lieutenant of the Tower, and promptly ordered to be also arraigned at the King's Bench. 'The public judgment,' says C. D. Bowen,[1] 'preferred Ralegh's bold evasions, to protect his friends, to Cobham's "truths" against them, in hopes of his own life.' Carleton remarked in disgust that 'having thus *ac*cused all his friends and so little *ex*cused himself', Cobham was quickly found 'Guilty', and 'with much fear and trembling . . . exclaimed upon Ralegh as one who had stirred him up to discontent. . . . He begged a great while for life and favour, alleging his confession as a meritorious act.'

That should be the end of Ralegh's hopes from him. But there would still be his execution speech; and Ralegh could not believe that a soul could so perjure itself when actually at point of death. December 10th was the appointed day. Ralegh from his cell high up in Winchester Castle looked down on to the scaffold and the headsman's block raised in the courtyard, and the crowds that milled thicker and thicker around it, in spite of the persistent icy rain.

Cobham was to die after two others: the Catholic Sir Griffin Markham, and the gallant young Lord Grey, who had dared 'dispute with the Judges against their laws', so there could be no hope for him. But Markham had been promised a reprieve, and staggered as though stunned at finding himself after all led up on to the scaffold. A friend gave him a napkin to cover his eyes, and that pulled him up; he waved it away and said he 'could look on death without blushing'. He knelt and prayed, the headsman prepared his axe, when there was a sudden shouting and clamour, and one of James' Scots pages was seen pushing and struggling through the crowd as he yelled out to the Sheriff to delay the execution, by order of the King. It was 'a damned close-run thing,' but the page thrust his way through just in time to stop the axe falling on Markham's neck. He handed a paper to the Sheriff, who read it and told the victim, 'You say you are ill prepared to die. You shall have two hours' respite.'

So Markham was led back to be locked into King Arthur's Hall for his last two hours of life; and young Grey was next led out, knowing nothing of what had happened. He was gay and

---

[1] *The Lion and the Throne*, p. 220.

debonair among his friends, but turned the straw over with his foot to see if it were bloody from Markham's execution. He prayed together with the minister, then said he was ready for the heads-man—but again the Sheriff interrupted at the last moment. The King, he announced, had altered the order of the executions, and now wished Cobham to come first. So Grey too was sent off to Arthur's Hall, for one hour of life only; and Cobham now came on to the scene, as bold and cheerful as he had hitherto been abjectly craven.

Carleton, as a connoisseur of executions, evidently thought Cobham's quite the worst before-execution speech he had ever heard. Not only did it 'hold us in the rain more than half an hour', he grumbled, but everyone guessed it to be a fraud; with only Cobham, the chief actor, in the secret. It was plain that he had been promised his life, if he said what the King required of him. The spectators jeered openly at his long prayers, though his duet with his minister was voted not so bad. 'He has a good mouth in a cry, but he is nothing when alone,' was the criticism of the crowd, who had waited in shocking weather through all these delays, and not seen an execution yet. They began to boo and hoot at the back, and the Sheriff had to prompt the prisoner to come to the real point of the scene. So Cobham hastily 'protested before God and his Angels that his accusation of Sir Walter Ralegh was substantially true'.

All heads at once turned to look up at the barred window where Ralegh stood watching; and again missed their sport, for they saw him smile. The French Ambassador was astonished at his *'visage riant'*—but it must have been grimly tense, for he had 'hammers working in his head to beat out the meaning of this stratagem'. One thing was clear to him, as to the rest of the audience, that Cobham knew his supposedly dying confession would win his reprieve—if only James did not change his mind once again. For there came yet another move in this game of cat and mouse. The headsman again advanced, and for the third time was stopped by the Sheriff. And now Grey and Markham were led back to join Cobham on the scaffold, and all three stood 'looking strange, one upon the other, like men beheaded and met again in the other world'. There they were 'together on the stage as at the end of the play', but no one could guess now what that end might be.

The Sheriff asked the three if they agreed they had been 'justly tried and lawfully condemned to execution, now to be performed'. They humbly agreed. 'Then see the mercy of your Prince, who of himself hath sent hither a countermand, and given you your lives.' It was indeed 'of himself'. Alone the King, in the humour of a macabre clown, had planned this hideous sequence of surprise tricks. The grisly stunt had all but missed fire; Johnny Gibb, his page, had nearly failed to reach Markham's neck in time to save it from the axe; but no matter, since it had been saved. The King now delightedly received his ministers' applause for his 'marvellous clemency', and for his judicial awarding of first merit to Cobham for his 'penitence and gratifying humility' (his still more gratifying condemnation of Ralegh was of course not mentioned); and of lesser praise to Grey for his courage— but with a black mark for his arrogance in refusing to beg for his life.

The reprieved culprits were committed to the Tower of London, excepting Markham, who was banished, and so impoverished that he who had been Lord of Beskwood Forest had to sell the silver-inlaid hilt of his sword to get bread. He became a ragged soldier of fortune abroad, and got paid occasionally by Cecil as a continental spy. The gallant young Grey died after eleven years in the Tower, despoiled of all his lands.

So was Cobham despoiled, one of the richest men in England. He was released after fourteen years as a hopeless invalid, part paralysed, deserted by his wife, to die at last in a hovel: 'so poor a house as he was forced to creep up a ladder into a little hole for his chamber'. So Lord Pembroke tells us, and adds that he was half-starved and lousy—which last may not seem so startling when even such illustrious guests as the Earl of Cumberland and his family found 'we were all lousy' after a visit to the new King's Court; and remarked that it was 'a great change between the fashion of the Court as it is now, and of that in the old Queen's time'.

So 'the end of the play' staged by the royal puppet-master left his three victims limp and deflated, two never to move freely again, and one only in inglorious exile. And for Ralegh it removed his last hope of getting the truth from Cobham. His own death was to take place in three days' time.

CHAPTER TWENTY-FOUR
A Dream, a Dream

'A dream, a dream! else in this other world
We should know one another.'
'So we shall.'

FORD'S ''TIS PITY SHE'S A WHORE'

RALEGH decided that he at least would dance no longer to
the puppet-master's jig. He faced the Bishop of Winchester
for his last confession and preparation for death, and
showed himself unexpectedly orthodox and reverent; but admitted nothing that his enemies had hoped for. He made no confession of any value to them, nor any last-hour plea for mercy.
On the contrary, he wrote in urgent command to his wife to 'get
those letters, if it be possible, which I writ to the Lords, wherein
I sued for my life. God knoweth that it was for you and yours
that I desired it, but it is true that I disdain myself for begging it.'

He went on writing, through that long, last night, his truest
confession of faith in God, and in her. 'I would not with my last
Will, present you with sorrows, dear Bess. Let them go to the
grave with me, and be buried in the dust. And seeing it is not
the will of God that ever I shall see you in this life, bear my
destruction gently, and with a heart like yourself.

'First I send you all the thanks my heart can conceive, or my
pen express, for your many troubles and cares taken for me,
which—though they have not taken effect as you wished—yet my
debt is to you never the less. But pay it I never shall in this world.

'Secondly, I beseech you, for the love you bare me living, that
you do not hide yourself many days, but by your travail seek to
help your miserable fortunes and the right of your poor child.
Your mourning cannot avail me, that am but dust.'

The tenderness of his desire for her to break away from the
cruel conventions that commanded a widow to shut herself up
in a darkened room for weeks of solitary mourning; and his
beseeching her instead to bear his death 'gently, and with a heart
like yourself', shows their deep trust and understanding of each

G*   201

other. Yet they had been married only eleven years, and the first two had all but caused his ruin; and after them had come long spells of separation. In his protest against her mourning there is an echo of one of Shakespeare's most poignant sonnets; to which Ralegh's own poetry has been compared, as the only other of the time that is as personal and intimate, springing so directly out of the poet's private emotion:

'No longer mourn for me when I am dead
Than you shall hear the surly sullen bell . . .
. . . 'for I love you so
That I in your sweet thoughts would be forgot
If thinking on me then should make you woe.'

He had to remind her that he had no friend left to whom she could turn for help; yet could beg her, and without bitterness, to trust herself to 'the great God that worketh all in all. Love God and begin betimes to repose yourself on Him; therein shall you find true and lasting riches and endless comfort. For the rest, when you have travailed and wearied your thoughts on all sorts of worldly cogitations, you shall sit down by Sorrow in the end.'

He had learned at last how empty was ambition, whether for power, possessions or wealth; though he still knew the truth of his own saying, 'Poverty is an imprisonment of the mind.' If only she could be free of that—'If you can live free from want, then care for no more; for the rest is but vanity. . . .

'I cannot write much. God knows how hardly I stole this time, when all sleep. It is time to separate my thoughts from this world. . . . I can write no more. Time and Death call me away.'

He 'stole this time' hardly indeed, with numbed hands that shook in ague from the raw cold of that exceptionally bitter winter. Outside his freezing cell, where the stone walls ran with damp, the December stars looked down on the valley below, and wreathed in its ghostly mists, the sleeping town of Winchester. It had once been the capital of England, and before that of Wessex; William the Conqueror had been crowned there; and it had been called Camelot in King Arthur's day. King Arthur's Table Round was still in this very castle, in the hall below his cell. Time and Death had called away many since Arthur and then William had helped to make England a nation. And Ralegh had tried to help make it a great one; had planned and worked and

spent so much in doing so, though often in vain, that he had reason
to hope, in spite of his traitor's death tomorrow, he might one day
be counted among them. And that his wife and son would so
account him, whatever ill tales were told of him.

The boy was now nine, and growing very like his father, whom
he did his best to copy in all things, as can be seen in the portrait
of them together, painted a little time before. Ever since he had
been old enough to listen entranced to his father's stories of
Guiana, he had been passionately resolved to sail with him to the
New World and help him discover El Dorado. It had been cruel
to enflame his earliest hopes, now all cut off. The past was kinder,
because devoid of promises, except through inspiration. He
might instead have told his son more of the noble examples of
humanity as well as heroism in ages past; and now there was no
time. He could not now, as he had once prophesied,

> 'begin by such a parting light
> To write the story of all ages past.'

There was a silly riddle-rhyme he had made up long ago for
his 'little wag' while he joggled him up and down on his outstretched foot: 'Three things there be', intoned the deep voice
above the child:

> 'And they be these, the wood, the weed, the wag.
> The wood is that which makes the gallows tree,
> The weed is that which strings the Hangman's bag,'

And then came the final upkick with a sudden shout—

> 'The wag, my pretty knave, betokeneth *thee*!'

The romp would not seem so funny to his 'pretty knave' when
he came to remember it together with his father's execution. And
his father could do nothing now to help him in what was left of
this night. 'No man may deliver his brother', nor yet his son, nor
his wife.

But he went back to his letter for a last attempt to do so. 'Teach
your son to serve and fear God while he is young, that the fear
of God may grow up in him. Then will God be a husband unto
you, and a father unto him; a husband and a father which can
never be taken from you. . . .

'Remember your poor child for his father's sake, that chose you and loved you in his happiest times.'

To remind her of their happiness was a desperate attempt to cheer her. So also, for both her and Wat, to keep them from the despair of lost faith in him, he wrote, 'Know it dear wife that your son is the child of a true man, who in his own respect despiseth Death in all his misshapen and ugly forms. The everlasting, infinite, powerful and inscrutable God, that Almighty God that is goodness itself, mercy itself, the true life and light, keep you and yours, and have mercy on me, and teach me to forgive my persecutors and false accusers.'

For a man so proud and so ruthless, to learn humility and the wish to forgive his destroyers shows a new heroism in him. Few of those who bear resentment to former friends could pray thus, as Ralegh then prayed, to learn how to forgive his betrayers. No atheist could have written this letter.

'My true wife, farewell. Bless my poor boy; pray for me. My true God hold you both in his arms!'

Then indeed he could write no more to her. 'It was time to separate his thoughts from this world.' They entered into another, unknown to him, to find lines of verse pacing through his mind like a pilgrim's steps through the silent watches of the winter's night. They were like none that he had ever thought of before.

'The Passionate Man's Pilgrimage at the point of Death,' so he called this strangely happy 'dirge'. It is his strangest poem, and his most uneven. Much of it is quite unknown or else derided; while the first eighteen lines are quoted in most anthologies as a complete poem, and a supreme example of beauty. Yet they startle one as unlike Ralegh, as something written when outside himself.

> 'Give me my scallop shell of quiet,
> My staff of faith to walk upon,
> My scrip of joy, immortal diet,
> My bottle of salvation,
>   My gown of glory, hope's true gage;
>   And thus I'll take my pilgrimage.
>
> Blood must be my body's balmer;
> No other balm will there be given.
> Whilst my soul, like quiet palmer,
> Travelleth towards the land of heaven:

A DREAM, A DREAM

Over the silver mountains
Where spring the nectar fountains:
There will I kiss
The bowl of bliss,
And drink mine everlasting fill
Upon every milken hill.
My soul will be a-dry before;
But after, it will thirst no more.'

The child-like vision is that of the later mystics. Ralegh's diction was always direct, but his simplicity was never as innocently naïve as in this poem—nor as companionable. The voice in his former poetry is solitary, either in address or attack, or in introspection; in 'The Ocean's Love' it speaks a single soliloquy of five hundred lines, sounding as if out of some deep sea-cave the echoes of his sombre thoughts; they might have come from

'some old lover's ghost
Who died before the God of Love was born.'

In the 'Pilgrimage' that he wrote for his last poem, there is no sad ghost, but a new-awakened, friendly spirit. Traherne's joyful shout, 'Oh how did all their lovely faces shine!' was echoed half a century before, in this next verse of Ralegh's:

'Then by that happy blissful day,
More peaceful pilgrims shall I see
That have cast off their rags of clay
And walk apparelled fresh like me.
I'll take them first
To quench their thirst
And taste of nectar suckets,
At those clear wells
Where sweetness dwells
Drawn up by saints in crystal buckets.'

He might be promising these delights to his young son, and to himself too as a boy again. As their long-shared dream of the jewelled cities they would find together comes true before their eyes, the rhythm of his verse alters and rocks into that of a cradle-song:

'Then the blessed paths we'll travel,
Strewed with rubies thick as gravel,
Ceilings of diamonds, sapphire floors,
High walls of coral and pearly bowers.'

205

Had he, after writing and thinking so much of Wat, had a dream of heaven as shared with him, not as father and son, but as two boys together exploring the New World of Heaven? There is even a reminder of the grim riddle-rhyme they had laughed at together, in his grisly wit about his execution the next morning.

> 'And this is my eternal plea
> To Him that made heaven, earth and sea,
> That, since my flesh must die so soon,
> And want a head to dine next noon,
> Just at the stroke, when my veins start and spread,
> Set on my soul an everlasting head!'

This is thought 'too grotesque and bizarre'[1] for Ralegh; but it is not more so than his comparison of his own Trial with that in

> 'heaven's bribeless hall
> Where no corrupted voices brawl'

No need with that last word to mention Coke by name. But he strikes still more shrewdly home, and with an irreverent pun on the name 'angel' for a coin, which shocked Gardiner and other nineteenth-century historians, as much as his unseemly sarcasms upon his 'bribed lawyers' palms', outstretched for earthly gains, in contrast with the heavenly Trial, where there's:

> 'No conscience molten into gold,
> No forged accuser bought or sold;
> No cause deferred, no vain-spent journey,
> For there Christ is the King's Attorney,
> Who pleads for all without degrees,
> And he hath angels, but no fees.
> And when the grand twelve million jury,
> Against our souls black verdicts give,
> Christ pleads His death—and then we live.'

There is an unquenchable youthful vitality in this half-jesting picture of the Judgment Day; in the happy confidence that sees in it no 'Dies Irae', but the daybreak of hope and trust.

> 'Be thou my speaker, taintless pleader,
> Unblotted lawyer, true Proceeder!
> Thou givest salvation even for alms.'

---

[1] Philip Edwards, *Sir Walter Ralegh*, p. 94.

A DREAM, A DREAM

Some writers have thought it odd that so staunch a Protestant as Ralegh should use the Roman Catholic imagery of the pilgrims to Jerusalem, and their age-old device of the scallop shell in their hats. Such pilgrimages from England were as out of date as the Crusades. Yet they had remained as a fanciful convention in much of the Protestant poetry. There was more, however, in Ralegh's imagery. His line,

'Blood must be my body's balmer,'

is the life-blood of the poem; and suggests not only his own, that must be shed on the morrow, but also the great Catholic mystery of the Atonement, and the Eucharist; and an 'emotional response, and sense of personal relationship with Christ . . . not found anywhere else in Ralegh's work'.[1]

But custom and logic do not enter into such visions. Ralegh may for once have been thinking like a Catholic—if he were thinking at all, which is doubtful. He was writing outside time. His pilgrimage carried him into the distant past of the palmers' quests; of his own childhood's early mornings, looking up towards the Devon hills as the first pale light turned them to pearl. It carried him too into the future, among other visionary minds. His luminous world of 'silver mountains' and 'milken hills', where white figures roam in the crystal light of dawn, is shared later with Vaughan's 'white celestial thought' of his friends, 'all gone into the world of light', and even later yet with Blake's land of dreams 'Above the light of the morning star'.

Ralegh was not a mystic it is said, and therefore this poem must have been written 'outside himself'. If so, he found there a happier and warmer fellowship with others, and with Christ, and through it a self unknown before. At point of death, the Passionate Man was writing, not another poem, but his final Passion.

[1] Philip Edwards, *loc. cit.*

CHAPTER TWENTY-FIVE

The King's Counterblast against Ralegh

KING JAMES was not altogether happy about the impression he was making on his new country. For all his ministers' praise of his mercy, and of his judicial sermon about it, there was an undercurrent of awkward questions, even complaints. Foreign Princes made sneering remarks; the cynical Henri IV of France observed that the 'new English Solomon' had once again shown himself 'the most learned fool in Christendom'. The English themselves grumbled that they preferred fair play to an arbitrary mercy. If three convicted criminals were reprieved then why should Ralegh die, merely because he was the greater man? For nobody believed that he was the more guilty; and few that he was even half as guilty. His trial had shown everyone that 'he was condemned to death on nothing more than presumption and surmise', and if that were 'according to the laws', then it was high time they were changed so as to allow the prisoner the chance of a fair hearing. And after all the fuss about these horrible treasons, even the Judges could not prove them to be anything more than talk, and a question of who had started the talking.

Cecil's numerous enemies declared that he had most likely fabricated the whole thing himself, to clear the ground of his rivals, and make the King believe that he alone was indispensable. Nobody ever knew his mind; he had 'no windows in his breast'; but his secretary wrote that Cecil had wept when Ralegh was condemned, so at that moment at least there was a window in his breast, if anyone could have seen into it.

The Ambassadors at Paris and The Hague were given no chance to do so. Cecil's discreet letters to them told nothing of what he thought about Ralegh; only that there was no doubt that Aremberg, the Spanish Ambassador, had been angling for English spies for Spain. (As Cecil swallowed this bait himself within a few months, he had good reason to know about it.) But it wouldn't do, he explained, to say anything against the Spanish Ambassador at this moment when King James was urging on a peace treaty with Spain. He had great difficulty in dealing with all the foreigners. The French Ambassador not only protested openly himself against Ralegh's condemnation, but made it public both in England and Europe that even Ralegh's traditional enemy 'the Spanish Ambassador has spoken strongly to members of the Council on Sir Walter's behalf'.

And Cecil's King gave him more trouble than his critics, with the startling blunder he had made in his royal sermon of self-praise for reprieving three of the condemned men; because, so the English Solomon publicly proclaimed, they were minor conspirators, and 'the two priests and George Brooke' (all previously executed) 'were the principal plotters and enticers of the rest of the said treasonable machinations'. This flatly contradicted Coke's claim that it was Ralegh who had been the prime plotter and enticer. If Coke were wrong, and the King right, then why was Ralegh not reprieved also? Cecil had to point out to his monarch, as tactfully as he could, his awkward flaw in logic, and how it might jeopardize his popularity in his new kingdom.

There were other hints of this, not so tactful, that buzzed up in the newly relaxed atmosphere of the hunting field. For James was a steady sipper rather than a hard drinker, and kept on sipping from a flask even while hunting, and inviting his companions to do so. Only 'a wee twa-three spoonfuls' at a time he said, but so close together were the times that the English lords, though well used to hard drinking, found it difficult to keep up with this insidious new habit. It also loosened their balance on their saddles, and above all their guard on their tongues. James' ear was acute enough to catch any murmur which might imply that his standards were un-English. Even his silly but scornful Queen, Anne of Denmark, who had been against Ralegh till she came down South, was now worrying him for 'fair play', as though she had been born and bred in England. Reluctantly, James was made to realize that it would be a grave risk to his new reign if he killed Ralegh too summarily at its outset. Better 'bide a wee'.

He bided.

Ralegh was told on the day fixed for his execution (but without any clowning 'surprises' on the scaffold—the humourless English had discouraged them) that his life was reprieved, and he was to be committed to the Tower.

Three days later, December 16th, 1603, he was taken back there from Winchester, to remain in prison for the next thirteen years.

*　　*　　*

Strangely, his strongest ally at this time was Cecil. He had done most to save his life, and now set about saving some of his property, for Lady Ralegh and her child. Before her husband was condemned, or even brought to trial, more than a dozen noble Scots newcomers were vieing with each other to get hold of the Sherborne estates. Commissioners had begun to cut down his trees and sell his herds and some of the furniture in his castle. The Howards, even his old friend and extravagant admirer, Nottingham, rushed to snatch not only his wine patent but all arrears of payment owing to him before it was forfeited, and which were therefore legally his. As Lady Ralegh wrote to Cecil in a desperate appeal for 'compassion and justice', the Admiral gained '£6,000, and £3,000 a year, by my husband's fall', so could well spare the back payments due to Ralegh, which were all that could keep his family from abject poverty. 'Our debts are above £3,000, and the bread and food taken from me and my child, will never augment my Lord Admiral's table, though it famish us.'

If Cecil suffered remorse for his share in Ralegh's downfall, he did his best now to make amends. He called off the Howard pack, made the Admiral drop his theft of the last bone, stopped the despoilers of Sherborne, and ratified the deed of gift whereby Ralegh, some years before, had made the estate over to his son, appointing trustees on his and his mother's behalf. He even took the trouble (and a slight risk) to write Ralegh encouraging messages, anonymously and in a disguised handwriting; but Ralegh 'knew the phrase'.

His letters of deep gratitude and relief for his wife, and hers of thanks all the more touching for their spelling, show how they recognized Cecil as now their kindest and indeed only friend; and Ralegh's show also something of the humility he had longed to learn, expressed in half-humorous resignation to a fate no worse than many others, since 'men are but the spoils of Time . . . wherewith childish Fortune useth to play, kiss them today and break them tomorrow—and therefore I can lament in myself

only a common destiny'. His past 'happiness had found too much
too little', he admits, thinking he had now curbed the vast reach
of his demands on life. But *that* he would never learn to do when
in his true mind, for

> 'Contentment is a sleepy thing,
> If it in death alone must die.'

At the moment he was sleepy from exhaustion, and after
suspense. He had been relieved of his agonized anxiety for his
wife and child, lest his enemies, some of them his former friends,
should, as he had written to her, 'seek to kill you and yours with
extreme poverty'. They *had* sought, but failed to do so; and they
had failed to kill Ralegh himself. He thanked James for this, with
a dignified and curious simile of himself to a magnet whose 'body
of iron had moved towards the loadstone of Death and could not
be withheld from touching it', had not 'Your Majesty's mercy
turned the point' . . . an odd trope that would have pleased James
if he had thought of it himself.

The King had the irritable jealousy of the second-rate author
who cannot bear to acknowledge another author as first-rate.
He had hurried to show the world how much more learnedly and
originally he could write than this presumptuous prisoner. His
'Counterblast against Tobacco', published early in 1604, was a
crushing attack on the new-fangled vice that Ralegh had made
so popular. 'Is it not a great vanity that a man cannot heartily
welcome his friend now, but straightway they must be in hand
with Tobacco?' James had a superstitious belief in the habit's
connection with witchcraft and atheism; and a keen nose for its
'black stinking fumes . . . resembling the horrible Stygian smoke
of the pit that is bottomless'. His loathing of this 'filthy and
unclean' offspring of Ralegh's was largely because it had been
brought 'from the beastly Indians—the refuse of the world, and
as yet aliens from God', and, still worse, 'brought in neither by
king, emperor, nor learned doctor of physic, but by a father so
generally hated'.

And there he revealed his jealous hatred of the man who,
though neither king nor emperor, had enslaved James' subjects
to a custom the King detested. Ralegh never knew that James
was jealous of him. He did not understand jealousy, to his cost;
for it meant that he never understood James' resentment of him—

nor how it was that he aroused it again and again, when he was doing his best to prove himself the King's true servant.

That first winter of his imprisonment was exceptionally cold, and unhealthy. It would have been much easier, and more dramatic, for him to have had his unbowed head struck off, than to linger on, aching and shivering in a freezing cell where the foul river-water seeped with the fog through the stone walls, threatening him 'daily with death by the palsy, nightly with suffocation by wasted and obstructed lungs'. The privilege that allowed his wife and son to lodge with him in the Tower added a torment of anxiety to him, for the Plague was still infesting that insanitary fortress, and 'my poor child has lain this fortnight next door to a woman with a running plague sore and but a paper wall between them, and her child is, this Thursday, dead of the plague'. There is a horrible immediacy about 'this Thursday', as about the paper wall.

It was probably consumption that obstructed his 'wasted lungs', to judge by the portrait of him nearest this time, with its sunken cheeks and cavernous eyes; and also by his almost feverish resilience. For he began to work again, and at top speed.

And he could pull himself out of his weary despair and sickness to catch at his best chance of life and liberty, and also glory, since he had been clamped down in this dank prison. The chance came through his power to make a new friend, one warmer and more eager and potentially far stronger than Cecil could ever be. This new friend was a child, just the same age as Ralegh's little Wat. But he was King James' eldest son, the new heir to the throne, Henry, Prince of Wales.

CHAPTER TWENTY-SIX

The Prince's Counterblast against the King

KING JAMES was devoted to his children, doted on them, so the staid and elderly members of the Court complained who had never had such wild young animals as the royal children and their friends racing noisily up and down the Palace corridors 'like little rabbit-starters out of their burrows'. Contrarily they also complained that the youngest, Charles, when just four years old, showed no hope of racing, nor even walking nor talking properly, since he had inherited his father's weak legs, and possibly his over-large tongue as well, for he had a bad impediment of speech. James wanted to have the string under the tongue cut to see if that would free it, and to make him wear iron braces round his legs; but Charles' governess, Lady Carey, refused to allow any such 'conceited' experiments, and even the King's will had to bow before that of 'Mother Carey'. Prince Henry's solution was that when he was King he would make Charles his Archbishop and then the long robes would hide his legs.

Henry and his sister Elizabeth, two years younger and named in compliment to her godmother the late Queen, had followed their father South the previous summer, into a land flowing with milk and honey and, above all, money—so James had exclaimed on meeting them. The plain country gentry here were richer than any lords in Scotland; all his hosts on the way down had given him presents: horses, hounds and hawks, gold cups and gold pieces of money; the richest of them, Sir Oliver Cromwell, was appropriately called 'The Golden Knight'. And now his bairns should have presents from their dear Dad; here was a diamond for Harry's hat that had cost him three thousand pounds, *sterling*, mark you, not Scots—and anything else they asked for. Harry chose stud ponies and new Ferrara fencing swords, and Elizabeth, even more expensively, a whole 'Fairy Farm' of her own, stocked with the smallest cattle, ponies and poultry to be found in the world. Each was given a river-palace, one in Ham and the other at Kew, with their own households, and boats in which they could be rowed up and down on hot evenings to visit each other and hold water tournaments. And Henry would swim in the river for hours.

In his own eyes, James' most treasured and valuable gift to Henry was his recent book, the *Basilikon Doron*. Written specially for and dedicated to 'Henry, my dearest son and natural successor', it was a learned homily to teach him how to be a King as wise and worthy as his father. The teaching was questionable, for it declared a King to have been created by God before, and therefore above, the Law; and to be 'a little God to rule over other men'. If he happened to be a tyrant, 'monster and idolatrous persecutor', his subjects must endure him 'without resistance'. Fortunately Henry found the book boring. James consoled himself with the reflection that he was not quite ten, and would come to appreciate it, and all his father's many books, as he grew older. The hope soon faded.

As a lighter treat, James took Harry with the Queen and the Venetian Ambassador to see the lions in the Tower, which housed a small zoo, kept by the Master of the Bear Garden, Edward Alleyn, famous as the chief actor in Marlowe's plays. His rival Richard Burbage, still more famous in Shakespeare's, was the son of a performing bear-owner in Birmingham; evidently it was a natural step from bear garden to stage. Alleyn produced bull-baitings for the royal party and then as a novelty a fight between three of his mastiffs and two lions. The dogs fought valiantly; when two were killed, the third, though badly mauled, flew at the biggest lion and bit him in the belly, so that he gave the splendid spectacle of a living Lion Rampant, roaring round the pit.

James' 'great but unmanly pleasure' in such sports, as even some contemporaries thought it, was at its height when suddenly Prince Henry shouted out that the show must be stopped. James protested fretfully that such a bonny fight should be fought to the finish, but the child insisted that the gallant mastiff's life be spared. Rounding on Alleyn, he ordered him to take the mastiff home, nurse his wounds and 'make much of him'; and never to put him into any other fight, since 'he had fought with the King of Beasts and should never after fight with any inferior creature'.

It was an eye-opener to many, including the King, and in it a warning to him that the will of this wisp of a boy, as he then was, had already put his father in the position of an 'inferior creature'. James was soon to learn it in a way that stung him far worse.

Ralegh had been transferred temporarily to the Fleet prison during the royal visit to the Tower. If the King had a hope of keeping him away from the Prince, it was short-lived. Ralegh had become too famous to be kept hidden. The lions were ceasing to be the most popular attraction in the Tower. The public now flocked there, not to peer down into the beasts' pit, but to gaze up at the wide walls where, if lucky, they might see a tall thin man with a pointed beard taking the daily walk allowed him for the sake of his health. Luckier still, they might see him conversing with a friendly Indian chief who had followed him from Guiana. Often they waved and cheered, and showed themselves more honoured by Ralegh's grave bow of thanks than by any unwilling recognition from their King.

For James, though so chatty and homely and fond of lewd jokes among his intimates, had a nervous hatred of public crowds. He ordered his chariot to be driven at top speed through the streets, and his attendants to ride close around it, so that the people should catch as few glimpses of him as possible. He had almost to be forced into his duty of touching scabby paupers to cure them of their skin disease, the 'King's Evil', an unpleasant and insanitary job, and doubtless, as James said, a 'silly super- stition'. But it was dangerous to break a custom sacred for centuries among English monarchs, so he complied; but with obvious loathing, and muttered oaths of surprising blasphemy to be uttered in a religious ceremony; and so insulting, though practical, were his good wishes: 'May God gi'e ye better health and more guid sense!' that his wretched patients went out more resentful than grateful.

The ordinary people were badly in need of a royal figurehead whom they could admire and worship and yet think of as friendly to them. Queen Elizabeth had been that to them for the whole of her long reign and even before; and her father King Hal, for all that he was a terror to his nobles, had been so easy of access that any man, however poor and humble, might stop him out hunting, and stand and speak to him at his saddle bow.

But this strange Stuart king from Scotland was of an alien race, unfriendly to the common folk, and proud of it, according to the learned who had read his books and said he thought a king was a 'little God'. Everyone had called Elizabeth a Goddess, but she also had delighted to show herself, even to the meanest of her subjects, as a woman. They had tired of her after many years; but now, within a year, they had tired still more of their new king. The ghost of the old Queen had already begun to take his place, and those who had helped make her reign great were more honoured than any of James' followers. 'Bonny Scot!' was yelled after them in the streets, and rude songs sung, such as 'England made thee a gentleman!'

Even this seemed an overstatement to apply to the Scots monarch. The English turned from him, and towards the Tower walls to see the gentleman who was the Last of the Elizabethans. He was far more the fashion than in the hey-day of his envied success. It scored a strong point to say you had just met and talked with Sir Walter; still more to say you had seen or even been inside the tiny laboratory that he had converted out of a little hen-house on the garden wall for his scientific experiments; most of all (and too rare to be easily believed) that you had been invited to meet him at dinner by the Lieutenant Governor of the Tower.

Once again the Lieutenant had to be changed for someone less friendly to the prisoner. The meanest official mind was chosen for the post; that of Sir William Waad, one of Ralegh's judges. His chief claim to anyone's notice was as Ralegh's jailor, and he was furious to find in how much less account he was held than his captive. Court ladies, great ambassadors and their wives, even Queen Anne herself, would make themselves charming to him, and then, just as he was beginning to plume himself, would divulge that all they had come for was to coax his leave for them to have a few words with Sir Walter.

Then came the heir to the throne, a remarkably intelligent boy, already accomplished and recklessly daring in many sports. In his grave courtesy to foreign ambassadors he was 'ceremonious beyond his years', and he was passionately constant in his ideals. His precociously formal politeness, his loathing of foul talk and swearing, of bad manners and sloppy behaviour and drunkenness, and of most of the uproarious revelry always going on at his father's Court, show clearly, not that he was a prig, but that he had already long suffered from an early reaction of disgust against his father. The reaction grew deeper as Henry grew older and more able to compare James with others. In Ralegh he found at last a man he could admire and trust, and one who knew all the things he most wanted to know, especially about ships and seafaring. Their tastes were the same, in spite of their ages, and the boy took him at once for his true friend.

Also, and more dangerously, he turned to him instinctively as to the father he would have liked to have. His sense of the difference between Ralegh and James is summed up for all time in his famous saying: 'Only my father would keep such a bird in a cage!' There is hatred as well as contempt in that 'only'. James' strongest reason to hate Ralegh, and to wish him out of the way, lay in Henry's growing hatred of his father. The helpless captive had dethroned the King in the eyes of the King's own son. Even if this man had not been a traitor to James' throne, he was so now to his blood. His wife Queen Anne admired and believed in him; that could be discounted as she was only a woman. What mattered was that Henry, his chief hope in life, gave all his devotion to Ralegh; and his own father was accounted nothing beside this old magician who was also steadily seducing the hearts of James' new subjects.

James might have reasoned from his own experience with his mother that there is no natural law to make a child love and admire its parent; but his philosophy, for all his lectures on it, could not extend as far as that. It was easier to roll his eyes on to his 'Baby Charles' and reflect what an easy, douce, and above all kind little heir to the throne the child would have made, now that he was growing out of his infant weakness.

Unfortunately Charles also had a hero to worship in place of his father, and that was his brother, six years older than himself and so much stronger, braver and wiser, a keen sportsman excelling in jousting and fencing; who always knew exactly what he wanted, and got it; and knew what he thought, and said it. Charles wrote a letter to his 'Sweet, sweet brother', saying, 'I will give you everything I have, both my toys and my books and my crossbow. Good brother, love me and I shall ever love and serve you.'

Charles addressed no such early expression of devotion to his father. For a parent so exceptionally indulgent in that age of stern parenthood, there was good reason for James to feel aggrieved. A hint of his own wretched childhood, if they would

ever listen to it, might show his bairns how to appreciate such a
fond guardian as himself, who never thwarted them. But however
much he had come to wish it, it was by this time impossible for
him to thwart Henry. The boy had been spoilt not only by himself but by everyone.

The whole nation showed openly how they looked forward to
another King Hal, the Ninth, as handsome, resolute and high-
spirited as the Eighth Harry in his youth, but more humane and
constant. Those foreign-correspondence gossips, the Ambassadors,
wrote home in glowing terms of his popularity in his new country.
After only three years in it, when still but twelve years old, he
was causing in his father 'a reasonable jealousy of the rising sun',
so one of them wrote; and another added revealingly, 'Nor is the
King pleased to see his son so beloved and of such promise that
his subjects place all their hopes in him.'

But James' jealous resentment was as impotent as a crabbed
old woman's. He could not stop the crowds from cheering
themselves hoarse for 'Our Prince Hal'; and he could not, indeed
dared not, stop Hal from getting his own way—even when he
determined to adopt Ralegh as his chief tutor. Together with Wat,
Henry learned from Ralegh about the things he most cared for,
history and astronomy and above all seamanship and improved
designs for shipbuilding. Ralegh made a model of a new ship for
him which Harry could use for his navy when he was King—or
possibly as soon as he came of age and could take command of
the fleet, since his father cared little about it and continued to
give more and more time to hunting and gambling at card games.
No doubt Waad's spies reported the Prince's hopeful projects for
the navy to the King.

But worse, in James' view, was to follow. Ralegh not only
taught history to the Prince; he was now writing it for him. It
was to be a history of the whole world, 'Beginning with the
Creation', as his preface declared ambitiously, a work more vast
in its conception than any man had ever dared attempt, and
dedicated to Henry, as James had dedicated his *Basilikon Doron*.

This was poaching on the royal author's and parent's preserves
with a vengeance. If not actual treason, it was at the least *lèse-
majesté*. Nor did Prince Henry's historical interest confine itself
only to past ages. He wanted to know all that his hero could tell
him of his own adventures in the wars, both at sea and on land;

so that Ralegh introduced them as modern instances and comparisons which have illumined his tremendous work with delightfully personal and intimate touches. Henry's eager affection for him led to his doing some research on his own account; he looked up all the reports of Ralegh's trial, examined the evidence, and was old enough by now to understand fully the criminal absurdity of the proceedings. He found many to agree with him. His mother continually tried to secure Ralegh's 'pardon', if only in gratitude for his having saved her life, when she was ill, by his mysterious Elixir, the 'Balsam of Guiana', which had won him such fame as a physician. It can have won no gratitude from James, since his enmity towards Ralegh was growing more and more to include conflict with his wife and son.

His score against them all mounted higher. He complained there was no end to 'the lawless liberty of the Tower, so long cockered and fostered with hopes exorbitant'. Not only did the Queen and the Prince believe that Ralegh was innocent of any real offence; so did the nobles, even some of James' own trusted Scots. These went to consult Ralegh in his prison as though his were the most important opinion to be taken on affairs of state. They even asked his views on James' grandiose scheme to unite Catholic and Protestant Europe, with Great Britain (as it was now called, so as to include Scotland) by marrying the Prince of Wales to the Spanish Infanta; and his sister, the Princess Elizabeth, to a son of the Roman Catholic Duke of Savoy, the satellite of Spain. These were the two political plans nearest to the King's heart—a' Spanish heart', it could truly be called. But his eldest son would have neither of them. 'Two religions will never lie easy in one bed,' he declared. It is the second saying of this schoolboy to leave a mark on history.

Henry's great wish was to 'compose differences in religion', having learned from Ralegh's bitter experience as a soldier in France that 'all wars of religion are only civil wars, and by civil war no nation's condition was ever bettered'. But Henry was a far keener Protestant than his father, who had 'used his authority in most crabbed and choleric manner' against the Presbyterians in Scotland when they told him that 'the King was but God's silly (i.e. simple) vassal'. That had not encouraged him to support the Presbyterian attacks against 'these Amaziahs, the belly-god bishops in England'. But James had a reaction against his tolerance for the Catholic Church just after coming to the English throne: 'Na, na, we'll no need the Papists the noo.' This cynical throw-over of the Papists, when no longer considered useful, led directly to their Gunpowder Plot, a lot of horrible executions, and yet another street-song:

'Remember, remember
The Fifth of November—'

The authorities tried but failed to implicate Ralegh in the plot. His old friend the 'Wizard Earl' of Northumberland was charged with complicity in it, partly because he was Ralegh's friend, partly because he was a Catholic, mainly because he was very rich. He was clapped into the Tower (where he helped in Ralegh's scientific discoveries), while his estates had to bear a crippling fine for many years. When released long later, he was no longer rich.

James' oppression of his Papist subjects was no hindrance to his plans of Papist marriages for his elder son and daughter. But Ralegh was. For Prince Henry wanted to know if Ralegh's opinion agreed with his own on the proposed marriage unions with Spain. It did; and Henry then demanded that Ralegh should write his reasons for it so that all should know and understand them.

So Ralegh wrote his two 'Discourses' against the Spanish marriages. They are the most masterly exposition of the larger issues of foreign policy, composed without the smallest notion of how impolitic it was for him to write them. Both marriages, he wrote, would prove disastrous for this country, for 'Savoy from Spain is inseperable. Spain to England is irreconcilable.' He clinched it with: 'Whatsoever is pretended to the contrary, it is Spain that we ought to suspect.' If the Princess, 'the precious jewel of this kingdom', married Savoy, she must give up her religion, or else have her children brought up in one alien to her. If she had no children, the case would be worse still—as when Mary Tudor married Philip of Spain—and England might again be subjected to a foreign ruler of Spanish blood. Yet on the other hand no English prince could hope to annex Savoy, 'all France being interjacent', and Savoy always of necessity a servant of France or Spain, of no strength in herself.

He was even more forthright in his arguments against the match for Prince Henry, whom he advised to 'keep his own ground for a while and in no way to engage or entangle himself'. This delighted the boy, since he had been pestered about marrying the Spanish Infanta ever since his first year in England. Now Ralegh showed the futility of the plan, for Spain's past wounds from England had been too many and deep 'to be healed with the plaster of a peace'. Ralegh of all men now living had reason to mention those wounds with pride; but he went dangerously far in comparing them with Spain's immunity at the present day. Now she had been allowed to build up her once defeated navy to a strength greater than England's, which had as quickly deteriorated through 'our own fault; and the detested covetousness of some great ones of ours'.

Here was the old hubris: a prisoner, never yet cleared of his sentence of death, admonishing the great ones as though he were the greatest of them. And with equal indifference to the effect on himself, he reminded them of England's command of the sea, which they had lost: 'for whereas, in my time, I have known one of Her Majesty's ships command forty of theirs to strike sail, they will now take us one to one, and not give us a good morrow'.

This reckless magnificence, backed by the practical force of his argument, proved sound in the three and a half centuries that followed him. England, he assumed, was one of three leading nations, with no need to truckle to the other two, Spain and France, as the King was always trying to do. For James, and his Stuart successors, carried down into England the traditional policy of Scotland, a small and poor country, who had always needed the help of a Great Power. The 'Auld Alliance' with France had lasted more than six hundred years. And in England the Stuarts continued to believe it necessary to be dependent upon either France or Spain. But Ralegh insisted that his country was herself a Great Power. He declared that it was for England to keep control and hold the balance; and that she could only do so by friendly alliance with the Dutch seaports that faced her shores. We had left them in the lurch by compounding with Spain before the Dutch had done so, and 'since that time they have neglected us. Let us look to it with all the eyes we have', for whichever of the three powers have their support, 'whether England, France or Spain—he that hath them will become the greatest, and give the law to the rest'. He added scornfully, 'If any man doubt this, he knows not much!'

The arrogance that seemed vainglorious in his time of power is glorious in the condemned man, who refused in every word and act to acknowledge that he was a criminal. Ralegh never saw any occasion for a change in his style of address. His theme was all that he thought of, and anyone who failed to perceive its truth 'knew not much', whoever he might be that chose to fit the Fool's cap on his head. He did not pause an instant to reflect that the two first to do so would be the King and Cecil. He was simply not thinking of them, but of his Prince and future King, Harry IX. It was sound advice to tell the boy 'to keep his own ground for a while'; but in doing so Ralegh cut away his own ground from under his feet.

James was naturally enraged by the way his long cherished dreams for his children were blown to pieces by this irrepressible old man, who though fifteen years older than the monarch, was so much younger in the vitality of his arguments and direct, easy force in writing them. There was now no hope for James' plan, for Harry had got the bit between his teeth, and was threatening a point blank refusal at the altar, both for himself and his sister, if the marriage plans were continued. Ralegh had encouraged rebellion in its most unnatural form, in the King's own children.

Robert Cecil had almost as much reason to be angry. Ralegh wrote as though he, and not Cecil, were the Chief Minister of State and Lord Treasurer, and dared to rebuke the statecraft and so, by implication, Cecil. And his phrase, 'the detested covetousness of some great ones', must have gone unpleasantly near home, since Cecil had suffered many lampoons on that subject. It is however far more likely that Ralegh was thinking of James' succession of favourites, mostly from Scotland, who drained the exchequer as fast as Cecil managed to put it on a sound basis.

The latest of these gave James and Cecil their opportunity for revenge on Ralegh. This was Robert Kerr (spelt Carr in England), handsome and high-spirited, who had happened to break his leg by a fall from his horse in front of the King, and so re-awakened James' paternal tenderness for 'the young man I brought up from a child', as he wrote to Cecil, pleading for his help in advancing Robert's fortunes. He was given a knighthood, of course, then the promise of titles: Viscount Rochester, then Earl of Somerset; and eventually of a lovely bride who happened unfortunately to be the bride of the third Earl of Essex, an awkward, tongue-tied youth (literally so, because of his stammer) who had inherited none of the charm of his father. All that was now needed for Carr was a fine English estate, but there were not nearly enough of these to go round among James' favoured applicants from Scotland.

Cecil suggested Sherborne. True it had been definitely made over to Ralegh's wife and heirs, but it might be possible to ferret out some legal flaw in the agreement which could render it invalid. It was possible; and Cecil, with the help of Sir Edward Coke and Judge Popham, ferreted it out. The fluctuations in his treatment of Ralegh are extraordinary, but predictable. Fascinated by him as a companion, Cecil feared him as a rival, and could be kind only when Ralegh was down. Now he was rising again alarmingly, and must be checked. So Cecil quietly cheated him out of Sherborne. Pious onlookers observed that all Ralegh could say, in Job's words, would be: 'Naked I came into the world, and naked shall I go out.' But he said a great deal more, both through lawyers fighting his case (a sheer waste of time against the Crown) and in a fruitless appeal to the King. Finally he appealed to Carr himself, not proudly for his rights, but humbly reminding him of Scottish magnanimity, since Ralegh had already 'been bounden to your nation—for the true report of my trial to the King's Majesty'.

His bold reminder that even his former Scots enemies, with Lord Hay at their head, had been convinced of his innocence after his trial, and had publicly expressed this conviction to the King, had had no effect on James himself. But it might have on the chivalry of a young knight. 'seeing that your day is but now in the dawn, and mine coming to the evening. . . . I trust, Sir, that you will not be the first that will kill us outright, cut down the tree with the fruit, and undergo the curse of them that enter into the fields of the fatherless.'

The lovely phrases that he could not help using were not for himself, where 'there remaineth nothing but the bare name of life', but for 'the inheritance of my children'. But Carr was soon to be 'a fellow almost damned in a fair wife', whose greed, 'as restless as the sea and as insatiable as the grave', only mocked at any superstitious fears of the curses of disinherited children. She herself was indeed to bring down curses enough on all who had anything to do with her, even on her indulgent King.

Now for the first time Lady Ralegh's unswerving devotion, and even sanity, began to break down. She had lived with her husband in the Tower, except when chivied out of it from time to time to punish him for Prince Henry's friendship; and then had lived in a nearby house on Tower Hill (at great added expense) from which she visited him continually. Their second son, Carew, was born in the Tower about two years after the trial. The following year her husband's health failed, as a result of a punitive spell of close confinement. A growing palsy affected his left side, arm and hand and, more alarming still, he began to lose the power of speech. His physician managed to get leave for a little room to be built on to the henhouse which he had converted into a laboratory, so that he could live there instead of directly over the river; and there his astonishing vitality helped to restore him, though he never had his normal health again after his trial. But the agony of watching her husband's abnormal condition grow upon him, together with the fresh anxiety of a new baby rather late in life, and the constantly recurring terror of the Plague for both sons and husband, had taxed Elizabeth Ralegh's courage too far. What finally broke it was the long, losing fight for Sherborne, which she had thought safe for her sons and theirs thereafter.

Fear of financial ruin often has a worse effect than any other; it has been far the most frequent cause of suicide. And endless anxiety for another can seek relief in rage; as Elizabeth's did now, when she turned on her husband in fury at his not having discovered the legal slip in his deeds of gift for Sherborne. Ralegh was more distraught than he had ever been when fighting for his life. He wrote a painfully intimate appeal to Cecil, for whom his Bess had always had some tenderness (and therefore, as he could guess, Cecil had for her) to beg him to intercede for her sake, and also his own, for 'I shall be made more than weary of my life by her crying and bewailing . . . charging me with unnatural negligence'. He knew nothing of course of his friend's treachery. It gave Cecil himself no discomfort, for he carefully kept King James' letter of passionate thanks to him: 'The more I think of your remembrance of Robert Carr for yon Manor of Sherborne, the more cause I have to conclude that your mind ever watcheth to seek out all advantages for my honour and contentment.'

Cecil already had reason to doubt James' 'honour' with regard

Count Gondomar, Spanish Ambassador
to James I. By Blyenburg.
By gracious permission of Her Majesty The Queen

Frances Howard.
Married first to 3rd Earl of Essex, then to Robert
Carr, Earl of Somerset. Panel by an unknown artist.
By permission of the Trustees of the National Portrait Gallery

to Robert Carr and his prospective bride. But it was James' 'contentment' that mattered. This was only slightly shaken when Lady Ralegh, holding her younger son Carew, a small, grave boy by the hand, accosted the King in the gardens of Hampton Court, and though 'a woman of very high spirit and noble birth and breeding, fell down upon her knees . . . and beseeched God Almighty to punish those who had so wrongfully exposed her and her poor children to ruin and beggary'.

It was Carew Ralegh himself who recorded that bitter memory forty years later, and who told how the King shambled miserably past his mother as fast as his weak legs could totter, muttering in answer: 'I maun ha'e the land. I maun ha'e it for Carr.'

The King had repudiated his own promise. There was no hope of appeal against that, whether from Ralegh or his wife or their little Carew. They had all failed, and their oldest and supposed best friend, Cecil, had been the one to instigate the theft.

But suddenly there was a royal roar from their newest, youngest friend. The Prince of Wales had entered the arena. 'Hearing the King had given Sherborne to Sir Robert Kerr', wrote Carew Ralegh long later, he 'came with some anger to his father'. Prince Henry, 'in such language as sounded rather like a demand than an entreaty', commandeered Sherborne 'for himself'.

His father could see through that transparent device, but he was cowed into doing all that Henry demanded. His nervously anxious instincts were by now shrinking in actual fear of his son. 'Will he bury me alive?' he had exclaimed in peevish bitterness on finding that the Prince of Wales' levées were far better attended than his own. Now Henry would soon eclipse him, not only in popularity, but in power. The tall youth would come of age towards the end of 1612. He had already forced the King into a public promise that 'Ralegh should be delivered out of the Tower before Christmas'. John Chamberlain noted this, and how the prisoner 'was growne into speciall confidence with the Prince'. Once the Prince were of age, he would no longer need to extort promises from his slippery father. He would then insist on the King's 'pardon' for Ralegh (and an acknowledgment that there had been nothing to pardon); on his full freedom, and the restitution of his property. Sherborne, now bought off from Carr, would then be returned by Henry to its rightful owner.

'Come Christmas', and all this would come true. The eyes of

both Prince and prisoner were fixed confidently upon the blessed festival; and those of Elizabeth Ralegh in hope that was almost anguish, so often had it before been turned to despair.

Other eyes, those of the King, and his new creatures, were also fastened anxiously on the coming date, that would give both to his unnatural son, and to the man James most feared and detested, full freedom and power to work together; and relegate himself to a mere cypher.

But Christmas was not yet come, and there were still many months of 1612 to go.

CHAPTER TWENTY-SEVEN

A Deal of Cold Business

'What a deal of cold business doth a man mis-spend the
better part of life in—in scattering compliments—following
feasts and plays, making a little winter love in a dark corner.'

BEN JONSON

ROBERT CECIL died that same year of 1612, in early summer, an old man at forty-eight, worn out by painful disease
and money worries, not his own, for 'his wealth passes all
belief' wrote the Venetian Ambassador; 'he guides the Council
as he likes—and is the real Prince of this Kingdom'. But he
couldn't guide James' extravagant tastes in young men; and his
financial genius had failed to keep the treasury from bankruptcy
again. As death grew certain, his friends 'fell from him apace',
scuffling at Court to grab what plums might fall to them by his
death. The King had owed everything to him, and acknowledged
it while Cecil could still be of use, but now could hardly be
induced to send him a consolatory message that barely disguised
the irritable protest spilling out with the wine at both corners of
his mouth: 'Na, na, we'll no need the little man the noo.' Anger
roused the sick man to a supreme effort; he would return to
Court from his 'cure' at Bath, and show James and his base pack
of hangers-on that he could still be 'haughty and terrible'. He
over-ruled his doctor, ordered his coach and litter and carrying-
chair so as to be shifted from one to the other to ease his agony on
the journey, and swore he would 'countermine his underminers
and cast dust in their eyes'. But on the journey across Wiltshire
he became so weak that he had to be carried into a strange
parsonage, and there died, 'his memorie perfect to his last gaspe'
—a gift hardly to be envied, in him. What did he remember?
That he and his only son, Will, 'his jewel', had enjoyed country
holidays with the Raleghs at Sherborne, which he had tossed
over to Robert Carr?

Robert Carr would now be the ruler of the country, at least
until Prince Henry should be strong enough to pull him down.
There was a spark of sexual jealousy in the latter's detestation of

Carr, for the only time the austere Prince had begun to fall in love was with the beautiful young Countess of Essex, until he suspected that she was Carr's mistress. Her glove, dropped at a ball, was handed to him as a favour, and he threw it aside. 'I'll have none of it', he said in his disconcertingly pungent fashion, so like Ralegh's that it shows how he imitated his tutor; 'it hath been stretched by another'. This third of his well-known sayings was more dangerous than even the two that had defied his father. For it was dangerous to offend Frances Howard, even at seventeen. The great-niece of Lord Henry Howard, now Earl of Northampton, who had undermined Ralegh's chances so long before his Trial, she had learned her uncle's technique in intrigue and enmity. She had long been conducting a ferocious campaign against her shy, clumsy young husband, the third Earl of Essex, to prevent his consummating their childhood's marriage and so enable her to get a nullity divorce that would set her free to marry her lover. The King would give full support to it, since he would do anything for Carr, who had infatuated his royal master to the point of slavery.

Already Knight of the Garter, Privy Councillor and Treasurer of Scotland, Carr now actually stepped into Cecil's shoes as First Secretary, though neither his education nor his intellect was equal to the work. But the King delighted in giving him lessons in Latin and politics every morning; and Carr had a very clever friend at Court in the young Sir Thomas Overbury, who had first helped him to the King's intimacy, and now took all the heavy work of State off his shoulders.

Cecil's death was welcomed by 'all men's rejoicing' and in a spate of venomous lampoons, some repeating gleefully the report that he had died of the pox, some calling him Herod, or Judas the Second, and all agreeing that 'The Devil now hath fetched the Ape'.

Sir Francis Bacon was more subtle. On return from the funeral at Hatfield (Cecil had left only two hundred pounds for its provision—a great shock, especially to the guests) he wrote the famous Essay on Deformity, which was printed before the year was out, so that the whole world 'takes notice that he paints out his little late cousin to the life'.

'Deformed persons are commonly even with nature, for as nature hath done ill by them, so do they by nature, being for the most part (as the Scripture saith), "void of natural affection"; and so they have their revenge of nature.' Deformity 'stirreth in them industry and especially . . . to watch and observe the weakness of others, that they may have somewhat to repay. . . . So that, upon the matter, in a great wit, deformity is an advantage to rising.'

Bacon's stunted heart was at least equal to his cousin's stunted body as a spur to rising. Even before the funeral he had written to assure the King that he was all agog to take Cecil's place with him, as 'ready as a chessman to be wherever your Majesty's royal hand shall set me'. A still more deadly rivalry ended tragically and, it was thought, mysteriously.

The King and Carr, and his mistress the Countess of Essex, had of a sudden no more reason to fear the Prince of Wales. He had not yet come of age on his eighteenth birthday when he had urged on the betrothal of his sister Elizabeth, two years younger than himself, to the equally young Frederick, Elector Palatine, so as to help weld the Protestant powers together. Elizabeth, like Charles, would do anything that her elder brother told her to do; but her father, in his disappointment of the Spanish match, did not think one of these little German provincial states good enough for her; and for once his wife agreed with him. Her maternal snobbery teased her daughter with jeers of 'Goody Palsgrave!' for that was all her marriage would make her—a German hausfrau! It was bad prophecy, for Elizabeth became the most undomesticated mother of thirteen children in history.

Very small and shy, Frederick arrived that autumn, belatedly, for his ships had been driven back by such appalling gales that three big English ships had finally to go and bring him to Gravesend. By some mismanagement he became separated from his baggage, so that he had to make his first appearance in travelling dress at what was the most showy and fashionable Court in Europe. His dark, anxious eyes fastened on an old man like a seedy badger with frayed fur, who was his future father-in-law, the King of England. All round him were figures as fantastic as puppets in a show, gallants whose breeches stuck out almost as widely as the skirts of the ladies, that made each one of them the centre of a little round table, while their ruffs soared up from their bare necks like the transparent plumage of some exotic bird. Jewels winked everywhere, and they were real. He saw the fair hair and long smiling face, kindly and quizzical, of his mother-in-law the Queen from Denmark; and her grave elder son, as tall as she, and far more beautiful; and his little brother Charles, who came forward to pay his stammering honours to him, with backward glances at his elder brother, always so courteous to foreign guests (and who had done the most to bring about this alliance) yet who stood so still and silent that everybody stared at him in wonder. And then Frederick saw his bride, whom he was to make Elizabeth of Bohemia, the 'Winter Queen', from whose rich power of creation was to come the lines of Kings and Queens of England down to the present day. He fell in love, and never regretted it; though it was to be his ruin, and hers.

Henry had been in a high fever at that reception, but would not admit that he was ill. He recovered his spirits the next day, and insisted on riding at the ring with Prince Frederick. He told his sister how much he liked him, though he wished he were bigger; but there was time yet for him to grow, said Henry, just two years older, and so much taller, that Elizabeth, outrageously, called Frederick her Nigger Duckling; her nicknames were even ruder than those of her late royal Godmother. People said it was because Henry had outgrown and overworked his strength when a few days later he fainted at a banquet. He rode and played tennis too hard, they said, and would walk for miles by the Thames in the dew of the evening, and go for long swims, delighting to hear 'the sound and echo of the trumpets over the water in the moonlight'.

The doctors got him to bed and reported 'a malicious extraordinary burning fever—a putrid fever'; but the wedding entertainments had to go on; they had cost so much to prepare. Nine thousand pounds were spent on fireworks alone; a river pageant for the Lord Mayor's Day was ruined by storms; there were masques by Bacon, by Thomas Campion on the Marriage of the Thames to the Rhine, to symbolize the bride and bridegroom, and by Ben Jonson, who turned the sixteen-year-old Elizabeth into the goddess Diana.

'Queen and huntress, chaste and fair,' he wrote of her, and

> 'Thou that mak'st a day of night,
> Goddess excellently bright.'

She certainly did that at her wedding (and ever after when she could). Her father, after two whole nights out of bed, told Bacon to take his masques away. But he had to endure a new musical play by Will Shakespeare, who was fetched up from his country retirement by special request. It was said that he died of the sack and supper celebrations with Ben Jonson at their old haunt the Mermaid. But first he managed to give *The Tempest* at the Cockpit in Westminster, with magnificent scenic effects and fancy portraits of King James as a learned and magnanimous royal magician (whose tedious long speeches sent James himself to sleep) and of his daughter as a fairytale heroine who had never met a man. Elizabeth laughed at that, and at everything else; at the absurd long German sausages brought by some of Frederick's suite, in distrust of the foreign English food; at the crowds squashed so tight that farthingales got stuck fast in Whitehall's galleries, and a law had to be rushed through to restrict their size; at the bad French of the lawyer who read out the betrothal articles, when she infected Frederick and all their company with such wild giggles that the Archbishop had to cut the religious ceremony short. Her unnatural gaiety was largely hysteria; she knew that Harry had called for her in his delirium, 'Oh where is my sweet sister?' and she had tried again and again to get to him, once even in disguise as a page boy, but was caught and dragged away for fear of infection.

He called too, waking suddenly from a moment's real sleep, to his most trusted servant and friend, Sir David Murray, who was at once at his bedside to ask what he wanted, when the boy fell back with a sigh, 'I would say somewhat, but I cannot utter it,' and became unconscious.

There was a rainbow over the moon one night, just over St James's Palace where he lay: a fatal sign of 'the desolation of kingdoms', said the doctors, who had applied newly dead pigeons and a live cock cut in half to his burning head, without any success. Their despair gave Queen Anne the chance for which she had been waiting. She sent her own messenger to Sir Walter Ralegh in the Tower to beg him for his Elixir of Life, that he had not denied even to one of his worst enemies, old Justice Popham.

Ralegh sent it straightway, with a letter of urgent instructions that it be taken by the Prince at once without delay, and 'would certainly cure him or any other of a fever, except in case of poison'—a bold proviso that showed his suspicions. The Queen struggled to get the medicine immediately to her son, but all her efforts were frustrated. Her husband had gone on a hunting expedition for some days into the country. He feared infection, and the sight of sickness and death; in his son's case it would be too distressing for him, so his Privy Councillors and courtiers explained. Some of them were left on guard in and around the sickroom, and did all they could, by way of caution, to delay giving the Elixir to the patient. The doctors examined it but could not discover its ingredients, which were probably chiefly quinine, learned for the first time from the Indians. They tried it on a dog, then on some of the Privy Council, waited for results, and at last, as nobody was the worse for it, on the now dying youth. He revived; his eyes opened, unclouded, fully aware, and he spoke calmly and distinctly though very low. The fever had all gone; but he was by now too weak to recover. He asked again for David Murray, but once again lost consciousness before he could finish saying what he wished; and never recovered it. The Elixir had been withheld till it could add only a few clear moments to his life.

The 'English Marcellus', the most promising heir to the throne that England has ever had, now left his weak, nervous little brother to inherit it as Charles I, and with it the Civil War that Henry might well have prevented.

The Elector, already half ruined by his prolonged visit to this sumptuous Court, had to add the cost of mourning to that of wedding garments for all his suite; but at last escaped with his bride on a wintry stormy voyage into their stormy future. James lost none of his passion for festivities; the Court was as gay as ever after its brief mourning for Prince Henry. But the country was saddened by it, and full of strange rumours. The Queen believed to the end of her days that her son had died of poison. So did many others; within a few months the belief was strengthened by a split in the most powerful and unpopular faction at Court.

Robert Carr, Viscount Rochester, soon to be Earl of Somerset, had just kicked away the ladder that had helped him climb first into the King's favour, and then into the bedchamber of the young Countess of Essex. He had quarrelled with Sir Thomas Overbury, openly, even noisily, in the galleries at Whitehall; so that servants had heard Overbury call the Countess of Essex 'a filthy base woman—nothing but a whore', and say that if Carr were to let her persist in her divorce from Essex, and then to marry her, 'you will utterly ruin yourself; and you shall never do it by my advice or consent'.

Carr swore back: 'I will be even with you for this!' and swung off in rage, and fear, to tell his mistress. The divorce had been going forward moderately comfortably, though the Archbishop of Canterbury, who was in charge of it, had remarked 'These things please me little'; and greatly disliked the King's backing of it. But when he urged caution, James' only reply was to urge on the proceedings. Essex had denied that he was impotent, except with his wife, who had been determined to prevent his being anything else. A committee of ladies examined her to discover if she were, as she protested, a virgin, but as she insisted upon wearing a thick veil all the time, they could not be sure that it was indeed the Countess whom they examined. Nevertheless they said what was required by the King. The laymen in Court naturally said it also, and even the bishops who had formerly agreed with their spiritual Head now followed the royal lead.

The loving couple saw their course clear before them towards holy matrimony, when suddenly Overbury stood in their way. Nobody knew why he should oppose their marriage, when he had assisted at their liaison (it was probably because he had come to know the Countess better). But Carr and his bride-to-be knew that he had it in his power to stop the divorce. Their obedient King tried to send him on a mission to Russia; Overbury flatly refused to go. This was disobedience, so James made a show of anger and committed him to the Tower, though Carr assured Overbury that it would be only for a brief period. It was. In prison he soon became very ill and died in horrible agonies in less than five months. By then the divorce had gone through.

It was quickly followed by a wedding almost as princely as that of the King's daughter. The King gave the bride £10,000 worth of jewels; Bacon wrote and produced for them his exquisite Masque of Flowers, which cost £2,000, and insisted on paying for it all himself; John Donne gave them his beautiful bridal poem, *The Epithalamium*, which contained the doubtful statement:

'All is warmth and light and good desire.'

The bride wore her fair crimped hair down to her feet to show she was a virgin, and her rather sullen resentful stare outfaced any in the crowds who might be inclined to snigger at that, or at the unusually low-cut bodice that only just covered the nipples of her breasts.

There were whispers among the throng that she had procured Essex's impotence through witchcraft (no uncommon charge in such cases). From that it was an easy step to whispers of poison. What had really happened to Overbury? And why had Sir Henry Wotton, the Ambassador, written so assuredly on Overbury's departure to the Tower: 'He will return no more to this stage'? Had Carr's ally become an inconvenient confederate, who had jibbed when crime went too far—perhaps as far even as the poisoning of the Prince—Robert Carr's greatest potential danger? Nothing was yet said openly. For a little while the young couple could continue to be James' most intimate and pampered protégés.

Prince Henry's purchase of Sherborne reverted at his death to the King, who gladly handed it over once more to Carr. By Christmas, Ralegh and his family would have been living there, if Henry had lived, and Ralegh would have been free. But James saw no reason now to keep his solemn promise to release Ralegh by then, or indeed ever, without some sound motive of profit or revenge. The suspicions that the Prince had been poisoned, and Ralegh's cautionary warning of it, so incautious for himself, had made James implacable. All the prisoner's hopes and plans were destroyed yet again. His brand-new ship, the first three-decker in the English fleet, *The Prince Royal*, had been designed and named by him for Henry, and was now at last ready. It was to become famous in the future; but it was launched too late for Henry, and for Ralegh.

The King of Denmark had begged that Ralegh should be set free to become his own Chief Admiral. James had toyed with the request for a time, partly from courtesy to his brother-in-law, and partly from his irritated resolve to free himself somehow from this Old Man of the Sea, whom no one would let him forget. But James' mulish obstinacy, that had often worked successfully for himself, prevented his granting Denmark's demands. Let the King's heir, wife, brother-in-law, demand Ralegh's freedom; he should still be left with only the barren triumph that no other prisoner had had such pleaders.

Christmas had come and past, and Ralegh was still in prison, with nothing left to help win his release, yet he never doubted that it would come. His work as author alone should win it. Unlike most prisoners who try to sleep out their tedious days, he had cut his sleep to five hours a night, and studied and wrote incessantly. He

> 'could be bounded in a nutshell
> And count himself a king of infinite space,
> Were it not that he had bad dreams;'

So he saw to it that there was no time for them. He had written books on Navigation, new inventions and models of Ships, Anchors, Compasses, etc.; on the Royal Navy and Sea-Service, dealing with matters as small as the preservation of beer-casks, and as large as the Art of War by Sea; all 'for the Lord Henry, Prince of Wales'. There was also a study of Queen Elizabeth, and a 'Description of the River of the Amazons', and a Treatise on the West Indies (all three since lost). The sea-books alone were invaluable in their practical help on subjects 'never handled by any man, ancient or modern'; so also was the more philosophic essay on the causes of war in unemployment, discontent and overcrowded population, and the false lure of fine words such as '*Liberty*'; which 'is but a word in the mouth in the time of civil war'.

The magnum opus at which he had toiled these past years in prison was the million words of his first volume of the *History of the World, Beginning with the Creation, down to Rome in the Second Century B.C.* That too had been written and dedicated to 'that glorious Prince' whose death had fallen 'like an eclipse of the sun'. Ralegh later transferred the dedication to young Will Cecil, of whom he and his wife had always been fond. And he hoped that his scholarship and philosophy would win approval and also his freedom, from a learned fellow-author like his King.

Nothing could show more clearly that even when he was just over sixty, and after all his dealings with James, Ralegh was still as incurably guileless as in his aspiring youth, when he had written asking to buy back his old home, and had offered the owner whatever he thought it worth. And now, so wrote an ironically sympathetic contemporary, with his History 'he thought he had won his spurs, and pleased the King extraordinarily'.

The royal author endured it with difficulty when Bacon proudly presented him with his greatest work, the *Novum Organum*. Flicking over the pages, James complained that it was 'like the peace of God, which passeth all understanding'. And here was another vast tome, by James' most serious rival, in life as in letters. Ralegh's touchingly beautiful dedication to Prince Henry would alone ensure James' hatred of it, as did the fact that Henry had read and admired it. With jealous zeal the King searched for some offence in the Preface, since he could not trouble to read further, and was indignant at Ralegh's severe description of Henry VIII—whom James himself habitually abused. The author, he said, was 'too saucy in censuring princes', and, still more indignantly, that he had no right to have his name, and even his portrait on the title-page. He sent his royal orders to the Stationers' Company to suppress all copies. Its instant popularity prevented this. But the title-page was removed wherever possible.

The *History* had been baulked of its aim like all else that Ralegh had done. There were sheafs of notes, together with exquisite drawings of maps, and plans of battle, that he had 'hewn out', he said, all ready for the second volume; some thought the volume was even then ready written, but that under the blow of his disappointment he burned it, thrusting it into the fire with his boot. That one can hardly believe; 'as soon kill a man as a good book', he would have agreed. But he would never now finish it, as he wrote at the end of the first volume; the Prince to whom the huge labour was 'directed' had been taken 'out of this world', and so prevented its completion, 'besides many other discouragements, persuading my silence'.

Yet nothing could really discourage his unconquerable courage. He had had a dozen years in the Tower, from which so few prisoners had ever emerged. He had made a large room in his narrow cell for what many think the greatest works of his life. He had always known that life is;

> 'time's fool,
> And time, that takes survey of all the world,
> Must have a stop.'

He had acknowledged this in the two hours a day, or rather night, that he had given to reading, even in his most crowded busy-thinking time at Court; and in the trunk-loads of books carried into his cabin for his most venturesome and forward-reaching voyages. The time ahead could in any case stretch only a short way, and 'to spend that shortness basely were too long'. So he had kept always a line of escape to refresh his spirit in the springs that renew life in the mind; and it gave him life where others had come only to die.

But Ralegh firmly believed he would escape, and through no secret scheme, but with full recognition of his innocence. His time had taken survey of all the world; here in the Tower it had stopped, while he did all the things he had never before had time to do. These things had not after all brought him his freedom; but where they had failed, action might even now succeed. Old, and often ill, he was to be given a final chance of adventure, and to spring like a boy towards it.

CHAPTER TWENTY-EIGHT

The Throne of God

'Kings sit in the throne of God, and thence all judgment
is derived.'

KING JAMES' LECTURE TO
THE STAR CHAMBER

'THE curse of them that enter into the fields of the fatherless'
fell quickly upon the Carrs. For just under two years they
reigned supreme in Ralegh's home at Sherborne, and over
the whole country, as the newly created Earl and Countess of
Somerset. As with the late, the second Earl of Essex, Ralegh's
fortunes and Robert Carr's were balanced at the ends of a see-
saw; when one went down, the other went up. At his marriage
Carr was the richest and greatest man in the kingdom and the
most passionately pro-Spanish. His friendship with Spain's new
ambassador, that 'crafty Gallego', Count Gondomar, was closer
even than that of the King, who fawned on Gondomar with
presents as extravagant as if he were a new favourite, which the
Spaniard rewarded with the broad buffoonery so congenial to
James, and still more congenial compliments on his learning; he
lamented that he himself could 'only speak Latin like a King,
but the King like a Master of Arts'. Pocketing a gift of two
thousand ounces of gold plate at a moment when the treasury
was all but bankrupt, Gondomar blithely wrote home to his own
King that it was easy to get round James merely by pretending
to be his pupil, both in scholarship and statecraft.

He also wrote of his fear and detestation of Sir Walter Ralegh.
While the pro-Spanish party was uppermost there was no chance
for 'Guatteral' or 'Sir Vate Ralo', as they variously called him.
But the Spanish alliance was to suffer a set-back with the decline
and fall of its chief backers, the Carrs. The storm they had
brewed approached them gradually, but muttered its first warnings within a few weeks of their wedding. The curse of their
slowly poisoned victim soon began to plague them with hints of
coming danger. 'What secrets have passed between you and me,'

Overbury had written to Carr in his agony in the Tower; 'is this
the fruit of our shared secrets and dangers? Of all my care and
love to you?' He had even written all Carr's love letters for him:
'you used your own only for common passages', and now, 'notwithstanding my misery, you visit that woman, frizzle your head
—traffic with my enemies. You made your vow I should live in
the Court, was my friend—and stayed me twice when I would
have gone, on that day that I was caught in the trap.'

Carr might well come to repent of throwing away his counsel,
'in this very place where I now write this letter'.

The first part of that threat proved at once disastrously true.
Overbury had done all the work of the First Secretary; without
his counsel Carr could not manage even the pretence of it, and
had to agree to the appointment of another man to the post. But
he furiously disagreed with the King's choice. This was Sir Ralph
Winwood, a friend of Ralegh's, and deeply influenced by his
ideas on statecraft and foreign policy. It is an extraordinary
tribute to Ralegh's force of personality, and power to keep in
touch with the world outside his prison, that he should have been
mentor, not only to a young and idealistic Prince, but to a
remarkably astute leading statesman.

Winwood had proved his astuteness at Carr's wedding, when
the bridegroom found (rather oddly, in view of the fact that he
had spent at least ninety thousand pounds in the previous year,
largely in preparations for it) that he had no horses fine enough
to draw the new coach for his bride in the procession; and asked
to borrow four of Sir Ralph's famous stud. Sir Ralph promptly
insisted that they should be a gift. It was considered strange that
Winwood had, for no given reason, worn deep black without a
single jewel, among all the glittering coloured figures at the
wedding. Carr, who still spoke broad Scots, may have retained
enough native superstition from his home at Ferniehurst to shun
taking such a conspicuously valuable present for his bride from
a wedding guest who looked like a harbinger of death. He did his
best to refuse, but was overruled, probably by the bride's greed
rather than the guest's generosity; and everyone exclaimed that
Winwood's four horses were the crowning glory in the procession
through the December night, 'so bespangled with jewels that the
torches and flambeaux were but little light beside them'.

And now here was this fellow, who had had the bad taste to

wear mourning at his wedding, already standing in his shoes as
First Secretary, and being the cause of his first real quarrel with
the King; who for seven years had done everything Carr wanted
of him, but now actually refused to listen to him. Winwood, Carr
pointed out, was dead against Cecil's policy of appeasing Spain;
Winwood was hand in glove with that ruffian Ralegh, and
already working for his release. Winwood was personally abhor-
rent to Carr's useful uncle-in-law, Lord Henry Howard, who had
done more than anyone to engineer Ralegh's downfall and his
niece Frances' marriage to Carr.

> "Tis early to begin to fear
> The Devil at fifteen,'

sang Dorset in his charming verses, but Frances Howard's ferocious will had no fear of the Devil, nor need to learn from him.
It was well before the age of fifteen that she had begun to
sting Robert Carr with desire for her. Torn between her fierce
demands on him, and his new disgust for those of his elderly
monarch, Carr was driven to frantic irritation with the King on
whom his fortune depended. James was in increasing need of a
secure and docile friendship to reassure his shattered nerves; but
that very need only made Carr bully him the more.

The King had been in a state of panic for some time after
Prince Henry's death. He had a barricade of bedsteads placed
around the one he slept in, for protection against any sudden
attack; and an extra troop of specially fast runners to surround
his coach as it drove at a gallop through the streets. He even grew
to fear his gentle 'Baby Charles', then only fourteen, and to
suspect him of wanting to dethrone his unhappy father and put
him in a dungeon till he died. No reason was ever suggested for
this apparently insane new dread; but it is a fact that Charles
believed all his life that his adored elder brother had been
poisoned by Carr, and this must have added painfully to his
father's new discomforts in Carr's friendship. Carr himself
seemed bent on adding to them. James complained to him how
he was 'needlessly troubled with your desperate letters', and then
Carr would burst in on him late at night, to make an hysterical
scene and break away, so that not all James' barricade of beds
could give him any sense of security or hope of sleep.

Suddenly a face like an angel's shone on the King and seemed to promise all he wanted from a young man. On an official visit to Cambridge, where the Earl of Somerset and his Countess were taking all the honour and glory to themselves, James noticed a shabby undergraduate in a ragged gown who reminded him of the picture in the Banqueting Hall of the martyr St Stephen, his countenance radiating light. Who was that beautiful youth, he asked, and was told he was only the son of a poor country squire, his name George Villiers. He was at once Stephen, or rather 'Steenie', to James; Ganymede would have been more appropriate, for he quickly gave him the post of King's Cupbearer. With simple malice the King told him to ask for patronage from Carr, whose reply was still more simple: 'I will, if I can, break your neck.' But he only succeeded in getting his servant to pour a bowl of soup over Villiers' dazzling new white silk suit as he knelt to present a cup of wine to the King. Villiers hit out at the servant, and the official punishment for doing this in the King's presence was the loss of a hand. Carr's eager demand for the correct procedure was disappointed, but the King managed to shift the responsibility for forgiveness on to the Archbishop.

James was clearly very anxious to remain friends with 'his Robbie'. He wrote to him with a candour that approaches dignity, advising him to 'be kind', and warning him that if he tried to hold him by fear, then all his love would be changed to hate. He appointed him Lord Chamberlain and took pains to explain that it was because he was the man 'nearest him in affection'. He then attempted to confer on him a favour so extraordinary that it involved the Crown in a clash with the Law: for he actually demanded a pardon to be drawn up in advance for any crimes that Carr might be accused of committing. There was a long list of them, but the King found it incomplete, and added others, among them that of being accessory to a murder. This was too much for the Lord Chancellor, who protested that at this rate Carr had leave to steal the Crown Jewels with impunity. He refused, on his knees, to sanction it, and so did the Privy Council, when hastily summoned and stormed at by the King. So James failed to obtain his friend's *carte blanche* for crime.

Carr's need for it was coming very close. His marriage had been tormented from the start by alarms that had to be secretly suppressed. Even before the divorce, only three months after Prince Henry's death, a woman was publicly accused of the theft of a diamond ring and gold cup from the Countess. She had protested that they were merely her legitimate payment for the preparation of a slow poison for the third Earl of Essex. Her conscience had kept her from giving it to his Countess, but not from keeping her pay. The Countess dropped her charge like a hot coal, but its scald had scared her into paying continual blackmail to all the later agents she had employed for Overbury's murder.

The blow fell eventually from one who had never so troubled her, an apothecary's apprentice who had had the sense and tact to slip abroad, safely away as the Countess thought, and there die within two years. He had however made a deathbed confession to the English consul, who reported it privately to the First Secretary in London, Sir Ralph Winwood. And Winwood questioned the Lieutenant of the Tower, Sir Gervase Elwes, as to what he knew of the death of Overbury while in his charge.

Sir Gervase boggled, admitted there had been a plot to poison Overbury, then that he had been a party to it and that he had been given his recent appointment as Lieutenant for that very purpose by Lord Henry Howard. Lord Henry, with his usual sense of convenient timing, had lately died and so avoided these unpleasant revelations; but Sir Gervase was hanged on his own Tower Green, and so were three others of the Countess Frances' confederates who made full confession.

The chief of them was the fashionable milliner Mistress Turner, who procured the new French yellow starch for ruffs for her many Court clients. She also procured secret lovers' meetings, love potions, and poisons from a learned doctor ('sickness was his masterpiece'). The Countess wrote to her as 'Sweet Turner' and signed herself 'your sister, Frances'. Tastefully dressed in black, Mistress Turner made an elegant and pious before-execution speech, undeterred by the hangman's vulgar travesty of her, for he wore in mockery a huge ruff and cuffs, dyed with her yellow starch. It went out of fashion after that.

There were seven trials in all, culminating in those of the Carrs, and the result was to shake James' throne. His subjects were already disgusted with both Crown and Church, by James' indecent and imbecile interference in the divorce proceedings that he had forced through with the compliance of his bishops. They were to be appalled by the murder trial of his two chief protégés. He had realized that there was nothing to be done but command an open enquiry to 'search to the bottom of the conspiracy', conducted by the Lord Chief Justice. Sir Edward Coke had certainly understood and followed his King's wishes in conducting Ralegh's trial, and should do so here if he were wise.

But Coke had grown too powerful to be wise; his chronic state of bad temper, fostered by perpetual quarrels with his second wife, Lady Hatton, had become almost as much of a disease as James' state of terror. The seven murder trials were his greatest opportunity to date, and he fell on it with all his old gusto and dogged industry; wrote over three hundred examinations in his own hand, began to read aloud, quite irrelevantly and tactlessly, the full list of all Mrs Turner's distinguished Court clients in illicit love-affairs—and came to a dead stop on finding his wife's name among them, causing 'much mirth in Court'. He was to burn his own fingers far worse than that.

It was all very well for him to roast the small fry and thunder out his eloquent summing-up on Mrs Turner: 'Thou hast the Seven Deadly Sins, for thou art a Whore, a Bawd, a Sorcerer, a Witch, a Papist, a Felon and a Murderer.' But his furious attacks on a whole shoal of big fishes were far more rash and indiscriminate. He tried to net in everyone and everything, from another brand-new Popish Plot—'Remember the Fifth of November!' he fulminated—to spells for abortion—Remember the Queen's former miscarriages! (But it was many years since the King had given her the chance of one.) With ferocious glee he did his best to incriminate nearly all his colleagues, the Council and the Court, in this 'crime which slept two years, being *shadowed with greatness*'; a grand phrase and a true, but unfortunate in its suggestion that the crime had been covered up by the King.

Yet Coke proved an excellent detective. He exposed the late Lord Henry Howard's helpful part in the murder; also the fact that many leading English statesmen, including Henry Howard again, and the late Robert Cecil, had secretly received pensions from Spain. This was yet another of Coke's red herrings, and one that brought him the enmity of most of the Privy Council and the leading families of England. His most dangerous indiscretion was to insist that Overbury's murder was only one part of 'The Great Oyer of Poisoning', as he delighted to call it; and that a far greater victim had been that 'most sweet Prince' Henry, poisoned it was said, by a bunch of grapes. His 'discretion' over this reached its climax; 'I dare not discover secrets,' he said darkly in Court; and left it to be assumed that Carr had poisoned first Henry, then Overbury to keep it secret, and that the King had most likely had a hand in both crimes, or at the least knew all about them.

Scandal spread like the plague. It boiled up to such a pitch 'as it distracts everybody's mind from anything else'. But it provided much enjoyment. Nobles and gentry left their country seats in the height of summer to hurry back to town for the trial of the Countess. All who could push or bribe their way thronged into Westminster Hall; others waited outside all night, paid £50 or more for one of the boxes erected on scaffolding so densely packed that it cracked with a terrifying noise as the crowds all craned forward to see the horrible little instruments of magic the Countess had used to win her second husband and dispose of her first.

Coke's first-rate detective work had discovered these, and her letters ordering them: unholy aphrodisiacs and love potions for Carr, leaden images of him in the act of love with her, and of herself naked 'in her hair' before a glass; still more sinister, a small wax naked figure of Essex, 'in the privity of which a thorn had been stuck'. The thunder crack of the scaffolding was taken for the roar of the Devil himself, 'angry to have his workmanship shewed'. As the shrieking crowds of gentry jumped and fell from it, they saw Essex's tall form against the wall far at the back of the hall, watching this evidence against the woman that he had loved when she was a quiet, well-behaved girl of twelve, and he a clumsy boy of fourteen. He heard her faint voice plead 'Guilty', and heard her condemned to be hanged.

But not by Coke. The King had taken the case out of his hands and transferred it to the Attorney-General, Sir Francis Bacon, with special instructions that he wanted 'no odious or uncivil speeches'. Bacon quite understood. Coke had ruined the best chance of his career, and now it was Bacon's turn to seize his own by repairing the harm done; but, he sighed resignedly, 'Such it is to come to the leavings of a business!'

He had the most tricky part of the 'leavings' in the last of the trials, that of Robert Carr himself. On the evening his wife was condemned, Carr was told he was to be tried the next day, and still could not believe he was at last 'caught in the trap' that he had set for Overbury. He swore he would not go to his trial; they would have to drag him there in his bed; the King had promised not to bring him to trial; then, at the top of his voice, the King *dared* not do so. This sounded dangerous. Late though it was, the officer in charge, Sir George More, rushed by boat to the King at Greenwich Palace, where 'he bounceth at the back stairs as one mad', and insisted on James being woken up to hear how Carr had threatened him. The wretched King collapsed weeping and trembling on More's neck, imploring him to help him: 'On my soul I know not what to do.' More never told what else was said.

'What secrets have passed between you and me,' Overbury had written to Carr. No one has known what they were, nor how far they involved the King; that some of them were weightier than those of their sexual relations is plain from Bacon's words, 'Overbury knew more of the secrets of state than ever the Council did.'

There was no sleep for More that night; he was rowed back in the early hours, and went straightway to wake up and warn the Attorney-General. There was far more fuss over this; Bacon's servants, all elegant young dandies, protested in mincing tones that their master must never, never be awakened when he had given orders for his repose. More insisted that the King himself had had his repose broken, and far earlier in the night. The youths moaned and waved their hands. More noticed that they all wore long boots of the finest scented Spanish leather, an unheard-of extravagance in servants, but their master's sensitive nose could not endure the smell of plain neat's tongue hide.

More got his way. Bacon was woken up, and leaped out of bed to catch his opportunity. An expert in the art of hushing-up, he was as much in his element as Coke had been while exposing everybody he could think of. He appointed two servants to stand behind Carr at the trial, holding a cloak to throw over his head and carry him away 'hoodwinked' the instant that Bacon gave them the sign to do so. The indefatigable More had then to hurry off and warn Carr that if he tried to say anything unseemly he would only put his head in the bag, and eventually on the block.

At nine o'clock that blazing summer morning the trial began, with Bacon's 'viper eye', though somewhat docked of sleep, fixed unswervingly upon the prisoner for the first angry sign of his breaking out into any inconvenient disclosure. The King sent down messengers every hour to know if he had done so. He and

Bacon had already decided that Carr must not be driven to 'desperation and flushes'. But these came only from Coke, as in empurpled rage he insisted that the whole point of this trial was missed if they did not discover at least a dozen other murder plots at the same time. As Bacon agreed with the King, Coke 'marred' the trial.

Not so Carr. In a splendid suit of black satin, rich gloves, curled hair and beard, and round his neck the George and Garter, which only the innocent may wear, he swaggered to the prisoner's box, glanced at the two servants with the cloak waiting to muzzle him if necessary, and loudly pleaded 'Not Guilty'. The trial lasted thirteen hours and many fainted under the stifling ordeal, but not Carr. He was pronounced Guilty and sentenced to death. The chief evidence to condemn him came from his wife's uncle, Lord Henry Howard, in letters assuring him that Sir Gervase Elwes as Lieutenant of the Tower was an entirely safe tool for Overbury's death, that Carr need have no fears as long as Lord Henry were in town, and in a letter to Elwes, 'Noble Lieutenant, if the knave's body be foul' (from the poison) 'bury it instantly; I'll stand between you and harm.' But Elwes had been hanged, and Lord Henry lay in his grave, though even from there he could deal a death blow.

Both Carr and his Countess were saved from suffering the death sentence by the King's Prerogative, as everybody had known would happen. The crowds jeered that 'the Coke would have made white broth of them', like the white poison broth the Countess had sent to Overbury, 'but the Prerogative kept them from the Pot'. They hated and despised the King for it, and would have torn the Countess to pieces if they could, as they nearly tore the Queen when long later they mistook her mass of fair hair for that of the Countess, and mobbed her coach, shrieking for her death.

The Carrs' was to be a living death: for six years in the Tower and then at a remote country seat. Though always together, and seeing hardly anyone else, they never spoke to each other again in the sixteen years that they had still to live together. His release from her was to come only with her death at thirty-nine, from a noisome disease which made her mind as morbid as her body. Her heavy young first husband, the third Earl of Essex, became known as the 'Great Cuckold', and hid his humiliation in retirement from the Court that he loathed, until he had his chance in the next reign to lead the army of Parliament rebels against it. His infamous advice to slaughter the great Earl of Strafford whom they had failed to convict—'Stone dead hath no fellow—' shows how his wife had 'withered' him.

The Civil War, reaped by Charles I, was sown, and escaped, by his father; for James weathered the split with his subjects over the poison trials. They had a happy result for Bacon, in winning him his place in the Privy Council and in pulling Coke down from his post as Chief Justice, where he had been 'too busy in diving farther into secrets than there was need, and so risked seeing Diana naked'. To secure his overthrow James thrust himself into the Star Chamber, which no monarch had dared do since Henry VIII, and told them that the Royal Prerogative was above the Law, since 'Kings are properly Judges and all judgment properly belongs to them from God'.

He thus undermined his most treasured institutions; while 'Lord Coke is tossed up and down like a tennis ball, Lord Bacon is in slippery places' but gliding higher and higher; and the whirligig of time, that brought in its revenges on Ralegh's enemies, brought also his release, after over a dozen years.

Carr's pro-Spanish party had fallen with him into disrepute; it was no longer safe to be quite so openly kind to Don Gondomar. The political field was now led by Sir Ralph Winwood, whom Bacon called 'the boisterous Secretary'. He admonished him for familiarly leaning his shoulder against Bacon's at the Council table ('Keep your distance') and, in the still icier reproof of a true Englishman, when Winwood cuffed Bacon's little lap-dog off his Secretarial chair, 'Every gentleman loves a dog.'

Winwood was English enough to hate Spain, and did not fear to risk war with her. He had learned from Ralegh that there could be no cheap 'defence of nations', and agreed with Ralegh's passionate conviction that when Englishmen did make war they should do it 'as warriors and not as hucksters'. The Secretary had long urged Ralegh's release to James, and so did more and more of his colleagues as the Carr faction crumbled. The King's new favourite, George Villiers, and his brother and half-brother, pleaded and collected money to buy his pardon, in addition to the fifteen hundred pounds Ralegh paid for it. His house of Sherborne, confiscated from Carr, was offered to Villiers, this time with no violent protest from its owner; and 'Steenie' had long and effective talks with his King.

The most powerful argument in the prisoner's favour was James' now desperate need of money, and the confident belief of Ralegh and his friends that he could find gold for him in Guiana. That would be, as Ralegh wrote to him, 'a most easy way of being enriched, despite your grunting subjects'—for they had been grunting loudly against James' ideas, not only of Divine Right, but of Divine Taxation. But James grunted louder that they had not given him a subsidy for years, and he was sick of 'living like a shellfish upon his own moisture'.

Guiana was a hare-brained scheme, he thought. Every safe-guard must be provided—for the adjacent Spanish colonies, not for Ralegh. But if it succeeded, he would replenish his Exchequer; and if it failed he would have his best chance to rid himself finally of this Old Man of the Sea who out-did him at every turn, even with his own sons, his own Councillors; even with his books.

So he at last signed the Order for Ralegh's release; but actually let him out nearly a year earlier than the date stated for it. The reason was that yet once more the drama of Ralegh's fortunes was entwined with that of Robert Carr and his wife Frances. She had been ordered to the Tower towards the end of March 1616 to await her trial, and told that she would be lodged in the Bloody Tower, where Overbury had died in such hideous torments. For the only time in public she broke down, and in paroxysms of hysteria shrieked: 'Not that! Not that!' till it was thought she would run mad. So Ralegh was hurried out of his rooms in the Brick Tower on March 19th, 1616, and a week later the Countess was locked into them. She too was given permission to walk where he had walked on his wall above the Thames, but even she was not bold enough to attempt it a second time, after the yells of hate and derision that greeted her from the crowds that had been wont to wait for hours to show their love and admiration for Ralegh.

Ralegh's earlier lodging in the Bloody Tower was reserved for Carr himself, with all doors open between it and his wife's, but, like her, 'he useth the liberty of the Tower very sparingly'— small wonder, as they did not speak to each other. Ralegh returned to collect the remainder of his books, and for the first time the tall thin old man with the keen eyes confronted the young Scot, his florid beauty grown flabby with soft living, who had turned Ralegh's family out of their home, and worked persistently against him. For an instant there was a sharp duel of words, ended by one of Ralegh's mocking thrusts—that in his whole *History of the World* there was no precedent for their situation, except that of Mordecai and Haman, when the King's chief prisoner had his freedom at the same time as his bosom favourite had the halter! Once again he set 'the common world wondering at this man's wit, who had a way to break Jests, though to hazard his head again.'

CHAPTER TWENTY-NINE

The World's Bright Glory

'The world's bright glory hath put out the eyes of our minds.'

RALEGH'S 'HISTORY OF THE WORLD'

At first it was bliss just to be free to walk up and down in the streets again to see so many people, and so many more than in his day, jostling each other into the muddy gutters and garbage heaps. They did not jostle him; but some stared at the tall gentleman who gazed about him with the wonder of a raw countryman, or, rather, of a distinguished foreigner, yet without any retinue.

They looked at him as at a ghost; and so indeed he felt himself to be. His once familiar town had burst into a crazy chaos of traffic. The chorus of the hawkers had swollen deafeningly; they pushed their barrows like battering rams through the milling crowds, bawling their melodious street-cries to advertise their Spanish gloves and fine-cut pins. All must eat their 'lily white mussels' and 'quick periwinkles, quick, quick, quick' all alive-oh!, and oysters at fourpence a bushel. It was good to smell again their smoking-hot pippin pies, their bunches of juniper and rosemary, and even their garlic—'the only physic 'gainst all the mal-a-dies'. An outlandish novelty to him were the long red sausages introduced by the Elector Palatine's German suite at his wedding three years ago. The costermongers brandished and waggled them with ribald jokes in the faces of the passers-by, especially the women, who screamed and tittered.

The clearest singers were the chimney-sweep boys, black as negroes and chanting like choirboys: 'Soope chimney, mis-te-ris soope, with a hoop de-re de-re de-re soope, from the bottom to the top, there shall no soot fall in your por-ridge pot.' The cheeriest were the coopers, clanking pails to mend in a piercing cacophany that could not drown their irrelevantly happy boast, 'Married I am to as pretty a wench as ever God hath made, Have ye work for a coo-oo-ooper?'

He listened with grim interest to the ballad-mongers proffering the latest disclosures on the horrible murder of Sir Thomas Overbury by the Wicked and Beautiful Countess and her minion Mrs Turner, the procuress of fashions from France—and of other merchandise.

He smiled at the high hats of the gallants thronging the streets like moving chimney-pots; no doubt the tiny feathered caps that he remembered clamped to one ear 'like an oyster patty', as if with glue, would now seem as ridiculous to these modern young men. Their dress was as rich but not as gay; the colours were darker and aimed at a perverse and sinister note in extravagance. They wore nothing as fantastic as the Elizabethan peascod-bellied doublets or their monstrous cod-pieces, swollen as if in boast of a preposterous virility—a quality that seemed to have gone out of fashion. Many walked delicately with a kind of mincing disdain, and wore no swords out of deference to their King's aversion to the sight of them—not that he ever drove through the streets if he could help it. And even the younger nobles often drove in coaches like their elderly King, instead of riding on horseback; a sign of effeminacy to Ralegh, who would have scorned to take a coach instead of a horse.

'Paul's Walk' was still the smart rendezvous for strolling and scandal-mongering and business-dealing in the greatest and grandest of English cathedrals, which still towered above the City, though lightning had long since docked it of its lovely spire. It was a shock to notice how the slums had spawned to keep pace with the teeming population. They had begun to do so in the old Queen's day, in spite of the laws against new houses, and by now had cropped up everywhere like toadstools, mean little sheds over stables, in gardens and any odd corner; and her attempted ruling of 'One house, one family,' was everywhere ignored. Decayed houses were turned into swarming ant-heaps of stinking tenements. More than ever he longed to make room for his countrymen to live in new lands beyond the seas, now that he saw what he had always foretold—a London glutted to choking-point, and belching out its suburbs further and further into the country beyond, their filthy alleys and little shops infesting the green fields 'which ought to be open—and free for all men'.

To that demand of his, he was told, 'You will have to walk as far as Islington to hear the cuckoo now.'

He could not walk very far, for his lame leg tired easily after so many years of cramped inactivity. But he showed all his youthful zest in exploring this strange London, its novel splendours more than its squalors.

In the grounds of his old home of Durham House, where he had held court for princes and their ambassadors, for explorers and adventurers, he was amused to see the grand New Exchange that Robert Cecil had raised to dignify the power of money; a just tribute, since no one had done as much against heavy odds for English finance.

In Westminster Abbey he gazed long on the new effigy of his Lady; and the inscription that united her and Mary Tudor who as 'sharers of kingdom and tomb sleep here, Elizabeth and Mary, sisters, in hope of the Resurrection'. Just lately he had written, 'our bed is made ready for us in the dark'; this was one they could never have thought to share. After all their bitter rivalry, Time had surprised them both, in the concord of a single tomb. It was a fitting comment on the most famous passage in the whole of his *History of the World*: 'Oh eloquent, just, and mighty Death! Whom none could advise, thou hast persuaded; what none hath dared, thou hast done; and whom all the world hath flattered, thou only hast cast out of the world and despised. Thou hast drawn together all the far-stretched greatness, all the pride, cruelty, and ambition of man, and covered it all over with these two narrow words— *Hic Jacet*.'

He visited the Society of Antiquaries which he had helped to found, looked at new buildings of great beauty designed by the latest Court architect, artist and stage designer, Inigo Jones, whom Ralegh's old friend Ben Jonson called Iago, or 'the Villain Iago', for his presumption in having his name put on the playbills above those of the playwrights. He dined again with Ben, after so long, at the Mermaid Tavern, which they both had made the most famous London club for wits and writers.

Ben Jonson also grumbled against his old friend's son. He had gone with young Wat Ralegh to Paris as his tutor, got dead drunk, while his pupil, dead sober (as was his wont in imitation of his father), laid him sprawling in a hand-barrow to be trundled through the streets as a 'living image of the Crucifix'. His adoring mother tried to laugh it off with the old defence that his father when young had been much the same: a fondly maternal lie, for

Ralegh's roughest sport had never been as crude or blasphemous as this of Wat's; 'his father abhorred it,' so Aubrey tells us. The most thwarting part of Ralegh's imprisonment lay in preventing his bringing up his son as he could have done in liberty. This shows with odd perversity in his minute book of 'Instructions' to him, which are utterly unlike himself, as though in desperate attempt to teach Wat the worldly wisdom he himself lacked. Yet he took great pride in his bold, handsome son, and did all he could to correct the impression of his Oxford tutor that Wat was 'addicted to strange company and violent exercises'. As soon as he was free, he took him into the best company at an important dinner party with strict injunctions to be on his best behaviour. These were apparently too strict for Wat's contrary spirit, for after sitting very quiet and mum he suddenly produced an outrageously improper tale, which Ralegh stopped with a quick box on the ear. His irrepressible son swung round and 'rude as he was, he would not strike his father, but strikes the gentleman who sat next to him, telling him to "box about; 'twill come to my father anon"'. 'Tis now a common used proverb,' so Aubrey tells us, echoing the indulgent pleasure so many men took in this quick-witted youth, who was so like his father.

It had always been Wat's great ambition to be like his father. The portrait of them together, painted years earlier, shows that; the boy is in exactly the same stance as the man, his left arm, like his, akimbo, the hand resting on his hip, his right hand firmly holding the fringed garter at Ralegh's knee, and his watchful, direct gaze striving to be as penetrating as his father's. It is in fact even graver, for there is a slight smile lurking in Ralegh's black beard, while the curve of the child's long upper lip is as solemnly resolute as it is sensitive—the last an odd attribute in one who was to be chiefly known for his invention of an impudent proverb.

His resolution and wild courage were certainly like his father's. He had lately wounded a man in a duel, and as soon as he had recovered they had both gone to Holland, 'eating together in outward amity to cover their intent', which was to fight it out again in peace and quiet abroad. The English Ambassador, Sir Henry Wotton, wrote this to Ralegh, and how he had sent for young Wat, whom he obviously liked, and had done his best to talk him into sense, but found interference only made him the more obstinate.

Ralegh was certain that all Wat needed was some real action and adventure; in fact to sail with him for Guiana. For Wat, this was the dream of his life come true; for his mother, the dread of hers; for his quiet little brother Carew, born in the Tower, it was agony that he was still only eleven and could not go too, but must stay at home and look after their mother, who try as she would could never spoil him as much as she did Wat, for he never gave her so much chance to do so. For Ralegh's friends, it was a major anxiety that he should take such a firebrand as his elder son on an enterprise whose only hope for him depended on keeping the peace.

But the father's own recklessness made them fear the most. With his eyes open he was taking on a mad gamble, with the dice loaded against him by a King who hated and feared him, and who refused him an official pardon even when appointing him Admiral-in-Command of a fleet with powers of life and death over it—a sinister anomaly that most younger men would have the caution to avoid. And he was sixty-four, a much older age then than now, and weakened by thirteen years of persistent sedentary work within damp prison walls.

That work was recognized by many to be his greatest achievement; they implored him to continue it even at the cost of his freedom. One Sylvanus Scory, who did not know him personally, was inspired to unwonted poetry by Ralegh's amazing courage in facing open-eyed his foes' rebuffs and friends' discouragements:

> 'Scorning the sad faces of thy friends,
> Thou smil'st at Fortune's menaces and malice;'

yet entreated him to abandon his adventure and

> 'Hold thee firm here; cast anchor in this port.
> Here art thou safe, till Death enfranchise thee,
> Here—though enchained—thou liv'st in liberty.'

'That villainous adventurer,' as Lord Acton called Ralegh even while admitting that he venerated him, had known all the hollowness of ambition, and exposed it in his *History* as merely 'damnable pride'. He had shown that even valour 'taken by itself, is not much to be admired', but 'praiseworthy only in daring good things'. The Pagan Gods had passed away; 'Jupiter is no more vexed with Juno's jealousies, Death hath persuaded him to chastity and her to patience. The great god Pan hath broken his pipes.' Idols may pass, but idolatry never dies; he acknowledges this, and proves it against himself. For Ralegh's *History* is not only of the world, but of the world in himself; and no man ever wrote of himself with clearer eyes, and yet unconsciously. His chapter on Alexander the Great is thought the best in the whole book, and no wonder, for in Alexander he comes closest to himself; but remains undazzled by the romance of his greatness, and condemns him as one of the 'troublers of the world'.

This is one of the great books of all time. Milton was to learn profoundly from it in his poetry as well as his prose, and to write of it as 'the precious life-blood of a master spirit embalmed and treasured up on purpose to a life beyond life'. How then should such a master spirit as Ralegh's bow his head again before 'the high and shining idol of glory' and turn away from his treasure of 'life beyond life', to pursue once more 'the all-commanding image of bright gold'? Ralegh himself has asked this, and given the answer.

'But what examples have ever moved us? What persuasions reformed us? Or what threatenings made us afraid? We behold other men's tragedies played before us; we hear what is promised and threatened; but the world's bright glory hath put out the eyes of our minds.'

Yet that was not the whole answer; and he himself could hardly have given it, so deep did it lie within the truest part of him, never to be changed nor taught, not even by his own philosophy, learned so cruelly from his own experience. It is that part of him that has made him immortal.

Would Ralegh mean as much to us today if he had been content, as his friends and biographers have wished, to back out of his mad new endeavour, and cry with Lear,

> 'Come, let's away to prison . . .
> so we'll live,
> And pray and sing and tell old tales . . .'?

His value to us is more than the achievement of a great book,

or indeed than any of his achievements; for it lies in the unconquerable spirit that essayed them, whatever the outcome. Not the
brightness of gold nor of glory, nor even the fortune of his family,
was the mainspring of his last quest; but the vision and impulse
of his whole life since childhood, as fresh now in his old age—but
there was no such age for one who like Froissart's Percy, slain in
the Wars of the Roses, had 'saved the bird in his bosom'. In
Ralegh's it lived uncaged through all his years of prison, its song
as clear and instinctive as when Spenser acclaimed him 'the
Summer's Nightingale'. To deny its call would have been to belie
himself.

When there was no alternative, there was none 'that knew so
well how to advantage himself and his country in Imprisonment';
to turn defeat into victory, and carve out a new conquest of the
World in the liberty of his mind. But when given his choice, it
was not in him to play for safety—that sleepy and doubtful
benefit, for it cannot remind one that it is good to be alive. His
forefathers had scorned a 'straw death', that of a cow cooped in
the straw of a byre; and so did he when the chance came at last
of such risks as he had once shared with his men on the unknown
Orinoco. 'Let us go on, we care not how far!' had been their cry;
it was to be his own to the end.

CHAPTER THIRTY

The Mischief of being Wise

'He attains not to the mischief of being wise.'

BISHOP EARLE'S 'MICROCOSMOGRAPHY'

NONE of his contemporaries ever thought of Ralegh as old. Ambassadors from Venice and France and from Savoy, now at war with Spain, eagerly sought his services and offered him command of a fleet, if only he would consent to use his strength to help their Sovereigns. Even his own Sovereign of England found it useful on occasion to prod Spain, when too insolent, with the threat of their still most dreaded foe, 'Gualteral'.

The Spanish Ambassador Gondomar was frankly terrified by Ralegh's release; he wrote to his King to urge repeatedly that he must strengthen all his navies against him; and that no Spanish ships must now dare sail except under guard of a convoy. Finally he demanded leave to return to Madrid himself to impress on his master how serious was the danger from this 'great seaman, who took many prizes in the time of Queen Elizabeth, and who first colonized Virginia'.

He feared 'especially the formation of another company for Guiana and the river Orinoco . . . the prime promoter and originator of which is Sir Walter Ralegh. . . . He has already been in the country, and assures people here that he knows of a mine that will swell all England with gold.' This had at all costs to be prevented. Gondomar had actually managed to interfere with the English Admiralty, and forced them to 'act properly, by condemning as pirates the English ships that had long been accustomed 'to go to Brazil for wood. This has caused great annoyance.'

It certainly had, not only to the 'pirates', but to the Courts of Admiralty and their supreme Judge; they at first flatly refused this meagre, thin-haired, tight-lipped foreigner who dared meddle with English rulings, until they were driven by their own King to yield to him. What odds between a Scot and a Spaniard

they snorted; and Gondomar clinched it by finishing his report
on the wood-shippers as if he were himself the Lord Admiral: 'But
I have prosecuted them criminally as disturbers of the peace. . . . I
am trying to do the same with Ralegh.'

So the swords were drawn for the last of Ralegh's duels, his
death-struggle with Gondomar. Never to the end did Ralegh
admit Gondomar's accusation of his invading any soil of Spain's.
'That Guiana be Spanish territory can never be acknowledged,'
he wrote, 'for I myself took possession of it for the Queen of
England, by virtue of a cession of all the native chiefs of the
country.' Those chiefs had come to him of their own free will, to
swear loyalty to him, which he had accepted in the name of
Elizabeth. His claim to it as tenure of the English Crown was
never relinquished by James, who would argue his right to it by
the hour together, though he would not act on it. Nearly three
centuries later the boundaries between British Guiana and Venezuela were settled by neutral arbitration; and this proved
incidentally that Ralegh's last expedition had committed no
trespass.

It is no consolation to wait three hundred years to be justified;
but Ralegh, the most impetuous of men, was doomed to delays.
For the past twenty-one years, thirteen of them spent in prison,
he had worked at his dearest dream of planting a colony from his
struggling, often starving country of overcrowded England, in
the spacious and healthy land of Guiana. He had advertised its
lure as an untouched 'magazine of all rich metals', but did not
mention gold and diamonds as its chief attractions. To him these
lay in the friendly peace and happiness of its way of life; and in
common industries, its cottons and silks, and precious gums,
ginger, sugar, and Indian pepper, that rare treasure in search
of which men for centuries had died by thousands in their desert
voyages. In Guiana it grew at hand for the picking, along with
delicious new fruits such as the Pinas or pineapples, 'the princesse
of all fruits', which King James declared too perfect for any
subject to be allowed to eat.

A typically practical point which Ralegh made in Guiana's
favour was that the land was so defensible that it needed only two
strong forts to guard it from invasion; and the two places he
suggested for them have been confirmed to this day as the
strategic points that command the country. But his 'Lady of

Ladies' had been too old and weary for new adventure; and his Court rivals, delighted that he should fail, put all the objections that they could in his way. Impatiently he had fumed that 'we must cast so many doubts, and this dolt and that gull must be satisfied', and had had to watch, just as he had feared, how the Spaniards showed they were not so 'blockish and slothful'.

His book on his *Discovery of Guiana* was smiled on at home, and chiefly 'made a stir among poets and children'.[1] But abroad his book aroused great interest and at once stimulated the Dutch and French as well as the Spanish to follow his lead in Guiana. And all the while he chafed and pleaded in vain that 'no one be suffered to soil the enterprise'; to harry and exploit the native kings whom he had 'won to love and obedience', and to snatch from England's Queen 'that which she shall never find again'. His labour in the lost enterprise had been at his own cost, and again and again (even when he was in the Tower it was every second year) he fitted up and paid for a ship to go out to hold the tribes to their allegiance, and 'comfort and assure the people that they despair not'.

They needed it. Ships from Holland had been shunned by the natives until it was found they were not Spaniards, and then they were greeted with glad cries of 'Anglees!' An Indian chief had been hanged by the Spaniards and had prophesied at point of death that the English under their chief, Ralegh, would come to free his people. Other Englishmen belatedly took up Ralegh's venture; Prince Henry at fifteen, fired by his vision, actually induced the King to despatch an expedition under Robert Harcourt. He declared that if a mere hundred farm workers were sent out to work the crops for flax and cotton and sugar, it would pay in a few years beyond all expectation. The tribes gave him a great welcome, but asked eagerly always for Ralegh, and Harcourt tactfully invented other reasons than the Tower to 'excuse his not returning according to his promise'. The memory of him remained their greatest hope. A hundred and fifty years later they still looked for his return, as for that of a god.

His own hope even in old age may still have been 'to govern that country which I have discovered'. Its good government, whether by himself or, he wrote modestly, 'by some other, of better sufficiency', was his ultimate aim in returning to it. It was

---

[1] Sir Philip Magnus, *Brief Lives: Sir Walter Raleigh.*

more important to him than the rich gold-mine which Keymis was so sure he had been on the point of discovering. But gold 'to swell all England', and immediately, was the only thing that interested James. It would set him free from his 'grunting Parliaments,' and he need never call another to squeeze a subsidy out of them.

Yet Ralegh's vision of the future, dismissed from its birth as merely visionary, was to prove itself of infinitely more practical value. If he had had his way and annexed all Guiana, Venezuela and most of North Brazil for England, as well as Trinidad, they would later have brought his country great wealth from the gold and diamond mines that are worked there profitably up to this day; and, far later and greater in importance, from a mineral, then undreamed of, which has turned Columbus' discovery of 'little Venice' (hence the name, Venezuela, from its houses built on water) into one of the most valuable of the world's territories. The power of petroleum was something even Ralegh could not foresee. His belief in future possibilities as yet unguessed at, shows the genius of a scientist. But it was genius for which the world was not ready.

*   *   *

Ralegh told James in a frankly explicit letter that 'those Spaniards which dwell upon the same river' of Orinoco were already looking for Keymis' mine, though it was not in their part of the district, and 'have tormented an hundred of the natural people to death to find the place'. It was a warning that Ralegh needed to take to himself; it was ignored by James when he later accused Ralegh, and made it a capital charge, of deceiving his King—who, in spite of Ralegh's letter, pretended to think there were no Spaniards in Guiana. But nobody quite knew what James thought he thought; he cultivated a convenient muzziness when he chose. His rule for this was 'Heads I win, tails you lose.'

Gondomar had returned from Spain to goad him into fretful agitation; to threaten him with his master's rage at this unleashing of the last of Elizabeth's pirates, 'fleshed by her in Spanish blood and ruin'; to insist on knowing all the 'pirate's' plans, and seeing all his papers, and to object and interfere in all of them; to make James erase the accustomed words 'Our trusty and well beloved' from Ralegh's commission as Admiral; and worst of all to examine the Admiral's private list of his ships, armaments and proposed ports of call, which James had forced Ralegh to hand over to him, but given his sacred promise to hold secret 'on the hand and word of a King'. Whereupon he promptly handed it to Gondomar to inspect, and copy, for the Spanish Government.

To him, too, James gave a promise, far more sacred, that if Ralegh dared even look at any Spanish property, James would send him to be hanged in chains at Madrid. And to Madrid Gondomar sent express all this information, to be at once forwarded to all the Spanish authorities in the Indies, with orders to be in readiness to wipe out the English fleet as soon as it should appear.

Ralegh did not know of course how he was being double-crossed; even the First Secretary, Sir Ralph Winwood, was kept in the dark. Winwood was his staunch friend, and would back him against all Spaniards; and since the very essence of the plan lay in surprise, he helped keep up the pretence that the expedition was intended for Virginia, the scene of Ralegh's first and constant attempts at colonization. James had graciously given his name to the first chartered settlement at Jamestown, ten years before in 1607, when Ralegh had been four years in the Tower. The settlement had since been having a rough time and was asking for the support of Ralegh's presence. But this feint of Virginia, betrayed from the start by James, was only a joke to Gondomar and his Government, who were in full possession of the true facts.

Ralegh's friends in Devon were loyal to him as ever, and helped him raise a joint stock of thirty thousand pounds to build seven ships on the Thames, of 1,215 tons in all, to be armed with a hundred and twenty-one pieces of ordnance and manned by four hundred and thirty-one men, with ninety gentlemen volunteers amongst them. His own ship, the *Destiny*, was the show-piece of the little fleet, with its splendid equipment and latest practical inventions by the new Admiral, so long famous as a shipbuilder and navigator. It had become a more 'fashionable lounge' even than Paul's Walk; everybody went to see over it, except the Queen, who had asked but been refused leave to go by the King. She remained Ralegh's admiring friend, but could not help him, though she did her best by making friends with George Villiers, now Earl of Buckingham, whose power over the King was paramount. 'Christ had his John, and I maun ha'e my George,' was

James' explanation. So Queen Anne wrote to George as 'my kind Dog', and found him generous and charming; but as he had not taken up the offer of Sherborne, James handed it instead to Sir John Digby.

The French Ambassador, on hearing this, at once took the opportunity to go and admire the *Destiny* again, walk on deck with its Admiral and express his deepest sympathy with this new 'confiscation of his property' following on all the 'sufferings inflicted on him by his long and unjust imprisonment'. He then renewed the pressing offers for his services from his great minister Richelieu, who called Ralegh *'un grand marinier'*, and now authorized him to take any prizes he captured into the shelter of French ports—as a free concession without any conditions attached.

Such substantial appreciation was very pleasant after the cruel disappointment of his fresh hopes for Sherborne, a renewed punishment wantonly inflicted for no pretext. 'Seeing myself so evilly and tyrannically treated by my own King', as he said later, he began to see also that he might be in a trap, and James only waiting to spring it on him. So he did not refuse to consider any possible means of escape to France, should this prove necessary.

He also considered his legal position, and took legal advice on it—the highest in the country—from an old comrade whom he looked on as his friend. Francis Bacon, now in the full flush of splendour and power, Lord Keeper of the Great Seal, Lord Chancellor, Baron Verulam and Viscount St Albans, was indeed very friendly and had been for some time. It is he who tells how he 'continued walking with Sir Walter Ralegh in Gray's Inn Walks a good while', and how he gave him the best professional advice.

The two thin elderly men strolling up and down together, in nature so opposite, were akin in their enquiring minds, and for sheer intellect the greatest of their day. They had long shared a host of scientific and scholarly interests and eager experiments; Bacon had helped with books and information for Ralegh's *History* that had had perforce to be written away from all libraries and places of research. How much Ralegh had missed these is measured by his unexpected generosity, when impoverished in prison, in contributing fifty pounds to the Bodleian Library which he had helped to found.

Bacon's advice was just what Ralegh longed to hear; to go

ahead with his venture, and not waste the scanty remainder of his money by struggling any further to buy a formal 'pardon' from the King before he sailed; for 'Money is the knee-timber of your voyage', was Bacon's heartening phrase; and he declared the 'pardon' to be a mere formality and quite unnecessary. 'Upon my life, you have a sufficient pardon for all that is past already, the King having under his Great Seal made you Admiral, and given you power of martial law.'

So spoke the Lord Keeper of the Great Seal, and he should know. Then why did the King not add the pardon in words? Ralegh was still suspicious enough to ask it; and whether James' game was to hold him under sentence of death as a hostage, with which to parry Gondomar's protests against his voyage?

But the 'Lord Chancellor Verulam was no fool, nor no ill lawyer' (a striking understatement by Ralegh's son); and the Lord Chancellor repeated his assurance with all the weight of his legal knowledge and power. 'Your commission as Admiral is as good a pardon for all former offences as the law of England can afford you.'

Ralegh's confidence soared sky-high again. Bacon said casually, 'What will you do if after all this expenditure you miss the gold mine?' and Ralegh exclaimed, 'We'll look after the Plate fleet to be sure!'

'But then you will be pirates!' was the mock-solemn rejoinder.

'Oh no!' Ralegh laughed, 'who ever heard of men being pirates for millions?'

The cheerful irony had been taken literally enough in Elizabeth's day; and it certainly would be in James', if the two and a half million carried in one Plate fleet from Mexico were actually brought in to swell his bankrupt exchequer. But whether Ralegh really meant it, or, as seems far more likely from the light tone of the conversation, as reported by Bacon, he was only joking, to talk thus even to an old friend proves how incapable he was of learning even then to curb his reckless tongue. His careless remark that only poor 'mychers' and sea-poachers were hung in chains as vermin to warn returning sailors at London docks, astonished the successful careerist who strolled beside him, his narrow shoulders hunched against the nipping March air, while the elder man braced himself eagerly against the wind. This extraordinary fellow might even yet pull off his latest crack-brained escapade, as Spain so evidently dreaded. She never forgot what he had done at Cadiz. Ralegh was now twenty-one years older, but his 'Elixir of Life' seemed to have given him eternal youth; and he might do again what he had done.

Bacon weighed the chances carefully, and was far too tactful to hint at his doubts; but instead entertained Ralegh in comradely fashion with gossip of the world to which he had long been a stranger, since he was still forbidden to approach the Court or public assemblies. There had long been a happy link between him and Bacon in their common hatred of Coke, whose matrimonial quarrels had become a public scandal. Now Bacon was involved in the latest of them, and well aware of its advantage to himself. Coke had hoped to recover his lost favour at Court by marrying his pretty daughter, still only fourteen, to Buckingham's brother, Sir John Villiers. Coke's wife, as always, opposed his wish, so Coke broke down her door with a heavy beam and forcibly carried off their daughter, pursued by her mother till her coach overturned. Lady Hatton, as she still called herself, snobbishly abjuring the name of Coke, then rushed up to town to demand justice from Lord Chancellor Bacon, her former wooer. Bacon was 'laid at rest being not well', but she besieged his bedroom and 'bounced against the door and waked and affrighted him so that he called his men to him, and they opening the door, she thrust in with them' and complained 'she was like a cow that had lost her calf'. Her bellowing gave Bacon his best chance to bait her angry bull. He set up law suits between the elderly couple, both bringing the same charge against the other of 'Riot and Force'. Lady Hatton re-kidnapped her 'calf', then forged a proposal to her from young Henry de Vere, eighteenth Earl of Oxford (who was conveniently abroad), and made her daughter accept it with oaths scarcely becoming to a maiden not yet fifteen, to 'give myself absolutely to wife with him'. The letter greatly surprised de Vere, who had never seen his proposed bride nor heard of 'his' proposal.

Coke was safe game since his disgrace. He actually refused a bigger dowry for the Villiers marriage because he 'would not buy the King's favour too dear, it being so uncertain and variable'. What hope could there be after that of his ever winning it back? Bacon felt himself on secure ground in condemning this mad bull to Star Chamber and in backing the cow against him;

and she enjoyed over-playing her rôle of injured wife in so
'passionate and tragical a manner, Burbage could not have acted
better.'

But the play was to have a surprise ending. While Ralegh
walked down to the Thames again for yet another look at his
Destiny, Bacon went home to write with wise deliberation, and
care for his own affairs, the most tactless and unlucky letter of his
life. It was to the King's prime favourite, the Earl of Buckingham,
assuring him that he, Bacon, was doing all he could to prevent
the Earl's brother marrying into Sir Edward Coke's 'disgraced
house' and moreover 'troubled house of man and wife, which in
religion and christian discretion is disliked'; so that 'this match
. . . I hold very inconvenient both for your brother and yourself'.

Within a few days the curtain fell, on his own head. Secretary
Winwood at the next Council meeting pulled out of his pocket a
letter from the King which he passed round the table; it gave
James' consent to the marriage, his thanks to Winwood for helping it forward, and practically hissed Coke's wife off the stage.

Bacon had belied his own sly maxim: 'The Cat knows whose
lips she licks.' He had signally failed to know it. He could spot
the chances for treachery where Ralegh shut his eyes to them;
but Ralegh would never have been so blind to the affections,
especially of family feeling. These were a closed book to Bacon.
He had simply not noticed that Sir John Villiers was so much in
love with Coke's little daughter that he 'would be joyful to take
her in her smock' without any dowry; that Sir John's kind
brother Buckingham would be glad to please him; and that the
King would do anything to please Buckingham. Such stuff
meant nothing to Bacon, but now he had to swallow it though it
choked him, cough up all the clever letters he had just written,
and rush to write others, in cringing apology to Buckingham, to
the King, and even to Coke. He complained how he had been
'misinformed', so may 'God judge my sincerity'. He hastened to
drive off Coke's infuriating cow into a safe barn (in fact, into an
actual prison), and had to gulp down an icy draught of reproof
from the King, and from Buckingham, who told him 'in this
business of my brother's you overtrouble yourself . . . and have
carried yourself with much scorn and neglect toward myself and
friends'.

The King gave a gorgeous wedding at Hampton Court for

Coke's daughter; and her mother was not at the wedding. Coke was restored to his place on the Council (until his next quarrel with the King); Secretary Winwood was at the height of his favour; and all Bacon's 'Christian discretion' was needed to climb down from the 'slippery places' round which he had twined his hopes.

His absolute fall was not yet; he was to enjoy a few more years of wealth and comparative power, and the chance to deal the final death-blow to his old comrade Sir Walter Ralegh, in flat denial of the legal advice he had given him; 'Upon my life . . . your commission as Admiral is as good a pardon for all former offences as the law of England can afford you.'

'Upon my life' was not a lucky oath to the swearer, whose own life ended in ruin and miserable degradation, soon after that of his friend, which he had sworn away.

CHAPTER THIRTY-ONE

King of the Indians

'I might be here King of the Indians . . .
My name hath still lived among them.'

RALEGH'S LETTER TO HIS
WIFE FROM TRINIDAD

At last he was at large again, at sea again, for the first time
an Admiral on his own ship, and with a trunk-load of
books in his cabin, as always. The tangles and troubles of
the preparations were drifting fast behind him in the wake of his
ships, and the huge ocean rolled ahead to separate him further
from them with every mile they sailed.

Devon had given them a grand send-off, calling them with
drums and trumpets to farewell feasts at the public expense, and
greeting Sir Walter and Lady Ralegh as King and Queen of the
Western sea-coast. But she had to enter into a bond to meet the
grocer's bills for one of the ships; and another could not sail till
Ralegh had sold the family plate to pay for its provisions, and
had as well to borrow two hundred pounds more from his friends.
The worst delays were from the difficulties in collecting—and
discarding his followers; since there were few good men who
would choose to serve a leader still under sentence of death. Yet
some did so through devotion and belief in his genius; as with
Saul, 'there went with him a band of men whose heart God had
touched'. But the 'children of Belial' were his main rank and file,
men disgraced or out of a job: as he wrote himself, 'a mere rabble',
who had 'left their country for their country's good'. Even their
captains were scarcely such as he had been wont to command,
for the Navy had by now been subjected to fourteen years of the
new King's neglect of it, which had given small inducement to
men of honour and enterprise to serve in it. But the Admiral had
his son Wat and his nephew George Ralegh, and above all his
faithful friend Lawrence Keymis who had explored Guiana with
him twenty-two years before, and done so again the following
year without Ralegh. His report on the site of the gold-mine that

267

he had been shown by the Indians had remained ever since in his leader's mind as an article of faith. But Keymis also was now over twenty years older, and in ways that had left Ralegh's resilient spirit untouched. He was more nervous, and needed reassurance and commiseration.

'I know', Ralegh told him in sympathy, 'that, a few gentlemen apart, what a scum of men you have'; but he did his best to make them into a navy and, characteristically, to show them due consideration. He published his Orders to the Fleet: 'a model of godly, severe and martial government'; but also of respect to the men; for they were given sound reasons for all his rules. Drunkenness and smoking between the decks were forbidden because 'there is no danger so inevitable as the Ship's firing'; and so was blasphemy, because of the Bible's warning that the curse shall not depart from the house of the swearer, therefore 'much less from the ship of the swearer'. Thus, superstition should help piety. A coward would be punished with rational tolerance by being 'disarmed and made a labourer to fetch and carry for his comrades'. But the death penalty would fall instantly on any man who forced a woman, Christian or heathen; nor must anything, 'not so much as one pina (pineapple) or potato', be taken by force from the Indians. They must all, he emphasized in positive command, be treated with friendly courtesy, as he had insisted in his first expedition, 'rather than endanger the future hopes of so many millions'.

*   *   *

The storms of that summer of 1617 were worse than any since those that had wrecked the Armada galleons nearly thirty years before. Ralegh's fleet of seven warships and three pinnaces were delayed in leaving Plymouth till June, where they joined three more ships beyond the harbour, but were driven back by the gales, first into Plymouth, then south into Falmouth. At the third start, he lost a pinnace, sunk in a tempest off the Scilly Isles; and early in August he had to put in at Kinsale harbour in the south of Ireland for a fortnight to repair all the damage caused to ships and stores.

There Ralegh was entertained lavishly in his old home of Lismore by its present owner, Lord Boyle, the first and Great Earl of Cork. Of the new type of English settler, who waged big business instead of guerilla warfare, the once penniless lawyer had bought up half Munster and all Ralegh's Irish estates, and was very comfortably settled in the castle on the Blackwater that Ralegh had turned into so magnificent a fortress-palace. There was less need of it as a fortress since the rebellions, led by the Earl of Tyrone, had ended in the Flight of the Earls into exile. No longer did

> 'the ruthless vast and gloomy woods
> Resound with dreadful yells.'

Ralegh saw with satisfaction how the wildernesses that he had cleared for plantation were flourishing, and how even the pre-judiced natives were growing and eating their own potatoes, and so were the less eager to risk their livelihood in savage raids. On the lovely shores of the wide river where he had fished salmon and written and discussed poetry with his friend 'Gentle Spenser', now long dead, Ralegh rode out hawking, his favourite sport, with the Earl of Cork, a big jovial easy-seeming man who could drive a shrewd bargain in a pleasant way, but whose pride, as well as generosity, was tickled by giving the best of hospitality to the most magnificent courtier of the late Queen's reign, on his latest desperate venture.

Boyle had invested a considerable sum of private money in it, but actually ignored this point; for he urged his guest to abandon it and to use instead the commission presented to him by the King of France. Why should he not accept it by taking foreign service, as many other honest men had done, and won high honours abroad? It was in fact what nearly everybody expected Ralegh to do, once he was his own master on the high seas, where no one could compel him to return. But he could not be turned from his quest. The honour he might win in foreign service was not high enough for his intent. He was determined to restore honour to his slandered name in a harder way; to make his own country, not another, proud of his service, and acknowledge it for centuries to come. No lesser ambition could content him now. It was his destiny, and therefore that was the name he had given to his flagship. Queen Elizabeth had 'misliked' abstract names for ships, and had changed the *Repentance* to *Daintie*; but Elizabeth herself could not have dissuaded him now.

Certainly Boyle could not, who couldn't even manage his own

enormous family, of whom he pretended to have lost count; there were fifteen of 'em at least, he said truly, and far too many unbiddable little girls eagerly tumbling into love-affairs. Sarah and Alice got safely married before thirteen, but Mary, his eldest and favourite, refused all the fine matches he had arranged, and all for a mere younger son of a second Earl (said the first Earl of Cork) who was ill-tempered and already gouty. Her father stopped her allowance, and even deprived her of her horses; but she forced his hand by taking the young man in secret as her lover and then her husband, when only fifteen. Boyle might be the first and most successful business tycoon in Ireland; he could flick off a fine of £15,000 without blinking, and patronize the Archbishop of Canterbury with gifts of a 'runlet' of whiskey and a warm cassock of Waterford frieze; toss jewels to his friends and family; see ten of his children win a peerage, and the fourteenth and most famous refuse one—refuse even to be Provost of Eton or President of the Royal Society. Yet his ambitious father was so much in accord with this shy and scholarly scientist as to bestow on him his 'particular blessing'. And Boyle, beset with so many distractions, could feel a kind of envy as well as compassion for the old knight-errant Ralegh, whose single purpose gave him liberty to live, and if necessary die, in an exaltation above the common cares of most other men.

Boyle did all he could to show his sympathy for his guest at the end of the brief visit. He heaped gifts on the fleet: a hundred oxen, a handsome tip of £350, large stores of beer and biscuit and iron, and his supreme present to them, which he besought their abstemious Admiral to share, a thirty-two-gallon cask of his own home-distilled whiskey.

The soft Irish rain was falling again in a grey curtain over Kinsale harbour as the little painted ships weighed anchor and the sails were hauled up in huge coloured curves against it, flapping and filling with the salt breeze; when suddenly the grey curtain in the sky split asunder to show a stormy sunset, an unreal land in the West of floating islands and wings of fire. The other ships followed their leader in the *Destiny*; like the towering clouds above them they spread their bright sails to the wind, careening before it, dipping in magnificent obeisance to it, as they sped out towards the Atlantic.

The Earl of Cork watched the gallant procession until it was out of sight; then turned with a sigh to go on improving Ralegh's estates, and amass still more; to cuff his younger daughters for swearing to marry no one but young Wat Ralegh; and to die at last in safety, and lie stretched out in stone effigy on his magnificent tomb in the church that crowns the steep little hill climbing up from the fishing town of Youghal. He lies there in an uncomfortable position on his side, with his head on his hand, and a host of small stone children round him, his clever humorous face still rather fretted by all his business and domestic worries. The lasting memorials to Ralegh are outside the church, in the yellow scented wallflowers and Azane lilies that climb and shine all over the towering grey stone walls of garden and churchyard. But few who gather these no longer outlandish flowers remember that he had transplanted them from the jungles of an unknown world.

*   *   *

Refitted, replenished and rested, they had set sail again on the nineteenth of August, in good spirits—this with no reference to their parting present of thirty-two gallons of whiskey, for it was securely hatched below, and its presence kept secret from the crews.

Gondomar in England was told of their departure through King James' agents in Ireland, and gave reports of the fresh start to all the colonial ports of Spain, and with them the Spanish Government's commands 'to put an end to this enterprise, as well as to the lives of all who sail with Don Gualtero Rauli'.

For the moment 'Don Gualtero' had other enemies to fight. The weather seemed accursed. There were storms that drove them far off their course, tore away the sails, and once sprang a leak that drowned the men baling in the hold; it could only be stopped by treading down all the raw meat on board between the timbers, and nailing planks over it. Then at times they were smothered in a hot yellow mist, with the sun like a ball of blood and not a breeze to lift the heavy sails, nor a drop of dew nor rain in the empty buckets that gaped for moisture on the deck, as did the parched throats of the men.

A strange sickness fell on the crews and many died, forty in the *Destiny* alone. Among them were some of Ralegh's best leaders: Captain Pigott, his chief land-general and only refiner of metals; his Lieutenant Captain Hastings, and the fine scholar Master

Talbot. His second-in-command caught the sickness, then Ralegh himself, and while he lay in bed a hurricane whirled upon them, and he rushed on deck to give orders, and caught a chill that brought on a high fever. For weeks he was thought to be dying.

Some of his 'friends' proved as dangerous as his foes. One of the captains, Cyrus Bayley, a discontented boastful fellow in command of the *Southampton*, plumed himself on breaking the run of bad luck by capturing four French vessels and wished to plunder them, on the excuse that they were probably pirates; but to his disgust his Admiral forbade him, and paid the French the full market price of sixty-one crowns for three pipes of oil from them and a seven-ton pinnace.

Some of the fleet landed at one of the Canary Islands, Lanzarote, for water, and Ralegh visited the Spanish Governor, who obligingly agreed to sell him fresh provisions; but it was merely a ruse to gain time while he removed all goods away from the sea-board, set up fortifications, and then defied the English to do their worst. Needless to say the crews clamoured for leave to do so, especially when the Spaniards had murdered three of them as they walked alone. Ralegh had hard work to keep them from reprisals, especially his son, but his only retort was to send word to the Governor that if he had not been determined to respect the wishes of King James he 'would have pulled him and his people out of the town by their ears'. So, having lost three men and several days of wasted time, he sailed off again, and the churlish colony was left in peace—until the next year, when the Barbary corsairs did his job for him, and far more cruelly than he would have allowed.

Bayley was still nursing his grievance, all the more since it was discovered that the French ships he had captured really had belonged to pirates. He assuaged his sense of umbrage by deserting and sailing back to England to spread vague reports of Ralegh turning pirate ('as everyone thought he would') or, if he hadn't actually yet done so, Bayley was afraid he soon would; 'so that in the meantime there is a doubtful opinion held of Sir Walter, and those that malice him boldly affirm him to be a pirate, which for my part I will never believe'. So wrote that Carew who was 'Noble George' to his cousin Sir Walter.

But a Privy Councillor publicly expressed 'the great sorrow of all good people at what Ralegh has done', and added that 'the King promises . . . to remedy and redress . . . so atrocious a wickedness as this'. Bayley declared that Ralegh was landing in the Canaries to fortify himself for an attack there on the Spanish fleet; whereupon Gondomar told his government that Ralegh had already raided the Canaries, and demanded that a large fleet be instantly sent out to capture Ralegh's small one. Every English prisoner was to be put to death, except Ralegh himself and his officers, who should be taken to Spain for public execution. Such drastic measures would not offend the English monarch, he asserted; to prove it he enclosed a quotation from a letter from the English Viscount Fenton (now in Ralegh's shoes as Captain of the Guard) giving the comfortable assurance that King James 'is very determined against Ralegh and will join the King of Spain in ruining him, but he wishes this resolution to be kept secret for some little while, so that . . . he may keep an eye on the disposition of some of the people here'.[1]

'Some of the people' did in fact insist on a proper enquiry into Bayley's reports, and found them flatly contradicted by most of his crew. And just then an English merchant ship, which had been in Lanzarote harbour at the time of the unlucky visit, returned to England with a full account of Ralegh's extraordinary forbearance in the face of great insult and injury. Spaniards themselves went out of their way to praise his courtesy, and in letters to their Ambassador in England the Governor of Gomera, the furthest of the Canaries, stated how 'nobly' and 'justly' Ralegh and his fleet had behaved themselves in all their dealings with him and the inhabitants of the little island.

It is a relief to know of that happy interlude of real friendship between the English Admiral and the Spanish Governor and his wife. In a gallant gesture Ralegh gave her half a dozen pretty handkerchiefs and half a dozen pairs of gloves; and she gave him four large sugar-loaves and quantities of fresh fruit, oranges and lemons, grapes and figs and pomegranates, 'which I much desired to comfort and refresh our sick men', so he wrote, though not for her eye, and acknowledged that such 'trifles were better welcome to me than 1,000 crowns would have been'. He returned thanks with another present, of ambergris and 'delicate extract of amber, a great glass of rosewater, in high estimation here, a very excellent

---

[1] Hume's translation, 329 pp.

picture of Mary Magdalen, and a cutwork ruff'. To which she came back with more fruit at his departure and good white bread, two dozen fat hens and, above all, as much water as they could carry. The Governor's lady of Gomera waved him good-bye as he sailed away, and her husband wrote his testimony to the success of the English fleet's visit, 'without any offence given, or received, to the value of a farthing'.

This fairly disposed of all the lying reports of piratical raids on the Canaries. Bayley was summoned before the Privy Council, failed to substantiate any of his charges against the Admiral, and was sent to prison, whence after a few weeks he issued an abjectly apologetic denial of them. It was also awkward for King James, who had to admit to his Spanish Ambassador that they had snatched prematurely at their cue, but again assured him that he was only waiting for more reliable news, for 'he was anxious to proclaim Ralegh at once as a traitor, and to proceed against him and all those who took part in the voyage'.

But all this was happening back in England, many leagues behind Ralegh. That careless contempt of his detractors in his strong and insolent youth still held good now that he was old, at times desperately ill, and on a voyage, so he admitted in a letter to his wife, of such 'unnatural weather' that it had taken more than three times as long as usual. Characteristically he at once adds: 'By the next letter I trust that you shall hear better of us. . . . God I trust will give us comfort in that which is to come.' He is far more concerned with the deaths of his friends than with the slanders of his foes or treacherous followers. Bayley's desertion and lies he does not even bother to mention to his 'Sweetheart', but tells her she can hear about them from a letter of Keymis to a friend of theirs.

Equally casually he dismisses the King's machinations against him in a parenthesis, assuring her that in spite of their heavy loss of men through sickness his fleet is still 'reasonably strong—strong enough I hope to perform what we have undertaken; if the diligent care taken at London to make our strength known to the Spanish king . . . have not taught him to fortify all entrances against us'. But he shrugs off this quietly sardonic aside with a comment that sounds almost indifferent: 'Howsoever, we must make the adventure; and if we perish, it shall be no honour for England, nor gain for his Majesty.' The highlight of the letter is that 'Your son had never so good health, having no distemper in all the heat under the Line.' And he reassures her about his personal servants, who had escaped death, though all had had the sickness; and about himself, for he had recovered sufficiently to write her this long letter though 'with a weak hand . . . but God, that gave me a strong heart in my adversities, hath also now strengthened it in the hell-fire of heat'.

The extreme weakness from his fever in that broiling tropic damp, and from four weeks of starvation when he could take no solid food, nor anything except juice of the lemons given by the Governor's Lady of Gomera (but for which 'I could not have lived'), may seem a reason for his indifference to his human enemies; but it was not the chief one. That lay in his new liberty. He was his own master again, and on the high seas from whence none could pull him back except of his own will. He was free of time, and of space, as one can only be in a sailing-ship at sea. Weather alone could dictate to him, though it was often a cruel dictator, splitting the sky with forked lightning and tornadoes, or suffocating them with breathless fog so black that for two days they had to steer by candlelight, and the men cried out that they had reached the end of the world. Such horrible portents had good effect on their piety; they were the more obedient to their Admiral's Orders to hear Divine Service twice daily and to sing a psalm when the watch was set. And their wrangling and muttered threats of mutiny were hushed in dread as the 'fire-flags' of lightning played round the masts, and the sea swelled like boiling copper. Later, in a brief spell of fine weather, they could willingly sing a psalm of praise.

Ralegh's private Journal might well be called that; for the very fact of his keeping it is in praise of his new freedom and peace of mind. For five and a half months, starting at the end of August, ten days after leaving Ireland, he made minute, closely-written notes that paint vividly all that he saw, for his own pleasure alone. He had found his eyes again, and his ears, both dimmed so long by the narrow confines of the Tower. He could see with fresh wonder the white flash of the flying-fish over the waves, like the Spirit that moves on the waters; the swift onslaught of a sudden storm, the flight of fifteen rainbows off Trinidad that terrified the crews as another portent; and above all the huge spaces of the night sky, and the Southern Cross and the stranger stars, long ago familiar to him and now shining clear again above his head, instead of a stone ceiling.

'Thou servest only for moonshine in water', so Richard III had mocked Sir Henry Wyatt. A man might well serve for that reward who had for thirteen years been condemned, at curfew, to candlelight in a small room. After 'shut of eve in dull November' (as were indeed the evenings all the year round, inside the Tower) he now had his reward in the open night-sky above him, and the moonshine in the water below.

In mid-November there were other and human reasons for happiness: the coasts of Guiana were sighted at last, and with them the pelicans that mounted guard on the mooring-posts of native boats, as magnificently immobile as the stone King's Beasts at Hampton Court, until they flapped heavily away as the storm-battered fleet tacked and veered towards them. The paint blistered and peeling on their hulls, and their sails like the rags of a gypsy caravan, the little ships sailed into the mouth of the River Caliana (Cayenne) on the South American mainland. Vultures from afar sniffed the smell of sick and dying flesh aboard, and came wheeling on dark ragged-edged wings to get their pickings.

But others came also. Here Ralegh was at home again, and among his friends. Proud chieftains clad in jewels and parrot feathers, who had waited more than twenty years for this happy moment, now thronged eagerly to pay homage once again to their supreme Chief. He had sworn them to the service of his former Sovereign. It was only momentarily discouraging to learn that she had been so subject to human frailty as to die; for it was Ralegh they wished to serve.

Old as he was now, and wasted by fever, he was still the only Chief they longed for to protect them from the horrible cruelties they had suffered increasingly in these latter years, when many of their proudest chiefs had been hanged or tortured to death by the Spaniards in their relentless pursuit of gold. To Ralegh they came as their protector and refuge, their long-loved friend and long-wished-for Sovereign.

'To tell you that I might be here King of the Indians were a vanity,' so he wrote in mock-modesty to his wife; then had to admit in sincerity and pride, 'but my name hath still lived among them. Here they feed me with fresh meat, and all that the country affords; all offer to obey me.'

The first to welcome him was his old friend, the Indian Chief 'Harry,' who had chosen to live with him in the Tower for two years, till Ralegh had firmly sent him back to a happier climate and his friends. Now 'Harry' got him carried out of his crowded ship that was stinking with disease, and into an open tent and 'hamaca', where he could lie at ease, though still unable to swallow anything but the juice of the lemons from Gomera, freshly kept in sand. At last he was able to take some of Harry's presents, the pineapples 'which in especial had tempted me exceedingly'; and, gradually, 'divers other sorts of fruits' as well as some of Harry's 'great plenty of roasted mullets, which are very good meat, and great store of plantains'. He was able at last to eat a little of the fresh meat 'and began to gather a little strength'.

He still could not walk without help, and every time there was an off-shore wind his fever raged again. He would be a dead loss, and too soon dead himself, if he now started to make that terrible inland voyage up the Orinoco. Another, and to Ralegh more urgent, reason worked against it. His officers and men alike dared not risk going up-river unless their Admiral undertook to remain and guard the river's mouth for them against the Spaniards, who were said to be gathering an armada together to block their exit from it.

Only Ralegh would they trust to prevent this; 'when the time of trial came, they knew well enough what his value was,' says Professor Gardiner, though one of Ralegh's most persistent detractors. So Ralegh gave his pledge that on their return, 'you shall find me at Puncto Gallo, dead or alive. And if you find not my ships there, you shall find their ashes. For I will fire with the galleons, if it come to that extremity; run, will I never.'

The best officers next to him were dead. Keymis had to be given the general charge of the expedition, with Ralegh's son Wat as Captain, and his nephew George Ralegh as sergeant-major of the land forces. Ralegh's instructions to them were to avoid at all costs any landing at a point that might now be newly guarded by Spanish reinforcements of territory that had been neutral when Keymis had explored it. His anxiety was even more for their honour than their safety, 'for I would not, for all the world, receive a blow from the Spaniards, to the dishonour of our nation'; and since the English were not free to return the blow, they must run no risk of receiving one.

Keymis was confident. He had 'little fear of a Spanish attack—unless', he added in an uneasy afterthought, 'news sent from Madrid has caused them to guard all the waterways of the country'. That was the trouble. The Intelligence Service of Spain was working overtime to keep all her branches informed, while that of England was working only in aid of the Spaniards. Even Ralegh could only guess how much; the more unpractical Keymis could scarcely believe it; and young Wat and his cousin George would scornfully ignore it.

They set off in high spirits to play for the stake on which Ralegh's life and honour were pledged, while he had to stand aside, or rather lie, helpless, and watch the winged flowers of enormous butterflies flutter azure in the sun; the winged torches of fireflies flash through the murmurous dark; the whirr of wings, so swift that they seemed motionless, of humming birds poised to sip honey within the scarlet throats of hibiscus flowers. Even the exquisite orange tips at the ends of the many feet of the dreaded furry tarantula spider were objects of admiration, and the hummocked coils of a cobra springing, startled, into an emerald streak, then gliding away. These beauties did not usually attack unless attacked, nor did the many-toothed serpents, or crocodiles, whose main desire was to scurry back into the river.

Other phenomena had to be observed still more closely. With his skeleton crews of enfeebled men—for all the fittest had been sent up the Orinoco—Ralegh sailed to the appointed rendezvous of Puncto Gallo on the south-west coast of Trinidad, and there tried to enter into friendly trading relations with the neighbouring Spaniards. They replied with firing parties and sudden attacks, killing two of his much diminished forces. He ignored the injury as well as the danger; and nonchalantly turned his attention instead to botany, seeking and examining rare plants for their medicinal properties, and exploring the strange currents along the coast in short and careful cruises. On one of them he passed a canoe of Indians, who told him of a rumour from the mainland: it was said that the English, up-river, had stormed a Spanish town, and lost two of their captains.

His search was now in agonizing dread of any further news, however vague, worse still, belated. Whatever had happened must have taken place weeks before. Every day he sent out fresh search parties, and himself questioned closely every Indian that they found. His Journal shows the torment of his mind; but it is written only to himself.

Then on February 13th, 1618, the tiny crabbed writing of the Journal stopped; with no final statement to explain why. There is nothing to show what we now know, that it was on that day that he heard his son Wat had been killed in a fight at the Spanish village of San Thomé.

CHAPTER THIRTY-TWO
My Brains are Broken

'My brains are broken, and it is a torment for me to
write . . . it is the care for you that hath strengthened
my heart.'

RALEGH'S LETTER TO HIS WIFE

KEYMIS' letter about their fight with the Spaniards, and the
death in action of Wat Ralegh, took five weeks to reach his
Admiral; and it had taken nearly a week before that for
him to screw up courage to write it.

The fight had been unpremeditated and unprepared, at least
by the English, who did not know that the Spaniards had lately
expanded the Indian village of San Thomé from a cluster of
palm-leaved huts into a fortified small town, and moved it some
way down river. Keymis had sailed unwittingly past its forts in
the darkness, and landed in the morning, thinking they were still
about fifteen miles short of San Thomé; only to find that the
town was just across the river, and in a position to cut him off
from his return voyage. But friendly Indians in their dug-out
canoes had brought suggestions of some sort of 'gentleman's
agreement' from the Spaniards, that they might eventually open
San Thomé to the English, and trade some of their rich stores of
tobacco to them; as indeed Keymis had been instructed to do,
after he had found his mine. These overtures made him suppose
it must be some irresponsible action when two Spanish mortars
fired on them. After all, they had been sniped at here and there
all the way up the river, and had paid no attention to the
nuisance; for the Admiral's orders had been to avoid a fight
except in the last extremity. Keymis could continue to avoid one
now, by pushing on further up river. But two of his five ships
were still held up in the treacherous channels of the Orinoco, and
he waited for them for just that one day.

At about one o'clock the following night the Spaniards made a
surprise attack from the surrounding woods. It caused wild confusion for the moment in the English camp, and they were on the
verge of panic when young Wat rallied them. He scrambled a

company of his pikemen together somehow, and urged them on to drive the raiders back. In the blind rush, they pushed them as far as 'to the town, almost before themselves knew of it'. There they were confronted by the Governor at the head of a force of 'regulars' all drawn up ready for battle. The English were still short of two ships' crews and had none of their musketeers as yet to support them, and fell back in dismay.

But Wat dashed on, ahead of his handful of pikemen, shouting 'Come on, my hearts!' and attacked the Spanish line practically single-handed. He met his death almost at once from a dozen lance wounds in his breast, and fell, still calling 'Go on!' and then, knowing he was dying, 'Lord have mercy on me, and prosper your enterprise!' His pikemen, maddened by his death, charged without waiting for the support of the musketeers, or any further orders than the boy's death-cry.

'If the King of Spain himself had been there in person, they would have shown him but little respect.'[1]

The pikemen's headlong charge drove the Spanish garrison clean out of the town, and the English took possession of it. Five only had been killed on either side, all of them officers. One of them, the Spanish Governor, had been stabbed in the back, by his own men it was thought, since they had been on the point of revolting against the harsh cruelty of his rule. It was no triumph for Keymis, who now saw how heavily he had embroiled the expedition with Spain, before proving even the existence of his mine. He believed its position to be within about three miles of this new site of San Thomé; but he had far less chance to prove it now that he had boxed himself up in the town, with the enemy outside, most of them in the shelter of a fortified island in the Orinoco, and free to make sorties through the jungle to snipe at and ambush any search party he might send out. On one attempt alone up river he lost eight out of nine men in a single launch, killed or wounded in a sudden volley of fire from Spaniards hidden in the woods.

It was not only the danger that daunted him, but the difficulty. How could he be sure, after more than twenty years, of rediscovering landmarks that might have become densely overgrown in a few weeks? The officers under him knew nothing of the jungle

[1] Sir Walter Ralegh's letter to Lord Carew, Privy Councillor, June 21st, 1618.

and its insistent, overlapping waves of tangled vegetation. They called his delays 'mere illusions' and himself 'a mere Machiavel'. Keymis certainly seems to have invented some of the excuses for his hesitation. He had lost heart and now lost his head; he wavered and wandered, made night sorties to sift stones and pebbles which he brought back in childish triumph to be examined by the refiners, who tossed them away in scorn and pronounced them worth nothing. He was bewitched in this steaming, stifling, timeless world, among walls of towering trees where one could get lost in five minutes, and where the green flash in the gloom might be from a paroquet's wing or a snake poised to strike.

He managed at last, after some days, to write to Ralegh of his son's death, making the most of Wat's 'extraordinary valour and forwardness', which 'led them on when some began to pause and recoil shamefully'; and with no hint of how much better it would have been if they *had* all recoiled. It was true that Wat's heroism had been the one thing that had saved them in the Spaniards' surprise attack; but it was Keymis who had laid them open to that, and to their consequent dilemma. He had stayed on the river bank, instead of at once pushing on and avoiding any possible clash with the Spaniards, thus following Ralegh's last directions.

Many thought they would be indeed his last; for it had not seemed likely that he would live until their return, and Keymis may well have hoped this. His master's death, or his own, either would give him a way out from this dead end to which he had led the expedition. His only chance now was to risk everything in his power by going on and finding his mine—or any other. Young George Ralegh took a chance, and some of the boats, and searched for three hundred miles up the Orinoco, according to the Spanish report—an impossible distance in the time. He was looking not merely for gold, but for the possibilities of founding a lasting colony; and also of allying the Indians and the English in an effective rising against the Spaniards. But after three weeks he returned, having lost ten of his men from jungle fever alone, and having found that Ralegh's former greatest friend among the Indian chiefs, Topiawari, had died long since. The tribes were so weakened by war with the Spaniards that they dared not rise in revolt, even when backed by the English; who indeed could offer but poor backing. Spanish snipers had taken a steady toll of them, both of Captain George's expedition, and of the besieged and half-starved force in San Thomé.

There, Keymis made one important discovery. It broke what spirit remained in him. In the Governor's house was Ralegh's inventory of his fleet in his own handwriting. There were also copies of the plans of their voyage, down to every detail of their ships' crews and armaments. These had all been despatched by King James to the King of Spain, and thence to the Spanish colonial Governors. The dates on the letters showed that they had been written before Ralegh's fleet had even sailed out of the Thames; plain proof that the Admiral had been foredoomed from the start.

That settled the matter in Keymis' distracted mind. He finally argued, as Ralegh wrote later, that there were four reasons against his finding his mine: first, the death of his Admiral's son; second, the weakness of the English forces and the impossibility of getting victuals for them; third, 'that it were a folly for him to discover the mine for the Spaniards'; and fourth, last and chief, that his Admiral was still under sentence of death.

Keymis had held San Thomé just a month, and lost two hundred and fifty of his four hundred men, wasting his time in peace-parleys with the Spaniards, who preferred to continue in their much easier conditions of guerilla warfare. Then, in the frenzied irritation of a weak man determined on one decisive act, he committed his crowning piece of folly. He sacked San Thomé, seized all its stores of tobacco (his sole gain on the expedition) and burned the town. Then he sailed back, leaving his Captain, Wat Ralegh, in his grave before the high altar in the Spanish church, and wishing it were his own.

Indian chiefs came out to the ships in their dug-outs and implored him not to desert them to the horrible treatment of the Spaniards. They would bring him to gold-mines, to fabulous jewels, if he would but stay—and in only two hours march. But two hours were by now too long for Keymis' survivors; they had heard too many fairy-tales, and this latest was clearly prompted by the Indians' despair at their departure. For God's sake put an end to it, they said; and Keymis put an end.

*   *   *

He found Ralegh grown an old man in a few weeks; a white

283

eagle, his eyes wild and restless, enflamed from lack of sleep. The fever had burned up in him again ever since his frantic search to confirm the rumours from up the river.

Little was said at first; Ralegh seemed dazed with grief, and spoke gently, as though he were trying to put off the hour that would help bring the doom of both. Then later came his first and chief question, dangerously simple: 'Why you followed not my last directions for the trial of the mine?' before all else. San Thomé was no answer; Keymis had been ordered not to go near it, until after he had found his mine. He was on the rack; then suddenly he had to face a surprise attack. Ralegh accused him, rather strangely, not of dull irresolution and loss of nerve, but of 'obstinacy' and 'wilfulness'—the last things one would expect of Keymis. It was almost as though Ralegh were confusing him with Wat. But to his mind Keymis had shown rank insubordination in disobeying his leader's orders and then changing his plans.

It is the only time on record that Ralegh ever spoke harshly and unforgivingly to a subordinate. It was the worst time he could have chosen to do it. But there was scarcely more 'choice' in his sudden fury than there is in a hurricane that blows up out of the quiet air and destroys what is before it. Keymis did not hear the high ring of fever in that burst of rage; and Ralegh did not see that he himself was blinded by it. Keymis had been the wrong man for the job; he had grown too old for it. To Ralegh, an older man, that was no excuse. Once again, and once too often, he did not see the man, only the facts. Keymis' 'wilfulness' and 'obstinacy' had made the venture desperate; but that was no reason for abandoning it. And Keymis knew it.

Ralegh himself would not have abandoned it. 'Seeing my son was lost,' he cried out in his agony, he 'cared not if he had lost an hundred more' to prove he had not escaped from England upon a lie. He would have contrived somehow to gather the Indian tribes together and make a nation of them to defy and oust the Spaniards; his almost supernatural fame amongst them might indeed have done it. In any case he would not have returned until he had proved the existence of the mine, and so cleared his honour. Now there was no way to clear it.

Keymis still tried to believe he could save Ralegh's lost credit at home. He wrote a tedious, tortuous letter to Lord Arundel, as one of the chief promoters of the expedition, setting out the whole

Sir Walter Ralegh. By an unknown artist. Although dated 1598, the
portrait was most probably painted after his release from the Tower in
1616. Behind him is a map of Cadiz; his cane is another memorial of
his greatest victory, for his wounds in that battle lamed him for life.

By courtesy of the National Gallery of Ireland

case. He brought it to his master. Ralegh would not even look at it. He had had too much of Keymis' explanations.

Keymis left him, telling him he 'would wait on him presently and give him better satisfaction'. His tone was deceptively quiet. Ralegh heard him shut the door of the cabin; and then, the crack of a pistol shot over his head. He sent up to ask who had fired it, and Keymis' own voice, sounding quiet and natural, called back that he had merely fired off his pistol to clean it. In fact he had 'shut himself up in his cabin, and shot himself with a pocket pistol, which brake one of his ribs; and finding that it had not prevailed, he thrust a long knife under his short ribs up to the handle, and died'.

Those are Ralegh's own words, and not one of them in pity. Keymis had 'given better satisfaction' to himself, not to his leader and one-time friend, whom he now left to bear the brunt of his desertion. His suicide had removed the only witness for Ralegh's defence. It was the act, not so much of a coward, as of a deserter. Ralegh made no comment on it. People have thought this cruel of him; others may think it restrained. His own repeated words, 'seeing my son was lost', explain the cruelty of the despair that had gnawed at his heart, and now numbed it against any further feeling.

There was no more to be done. But he would still 'go on, he cared not how far'. Even up the Orinoco again, where he wanted to lead another expedition, under his own leadership this time, to seek the mine, though only Keymis had been shown the way to it. But his men banded together in mutiny against it. They knew their Admiral was desperate, and would be as glad to die, like his son, on that expedition, as to win gold for his false King. They knew that more and more enemy reinforcements were being poured into Guiana from Spain; worst of all, they knew now, from the papers found in San Thomé, that their own king was in secret league with Spain—and that soon it would be a secret no longer; that any failure of theirs would be judged as treason, to Spain; and those guilty of it would be handed over to Spain for punishment.

The suicide of Keymis, whom they had not liked, had fastened despair on their minds, more even than the killing of Wat Ralegh, whom they had loved. Keymis' suicide seemed a clear admission of guilt. People at home and abroad would take it as such, would hold his Admiral guilty, and all those who were concerned.

Ralegh set himself to fight for his case, and against his followers' sense of defeat, in the only letter he had written for weeks —to his friend and most influential ally, Mr Secretary Winwood. It is hard for us to realize what space and time signified only three and a half centuries ago; for Winwood had died suddenly half a year before, and Ralegh did not yet know that he had lost his best support in England. He wrote to his dead friend a carefully accurate account of all that had happened; then confided to him that he dared not write to 'my poor wife . . . for renewing the sorrow for her son'. He begged his friend, now six months in his grave, to do his best to comfort her.

By the next day he knew that he alone could do that, and forced himself to try. 'I was loth to write, because I knew not how to comfort you, and God knows, I never knew what sorrow meant till now.' He had to share his sorrow with hers, for her sake; but the first halting sentence shows with what difficulty he started. "All that I can say to you is, that you must obey the will and the providence of God'; and so he reminded her that 'the Queen's Majesty bare the loss of Prince Henry with a magnanimous heart'. Suddenly the letter brings him close to her. 'Comfort your heart, dearest Bess, I shall sorrow for us both. I shall sorrow the less, because I have not long to sorrow, because not long to live.'

Winwood would show her his letter to him; 'Therein you shall know what hath passed. . . . I have written but that one letter, for my brains are broken, and it is a torment for me to write, and especially of misery. . . . I have cleansed my ship of sick men, and sent them home. I hope God will send us somewhat ere we return. . . . You shall hear from me, if I live, from the island of the New Found Land, where I mean to make clean my ships and revictual; for I have tobacco enough to pay for it.

'The Lord bless and comfort you, that you may bear patiently the death of your valiant son.'

That was the end of the brief letter; but it had released the torrent of his emotion, so long pent up, and now it burst out at last, in a postscript over four times as long, telling her all he could. 'I protest before the majesty of God that as Sir Francis Drake and Sir John Hawkins died heartbroken where they failed of their enterprise, I could willingly do the like, did I not contend against sorrow, for your sake, in hope to provide somewhat for you, and to comfort and relieve you. If I live to return, resolve yourself that it is the care for you that hath strengthened my heart.'

He told her of the papers found in San Thomé, some in his own handwriting, proving that 'there was never poor man so exposed to the slaughter as I was; commanded, upon my allegiance to my King, to set down not only the country but the very river by which I would enter it; to name my ships, number my men, and my artillery—and all this' (which James had sworn to Ralegh 'on the hand and word of a King' to keep secret) the King had at once handed 'to the Spanish Ambassador to be sent to his master, the King of Spain. The King wrote to all parts of the Indies, especially to the Governor of Guiana, El Dorado, and Trinidado; and the first letter bore the date the 19th of March, 1617, from Madrid, when I had not yet left the Thames.'

Now he had certain proof that James had planned his death-trap even while giving him his commission as King's Admiral. It was enough in itself to 'break his brains'. But the treachery that tormented them worse was that of his former friends and followers.

For Keymis he makes some extenuation at first: 'It is true that he might have gone directly to the mine, and meant it. But after my son's death, he made the men believe that he knew not the way, and excused himself upon the want of water in the river and, counterfeiting many impediments, left it unfound. When he came back, I told him that he had undone me, and that my credit was lost for ever.'

Two of his captains had deserted with their ships, one of them, a friend Ralegh had treated with particular kindness, the very man for whom he had sold all his plate at Plymouth.

'So I am now but five ships, and one of those I have sent home —my flyboat—and in her a pack of idle rascals, which I know will not spare to wound my name; but I care not. I am sure there is never a base slave in all the fleet hath taken the pains and care that I have; hath slept so little and travailed so much. My friends will not believe them; and for the rest I care not.'

He breaks off suddenly in the midst of these broken hopes, to show his wife again what she means to him. 'I live yet, and I have told you why.' And ends, 'God in heaven bless you and strengthen your heart.'

*　　　*　　　*

Ralegh sailed for Newfoundland, still hoping to return to Guiana after refitting his fleet. The cold winds and snow and mountains of floating ice, gleaming like shrouded jewels through the freezing mist, cracking, roaring, howling in this silent land, where nothing living could be seen, were surely his best though painful allies to plead a return to his green land of Guiana. The frosty air had cured his fever, and though the men complained of rheums and agues, they were not dying like sick flies.

But Guiana meant the Spaniards, and the English King's monstrous alliance with them, and no one could hope to fight, with the promise of a stab in the back from their own liege lord. Rather than do so, two of the captains fled and turned pirates, seeing that they would probably be condemned as such anyway; and when Ralegh reached Kinsale harbour again, his remaining ships decided to stay there, feeling Ireland was safer. She showed sympathy in a way so extraordinary for that country that the traveller Lithgow noted in his *Rare Adventures* that in the length and breadth of the land he never met a single Irishman who could be induced to drink the King's health. They begged Ralegh to stay there too, as the Earl of Cork now did again; Ralegh thanked them warmly for it, but would not stay.

He sailed back alone to England in his last remaining ship, the *Destiny*, and landed on June 21st, 1618, at Plymouth, where he was met by his wife.

* * *

Gondomar burst into King James' closet at Whitehall shrieking "Piratas! Piratas! Piratas!"

James quietened him with fresh promises of sending Ralegh to a public execution in Spain; only there must be some sort of official enquiry first, for the look of the thing. He found Englishmen did not like the look of it; their country was not a subject province of Spain; so why should Ralegh be sent there, even if guilty? And few would agree that he was. His part of Guiana had been taken over by him long before, in the name of the Queen of England; it was the Spaniards who had since encroached on it; and it was the Spaniards who had attacked first, and had killed the English by murder or in battle, whenever they could. As Ralegh wrote succinctly, 'To break peace where there is no peace, it cannot be.' The case was so plain that even James found it hard to prove the contrary.

Also there was openly expressed sympathy for Ralegh all through the country. An order for his arrest had been sent out before he landed, but it was not at once acted upon when he did so. There was every chance for him then to escape to France. His foes as well as his friends would have welcomed it, to save them from their embarrassment. Public opinion was so strong in his favour that if James carried out his pledge to send him to Spain for execution, it might cost him his throne. He hesitated; but Gondomar insisted on his writing an official letter to the King of Spain promising that after some legal formalities, 'which cannot be altogether avoided', Ralegh and his remaining officers should be despatched in the *Destiny* to be executed in Spain. Gondomar hurried off with the letter to Madrid. Everyone expected Ralegh to sail for France; his wife and friends begged him to do so. He considered, but rejected it.

'The world wonders extremely', wrote a judicious contemporary, 'that so great a wise man as Sir Walter Ralegh should have returned to cast himself upon so inevitable a Rock.' As it wonders even today, and we seek out reasons for the 'strange fatalism' that made Ralegh 'cease for a time to value his safety'.[1] But when was he known to value it? Sir Philip Magnus has explained that 'he felt he was too old to start a new life in a strange land', which is scarcely likely, since he had known nothing of his own land beyond his prison walls for so many years. The appalling dangers of exploring the Orinoco jungle, now infested by Spanish foes, had daunted him so little, though still very ill and, at sixty-six, long past the age of contemporary explorers, that only the mutiny of his men had prevented his attempting it himself this very year. In France, there were friends awaiting him, a warm welcome from the French Court, and an honourable command as Admiral; it would have given him a new life indeed, and not strange.

But his life was not now the most important thing to him. He had come back to clear his honour before his countrymen. To fly the country before attempting this would be to acknowledge that he had 'abused the confidence and commission of the King. Before doing that, I would choose, not poverty alone, but death itself.'

He stayed to prove it, and so chose death.

[1] Sir Philip Magnus, op. cit., p. 144.

CHAPTER THIRTY-THREE

A Friend to the Spaniard

'Sir W. R. was condemned for being a friend to the Spaniard; and lost his life for being their enemy.'

CAREW RALEGH

JAMES was in a quandary. He had always acknowledged Ralegh's discoveries in Guiana as the possession of the English Crown; had openly boasted of it even to the Spanish Ambassador. More, he had officially declared it by granting royal concessions for English colonists there and by his commission last year to Ralegh himself to discover and take over a gold-mine in the name and for the benefit of his Sovereign. So if trespass could not be proved, then what was Ralegh's crime?

His real one of course was that he had failed to find the gold. And the real reason for his execution was that James sold him to Spain for gold. He had demanded a dowry for the marriage of the Infanta to Prince Charles, of 'two millions crowns, besides the jewels'; and Ralegh's head would be in payment for it. But, as James had to admit, the law 'cannot be altogether avoided'.

So the law had to make up a crime to fit the punishment. Five of the Crown's best lawyers formed a commission under the direction of the Lord Chancellor, Francis Bacon, and racked their brains for eight weeks to make out a case against Ralegh; but had to give it up. There was simply not enough evidence to bring him to trial, they complained, and suggested a 'private hearing' as the only way to condemn him. But one of the five came out strongly against this perversion of justice.

Sir Edward Coke had been Ralegh's most virulent enemy in his trial at Winchester in 1603; yet now it was Coke who demanded he should have a public hearing before all the forty-five Privy Councillors, some of the Judges, and with free access for any witness to appear. Let Ralegh speak in his own defence before them all and, this time, be allowed to face and question his accusers. Coke wrote this to the King himself, and urged him to 'let all witnesses be brought into Court, so that none might say' (as once they said) 'that proceedings were unfair'.[1]

From Coke this is an astonishing admission. If he had ever actually felt any remorse for his part in the Winchester trial, then he gave no other sign of it; nor made any attempt to save Ralegh's life. People were unimportant to him; even his own personality had faded slightly in the daunting light cast on it by his hostile wife, his distracting daughter, his deceitful king. He had come to value his own most sacred life's work, *The Institutes of the Laws of England*, above all else; even above his former loyalty to the Royal Prerogative. 'A word from the King mates him,' Bacon had sneered; but Coke had learned to put less and less hope in the King, and more in posterity's opinion of his own word as law. He himself had endangered that by declaring that the statute of Edward VI, which allowed the prisoner's right to face his accuser, had been repealed. In this he had lied against his own work; for in his 'Institutes' he states expressly that the statute had never really been repealed'.[2] There it was, in his own minute writing, for all lawyers in later ages to read and mark against his own ruling of the law against Ralegh. He had denied the truth of his own words; for the sake of a King whose favour, as he had now openly complained, was 'so uncertain and so variable'.

And there was the unpleasant report of old Justice Gaudy solemnly confessing to a crowd of people by his death-bed that English justice was 'never so depraved and injured' as in Ralegh's trial; and everyone was repeating it as the true legal opinion. Coke felt he owed it to the law to ensure Ralegh a trial this time that all men could call a fair one. But of what use to plead that to a King who openly preached that Kings are above the law?

James was of course infuriated. Here was this blustering old fellow interfering again to upset his plans. He was also badly frightened; for he dared not face a court case against Ralegh. Some of these 'fule lawyers' actually supported Coke in saying there should be some sort of public hearing before execution, in order to quieten public opinion; as if they could not see that it would be the very thing to enflame it in Ralegh's favour—just as it had done before. James hit the nail on the head: 'We think it

---

[1] C. D. Bowen, *The Lion and the Throne*, p. 415.
[2] 3 Inst. 26-27.

not fit, because it would make him too popular; as was found . . .
at Winchester, where by his wit he turned the hatred of men into
compassion for him. Also it were too great honour to him. . . .'
Thus ran the royal pronouncement to his lawyers.

Their dilemma was so obvious that public hopes ran high. An
acute observer even wrote that however much the King 'wished
to hang Ralegh, it cannot handsomely be done; and he is likely
to live out his days'. But it could *un*handsomely be done, and
it was so done; and Ralegh's former companion of many years,
Francis Bacon, was the man to do it. Yet again he saw his chance
to insert a spoke into Coke's wheel, and contrast that old medd-
ler's tactless rectitude with his own supple complaisance to the
King. And yet again, as with Essex, he seized his chance to give
the death-sting to one who thought him a friend. As a friend,
Bacon had given his best considered advice, that of the highest
lawyer in the land, that Ralegh need not be disturbed at
starting on his expedition before he had yet received a formal
royal pardon.

He now ate his words. He assured the King that the 'law of
England' fully justified his putting Ralegh to death on those very
'former offences' whose validity Bacon had denied, and 'ex
cathedra'. Now from the same pontifical chair he proclaimed that
for fifteen years Ralegh had been 'a dead man in law'; the King
could therefore make him one in fact, merely by revoking the
reprieve he had then granted him.

There were a few shuddering repercussions at this. The English
ear was not quite attuned to the Scots, and no doubt legal, custom
of propping up a corpse to answer charges of treason. But their
own English Lord Chancellor, Francis Bacon, kept reminding
them, and he the cleverest man in England, that this solution of
his was quite simple, and moreover legal; for the Common Law
did not allow a condemned man to be prosecuted on a new
charge. And so Ralegh's recent offences against Spain need only
be regarded as a side-line, to be given a strictly private hearing
behind closed doors; where it would be easy to suppress anything
that might seem derogatory to the King, or to Spain. And also of
course anything that might tell in Ralegh's favour. But it would
not matter whether the outcome proved his guilt or his innocence,
since they would only be 'hearing' a man already dead.

James snatched at this perfect solution, put forward so

smoothly by his supreme head of the law. It showed consummate ingenuity, of just the kind that James most admired, to execute Ralegh because Spain insisted on it; yet to 'make do' on the ancient charge of Ralegh's plotting friendship with Spain.

Others felt that such an anomaly was monstrous; worse, absurd. Coke, whose lifelong pride had been to 'embody the law', now had his cherished Common Law flung in his teeth, in contempt for his incompetence in failing to degrade it, as Bacon had done, into a trick to serve the King.

Coke's most deadly thrust of accusation in Ralegh's first trial had been his shout: 'Thou hast a Spanish heart!' Now that his victim was to die as an emeny of Spain, the recollection must have given a twinge even to his tough conscience. 'The most learned doubteth most,' he wrote; but he had never doubted himself. It was not in him to admit he could ever have been wrong; but he had begun to see that the law could be. It would be his business from now on to free it from his Sovereign's abuse of it. He himself had aided and abetted that abuse as slavishly as any underling in the law. He had done a great deal in like fashion 'to please the King', but James had proved, like his countryman John Knox, 'neither grateful nor pleaseable'; and it really was not worth while to go on trying. Far better to opt for posterity; to make the Common Law his god; to fight the Crown whenever it interfered with that, and so win 'enduring honour for his valiant assertion of the Rule of Law', as paid him by today's famous lawyer, Lord Birkett; who also tells us that 'Coke believed with passionate intensity that the King should be *under* the law'. Coke was, to quote Lord Birkett again, 'the narrow-minded, obstinate and fanatical lover of the Common Law; whilst Bacon was the true philosopher-lawyer'.

Bacon's philosophy was giving him every satisfaction. He had now made full amends to the King for his unfortunate misunderstanding about Coke's daughter and 'Steenie's' brother (whose marriage was in fact turning out almost as badly as her father's— just as Bacon had predicted); and he had once more saved the situation for the King from Coke's meddling, just as he had done in the Overbury trials. James must surely recognize him to be as eagerly useful to him as ever Cecil had been, whom he had affectionately called 'my little beagle'. We don't hear of his ever calling Bacon 'my little viper'; nobody indeed ever called Bacon by any nickname, however appropriate. But he could feel sure now of his King's affection.

As for Ralegh, here again Bacon's philosophy spared him any discomfort. He had long ago written in his famous Essays, read and quoted by all the wise men of his day, 'There is little friendship in the world, and least of all between equals.' All he had done was to prove this, with the only man equal to himself in intellect; the man to whom he had given his best professional advice, as lawyer, and as friend; and had now given himself the lie, in order to deliver that friend to his enemies.

CHAPTER THIRTY-FOUR

'Men are the Causes of their own Miseries, as I was of Mine'

SIR WALTER RALEGH

RALEGH'S sole purpose now was to make clear to all the justice of his case. But his exhaustion on arrival, and meeting his wife again after all that he and she had been through, prevented him from doing it straightaway. He could do no more than write to his cousin George Carew in explanation that 'want of sleep . . . has almost deprived me of my sight, and some return of the pleurisy I had in the Tower has so weakened my hand that I cannot hold the pen'. He would have to do better than that in writing to his enemies. It would be easier to speak to them face to face.

So instead of escaping to France, as he could have done so easily in the first fortnight after landing at Plymouth, he set out for London with his wife, confident of proving his case in person, even by putting his head into the lion's mouth. On his way there he was met by his young cousin, Sir Lewis Stukeley, the Vice-Admiral of Devon, with an order for his arrest, though no formal warrant for it. But Ralegh made no protest against this vague authority, and with humorous pleasantry remarked that he himself already 'had saved' Stukeley 'the labour, and done it to his hands' by setting forth for London of his own accord.

He had in the past given kindly service to Stukeley, who was the nephew of his admired hero, friend and cousin, Sir Richard Grenville; and he had always taken it for granted that this Devon man of his own kin was his friend. Sir Lewis' behaviour to him fully endorsed this; he had deliberately sought this office, he explained, in order to provide his cousin with a kind and easy jailor. He set no close guard on him, and delayed their journey to London by turning back to Plymouth to sell the cargo of the *Destiny*, the richest part of it being the store of tobacco on board. Stukeley pocketed all the proceeds, suggesting to Ralegh that it would be easier to share them with him as their rightful owner 'later on'. His profitable transactions were interrupted by a formal and urgent warrant of arrest from the King, 'safely and speedily to bring hither the person of Sir Walter Ralegh—all delays set apart'. Sir Lewis promptly finished off his sales of tobacco, and started for London with his prisoner.

But Ralegh had not yet written his defence, and his only chance to do so would be before he got to London. Once there, as he now at last saw plainly, he might well find himself on the scaffold before he could write or speak. To make delay, he shammed illness and delirium, and Stukeley, a rather nervous little man, was naturally terrified lest it should be some infectious tropical disease, or else a raging madness, for Ralegh threw fits, refused to eat anything but grass, like Nebuchadnezzar, and all so formidably that three important doctors at Salisbury signed a bulletin that the patient's condition, though mysterious, was highly dangerous, and he must not be moved. Having won his respite, Ralegh wrote with furious urgency all through the night, and at the same time made up for starving himself by devouring ravenously a leg of cold mutton and three loaves, smuggled in for him from the White Hart Inn.

There was no chance, and no need now, to think what exactly to say and how to say it. The words flew from his pen; and the result is a burning defence of his own, and of all great men's failures—that of the 'Unconquerable Emperor' Charles V's defeat ('I will not say dishonour') by the Moors at Algiers; of Spain's 'Invincible Armada' in '88; of Sir Francis Drake and Sir John Hawkins, 'men for their experience and valour as eminent as England had any';—and if all these had at some time failed in their enterprise and were yet condoned, 'then it is not so strange that myself, drawing after me the chains and fetters wherewith I had been thirteen years tied in the Tower, being unpardoned and in disgrace with my Sovereign ... I say, what wonder is it that I have failed, where I could neither be present myself, nor had any of my Commanders whom I might trust, living, to supply my place?'

The practical facts of his case were unquestionable; Guiana was a long-recognized English possession, won by the voluntary cession of its chiefs; and the English King had ordered him to go there. So how could he have committed any trespass, or any breach of the peace, since 'my men . . . were invaded and slain before any violence was offered to any of the Spaniards'.

His trick of feigned illness gained him the time and quiet he needed to make this statement. But the deception was of course used against him when discovered; and has shocked many since, as being disgracefully undignified behaviour, unbecoming to a true hero—an opinion that would have amused Ralegh, who 'was very jocund and merry' about it with his jailors.

Sir Lewis cannot have seen the joke in having been fooled and badly frightened, but he continued to show affectionate sympathy for his kinsman; and Ralegh did not guess that he was doing so under special orders from King James. He believed too that it was owing to Stukeley's good work on his behalf that when they reached London he was not put straightway into the Tower, but allowed to stay in his own house with his wife, with some appearance of freedom, and 'only' his cousin Stukeley on guard there, since someone naturally had to be responsible for him.

Others felt doubtful of James' show of considerate behaviour. His blonde Queen seemed a shallow, silly woman; but she had long experience of her husband and had lately warned her friend, the Lady Anne Clifford and Countess of Dorset, down at Knowle, 'not to trust your matters' (of business) 'absolutely to the King, lest he should deceive you'. Thus cautioned, the Countess had withstood a private talk of one and a half hours from the Archbishop of Canterbury 'persuading her both by divine and human means' to comply with the King's wish that she should part with her own property; and had yet managed to hang on to it.[1]

But there was all the difference in the world between the little dark ugly Countess of Dorset, the toughest of tenacious women, and Sir Walter Ralegh. There could be no hope for him against the Queen's uncouth husband. She saw that Ralegh's only chance was to get out of the country. The French were exceedingly eager to have him in their service. King James himself had given his official sanction to the project of an Anglo-French expedition to Guiana, and it would be entirely honourable therefore for Ralegh now to accept the repeated offers from the French Court of a safe shelter there and a warm welcome. Their offers were eagerly backed by the Queen, who also had her own reasons since, like most of England, she did not want her son Charles to

---

[1] V. Sackville West, *Knowle*, p. 70.

marry the Spanish Infanta. She would prefer a French princess for his bride, and a better understanding between the two countries. The French envoys again sought out Ralegh and urged him to escape to the high honour, and above all the freedom, that he would find in their country.

There was now every reason for him to accept. He had shot his final bolt, which he had come back to England to do in defiance of death. He had now put down his case for all to see. He had hoped to present it to the King in person, but James refused to see him. If France valued his services more highly than did his King, then it was plainly more sensible to render them to her, wherever they did not conflict with England's interests, than to moulder in his grave or, worse, in prison; where even the books he wrote were liable to be suppressed. So he finally agreed to his wife's and Queen's and friends' persuasions, and received the French envoys, Le Clerc and Chesnée, quite openly in a room full of his friends, and thanked them for all their kindness. He discussed their plans afterwards with Sir Lewis Stukeley and said he would rather escape in an English ship. Stukeley showed violent indignation and compassion for his kinsman and resolved to flee this ungrateful country with him. Ralegh thanked him warmly for his devotion.

So on a thick moist night of that August of 1618 they set out downstream towards the open sea. Stukeley gleefully boasted to Ralegh how he had now proved himself to him as 'an honest man', while from time to time he peered back through the mist at the shadowy form of a following boat. But he scoffed at Ralegh's anxiety about it; in a shrill defiant flourish, he called himself a fool to have risked everything to accompany such a timorous friend.

At Greenwich the dim shadow drew alongside them; it was a larger, stronger ship, and halted Ralegh's boat. Ralegh scented danger and, still believing in his friend, handed Sir Lewis some things from his pockets to keep safely for him. Sir Lewis promised to do so, and embraced him lovingly; while the dark forms of men from the other ship swarmed silently up over their boat's side, and surrounded them. Sir Lewis in a loud voice then arrested Ralegh in the King's name, and handed him over to the strange crew.

Ralegh looked down on his cousin in the flickering light of the ships' lanterns, his immense domed brow towering over him, the queer high pulse in it throbbing above the arched, questioning eyebrows. They did not question now; the piercing eyes that always watched so intently, yet could never recognize a traitor in a friend, saw at last who stood before him.

'Sir Lewis,' said his low voice, 'these actions will not turn out to your credit.'

The quiet dignity of the reproach seemed a mild return for black treachery. Sir Lewis thought he could well afford to 'shog it off' as he brought his victim once again inside the gates of the Tower. He assisted, at first eagerly, then contemptuously, while Ralegh was docked of his personal belongings—bright trifles such as an eager boy might treasure: a jacinth seal with Neptune engraved on it to bring luck at sea, and a lump of Guiana ore tied on to it with string; a little Guiana idol grinning like a devil; an ancient silver seal of his own arms; a scarlet purse with a lodestone inside and fifty pounds in gold; a captain's gold whistle set with small diamonds, and sixty-three sparkling buttons; an ounce of ambergris; a diamond ring given him by the late Queen; samples from silver-mines, and several charts of Guiana, Panama, the Orinoco and Nova Regina. They would be out of date in a few years, and so would their owner. It was a comforting thought for Sir Lewis as he pocketed all that he could of his old kinsman's fanciful relics of his crowded life; but not the most precious, a miniature of his wife set in gold and diamonds which Ralegh insisted on handing over instead to the Tower Lieutenant, who stood by in respectful sympathy.

Sir Lewis could afford to shog that off too, having safely acquired and kept all the rich proceeds from the sales of tobacco in Ralegh's ship. Even more profitable would be his claim for Expenses, which he had already put in to the Government, in the sum of £965, 6s. 3d., for 'bringing up out of Devonshire the person of Sir Walter Ralegh'—a fairly tall claim, but the 6s. 3d. showed it to be an exact calculation. And there was all the medical expense, and the anxiety, not to say bodily fear, that he had been put to over the shamefully shammed 'illness' which the prisoner had only laughed over. It was Sir Lewis' turn now to laugh, as he went freely out through the jaws of the Tower gates in the misty August dawn, and left his tall kinsman safely locked inside.

The Exchequer promptly paid him his blood-money, but he found that all men referred to it as 'thirty pieces of silver', and to himself as 'Sir Judas'. 'Shunned by every man', he dared not return to Ralegh's home county of Devon although he was its Vice-Admiral, and had to visit the Lord Admiral Howard of Nottingham on official business. He was violently prevented. The Lord Admiral had not always been a true friend to his old comrade at sea, who had so magnificently vindicated him in his command against the Armada; but now he remembered that once he had been proud to kneel and wipe the dust with his cloak from Ralegh's shoes. He roared at 'Sir Judas': "What, thou base fellow! *Thou*—the scorn and contempt of men, how darest thou offer thyself in my presence?" and picking up his staff he threatened to cudgel him out of his house. 'Sir Judas' fled; and complained to James that all men were reviling him for his loyal service to his King, so that he went in fear of his life. For thanks, he got a brisk rejoinder: James was not surprised, and anyway, 'What wouldst thou have me do? If I should hang all that speak ill of thee, all the trees in my kingdom would not suffice!'

Then an extraordinary spasm of truth shivered through the shabby form of the King as he shambled up and down. He stood still for an instant, and said: 'I have done amiss.' He could not face it. He shifted back into his typical shirking of responsibility, putting it on to the miserable creature that he had bribed to become his tool for treachery. Shuffling down the room again, clutching and hanging on to his 'Steenie's' arm, he flung over his shoulder at Sir Lewis, 'Ralegh's blood be upon thy head!'

Once again he slid out of what he had 'done amiss', and left another to pay the price.

'Sir Judas's' was heavy; he had to fly from England, and sought a lonely shelter in Lundy Island. But there was no escape from himself. He became a raving madman, and died within two years of his betrayal of Ralegh.

CHAPTER THIRTY-FIVE

'Love, and Time, hath given thee leave to rest'

'THE OCEAN'S LOVE TO CYNTHIA'

RALEGH's defence was thrust aside at the private enquiry as irrelevant, since he was to be condemned, not on recent events, but on the verdict pronounced fifteen years before. He replied with spirit that the King himself had proved he did not believe that verdict, or he would never have despatched him on this last important mission as Admiral in command of a powerful fleet. They could find no answer in law nor logic to this; only a superb piece of rhetoric as reason for his death.

'You have lived like a star, at which the world hath gazed. And like a star you must fall, when the firmament is shaked.'

*　　　*　　　*

Gondomar received some shaking. He had liked to ride about London in a litter, but the crowds threw mud and stones at him and yelled at 'the devil in a dung-cart', although some were flogged for it through Fleet Street at the cart's tail. He dared not venture into the streets, especially after he had tried to escape through the back door of Lady Hatton's house, and had it shut in his face. For even his success as a ladies' man was failing him. He had done his best to make love to Coke's wife, whose easy virtue was as notorious as his own; but 'the extraordinary lady will not allow her husband to come in at her front door, nor myself at her back'. He had to abandon his demand for Ralegh to be executed in Spain, lest the firmament be shaked too dangerously.

Young Carew Ralegh, now thirteen, wrote an appeal for 'my poor father, sometime honoured with many great places of command by the most worthy Queen Elizabeth . . . as a token of his loyalty'. But James had heard quite enough of loyalty to Elizabeth.

George Carew's appeals as Privy Councillor also failed, as did Queen Anne's. In desperation she wrote to the Duke of Buckingham, whom she had welcomed as a relief from Carr. In deep earnestness she begs her kind dog to 'deal sincerely and honestly with the King . . . that Sir Walter Ralegh's life may not be called in question'; . . . and so to 'prove yourself a true servant of your master. Anna R.'

She was ill and near death herself. Some prevision of it may have made her dread Ralegh's execution, not only for himself, but for her husband and their son Charles; her anxiety is shown in that ominous entreaty for a 'true' service to the King. But her warning went unheeded, and she seemed glad to die six months later, for it was 'the happiest going out that anyone ever had'.

James, flustered, frightened, irritated, sought escape in hunting expeditions, and in writing *Meditations on the Lord's Prayer* which he dedicated to Buckingham; then heard in alarm how people were thronging up to town from all over the country to see the 'great old wise Knight' before he died—or perhaps to see to it that he did not die. James quaked at the thought of that, then suddenly made up his mind once more not to go on being 'an irresolute ass who could do nothing of himself'; and at the last minute decided that as tomorrow was the Lord Mayor's Day, it would be the perfect moment for Ralegh's execution. Then all the pageants and fine shows would draw the crowds away from the scaffold, and take their minds off it. In any case it could be got over early, and with so little warning that there would be hardly any people about.

So he signed the warrant for the execution to take place very early the next morning, October 29th, 1618; the warrant itself being phrased in such hugger mugger haste that it hardly makes sense. 'Our pleasure is, to have the head only of the said Sir Walter Ralegh cut off, at or within our palace of Westminster . . . the said judgment to be drawn, hanged, and quartered, or any law, or other thing or matter whatsoever to the contrary notwithstanding.' The very secretaries who drew it up seem to have been 'shaked'.

Ralegh was taken to the old Gate-House of Westminster for his last night, and on his way through the Palace Yard met an old friend who asked what was happening. Ralegh told him, and advised him to get up early tomorrow if he meant to attend the execution. He added laughing, in a flourish of his old gay panache, 'You must make what shift you can for a place. For my own part I am sure of one.' He knew his power to outvie the rival attractions of the Lord Mayor's Show; as was overwhelmingly proved next morning. Some biographers have deplored the spark of youthful vanity that flashed out in his unquenchable vitality; they probably never learned by experience that the best command given to tired troops at the end of their march used to be, 'Swagger, gentlemen, swagger!'

Ralegh was very tired, and he had reached the end of his march; he had all the more reason to give himself the command to swagger. He had of late been too ill to have his hair and beard trimmed with his usual care; but now let his valet do his best for them, though laughing at him for his pains, which would shortly be wasted unless his man could also provide him with a plaster to set his head on again after it had been struck off. But he asked for his finest clothes, of a sober richness, to be put out for him tomorrow: a tawny satin doublet and ash-coloured silk stockings, black taffeta breeches, a long gown of black wrought velvet, and a laced skull-cap to wear under his hat lest the chill of the early air should bring on his ague and make him shiver, as if from fear.

Many friends came to see him that evening, hoping to comfort him, but it was not necessary. He smoked with them and gave them wine, talked easily and 'was very cheerful and merry'. They were astonished; and one or two, slightly shocked, advised him, "Do not carry it with too much bravery, or your enemies will take exception to it."

But his enemies had at last set him free from them. He had no longer any need to consider what they thought, nor even to keep his friends' counsel, though he answered their rebuke with a strange new gentleness. 'It is my last mirth in this world. Do not grudge it to me. When I come to the sad parting, you will see me grave enough.' And picking up one of the lighted candles he pinched it out, dipped his finger in the snuff, and scrawled an impromptu couplet:

> 'Cowards may fear to die, but courage stout,
> Rather than live in snuff, will be put out.'

The pride of life had been his more variously than in any man of his proud age. He had earned the right to pride in his death. But it was with none of his old scornful arrogance; not even when put through his paces by the brisk, rising young cleric, the consequential Dr Tounson, already at forty-three Dean of West-minster and one of the King's chaplains. He bustled in, though in the middle of 'a busy week with me', full of self-confidence, on his official mission of religious admonition and comfort against the fear of death. It was disconcerting that the prisoner 'seemed to make so light of it that I wondered at him', and he expostulated with him lest it should come from careless levity or vainglory.

To us today it sounds an intolerable impertinence to a much older man, so soon to die. But not to all of us; for a recent writer reproves, as harshly as any dogmatist divine of the seventeenth century, 'the essential frivolity of Ralegh's character . . . giving a lightness and gaiety to his courage before death', all the more reprehensible, apparently, because it 'deeply impressed contemporary opinion, and showed up James by contrast as a mean and grasping schemer'. But Ralegh can hardly be blamed because James suffered in contrast to him. It had indeed always been the deepest and worst complaint James held against Ralegh; all the more unforgivable because it must never be mentioned. As for Tounson, out of his own mouth he reveals himself as just the sort of whipper-snapper busybody that Ralegh and his arro-gantly intellectual friends used to mock at. But Ralegh did not do that now; he could discern some goodwill under the blustering exterior, and seek to meet it kindly. There was no 'frivolity' in his sincere and courteous answers to the Dean's rather truculent questions. He took pains to explain to him, and with humility and patience, that he 'gave God thanks he never feared death . . . it was but an opinion and imagination; and the manner of death, though to others might seem grievous, yet he had rather die so than of a burning fever'.

Too well he had known the agony of such fever, and of a lost and wandering mind, alien to himself. Now he was to be spared that frenzy, and the crippling pains and clouded thoughts of illness; and was thankful that his soul would be his own until the axe fell on him. He had chosen his own path to death, as in life; had flung to the winds the calm sunset of a safe old age and a final sick-bed. He had written how poor a thing was ambition, how vain was glory, and the 'humour of rags' (though now he wore his finest); how hideous, war; how small the world, and near its end. That was no reason why it, or he, should sink in flaccid despair to accept the worst at the world's end; since for us all, 'Death . . . doth pursue us and hold us in chase from our infancy.'

Envy, not pity, was the tribute of his friends; they saw in him no light play-actor, but one of 'those few black swans' who, as he had once written, 'behold death without dread, and the grave without fear, and embrace both, as necessary guides to endless glory'. Even the busy Dean could recognize something of that rare quality, and went away to write a warmer testimony than he could before have imagined possible. 'He was the most fearless of death that ever was known, and the most resolute and confident, yet with reverence and conscience.'

Ralegh had yet to face his worst ordeal, his farewell to his wife. Her heroic control broke down, and he could not catch what she was trying to tell him through her sobs. Then he heard how she had begged the Lords of the Council to sue for a pardon, but that all they would grant was the favour that she should dispose of his body. He answered tenderly, "It is well, dear Bess, that you should have the disposal of that, dead, which living was so often denied to you."

It was a surge of remorse for all that she had had to suffer for him, and especially for the long times of absence on his wanderings, when they might have been together. He sought refuge for them both in talk of the future of their young son Carew, and plans for his education; tried to fasten her mind on things that she could still do for his sake, to clear his name and honour after his death; and gave his papers into her care. At midnight she had to leave him, and went without protest or more tears, looking back only once at 'the tumultuous adventurer who had been her life'.

He had still a few hours and must use them quickly and coolly. He wrote his testamentary notes. They show an extraordinary consideration and care for his dependants, as well as his clear head for business, even at this moment. He gave nine brief denials of the recent charges made by James against him; and at the end summed them up in one terse answer: 'No; if I had not honoured the King truly, and trusted in his goodness somewhat too much, I had not suffered death.'

Yet there was still room in his keen mind for a love song that he had written long ago, whose last verse chimed with this hour more deeply than when it had been written in his burning youth. 'Oh cruel Time, which takes in trust', so it began, but he did not rail at Time now. He scribbled the verse on the fly-leaf of his Bible, changing the first words to:

> 'Even such is Time! who takes in trust
> Our youth, our joys, and all we have,
> And pays us but with earth and dust ;
> Who in the dark and silent grave,
> When we have wandered all our ways,
> Shuts up the story of our days.'

Then he added the two new lines that had now come into his head:

> 'But from that earth, that grave, that dust,
> The Lord shall raise me up, I trust.'

It was in that mood of serene confidence that Dr Tounson still found him when he came again before dawn to give him the last Sacrament, and tried once more to make him acknowledge his guilt, if not 'for that particular for which he was condemned, yet for some other matter it might be he was guilty'. But the prisoner obstinately continued 'very cheerful and merry', and when breakfast was brought in he ate it with a hearty appetite, and then produced his elegant long pipe for his last smoke, which he took leisurely and casually, and 'made no more of his death than if it had been to take a journey'. Not only did the pipe rather shock the Dean in itself, but so did the thought of how his tobacco-loathing King would be sure to take this for a last carelessly defiant gesture.

The Sheriffs and their men came to lead him out. The jailor of the Gate-House brought Ralegh a cup of sack against the early morning chill, and asked anxiously if it were as he liked it. He drank it gladly and said smiling, "I will answer you as did the fellow who drank of St Giles' bowl as he went to Tyburn, "Tis a good drink if a man might but tarry by it'." There was a great roll of drums, and at their summons he strode firmly towards the scaffold, in spite of the limp from twenty years ago when Spanish guns had riddled his clothes with bullets and 'interlaced and deformed his leg with splinters'. The people swarmed like bees; he and his company had to push and struggle through them till they were out of breath, for all the barriers set up had been swept away like straws. The city bells pealed in the distance, unavailingly summoning the people to the Lord Mayor's Show; but

306

nobody heeded them, and it must have been an empty show indeed. All London seemed to have thronged into Palace Yard, and many from far off, especially the West Country, not only nobles and gentry who could travel at ease, but rough Cornish miners and Devon sailors, unemployed by the new régime, who had set out as soon as his death was certain, to tramp all this way for a last sight of the leader who had served them well.

It was his first appearance before the general public since he had walked in sombre magnificence at the old Queen's funeral fifteen years before. They had had time to realize that it had signified the passing of the greatest age England had ever known; and now its last splendid embodiment was to pass also. Sorrow and admiration and a deep, abiding anger showed in their faces as they gazed at the frail, white-haired old man who stood tall and erect above them, with 'that Awefulness and ascendency over other mortals' that had so often made men fear and therefore hate him.

But now these were tempered with a rare sweetness. A very old man stood with his bald head bare at the foot of the scaffold, and must have been there since very early to have got so good a place. Ralegh asked him why he had ventured out on so cold a morning, and if there were anything he wanted. 'Nothing,' was the answer, 'but to see you, and pray God for you.' Ralegh thanked him for his good will and, as the only return he could make for it, took off his laced cap and flung it down to shelter his head, 'for thou hast more need of it now than I'.

Then he strained his voice to reach his many personal friends in the balconies and windows around the Yard, and thanked God 'that he Hath sent me to die in the sight of so honourable an assembly and not in darkness'. But his voice was hoarse and weak from the effects of his feverish ague, always worse at this hour, and he apologized for it, regretfully, 'for I would willingly have your Honours hear me'. From his balcony, Lord Arundel called back 'We will come upon the scaffold.'

The Sheriffs dared make no protest at the delay, as his friends struggled with difficulty through the crowd, up on to the scaffold one by one, and shook hands with him, and stood round him. Over the multitude fell a hush of deathly stillness as all strained forward to catch his quiet tones.

This was his only chance of the 'public hearing' that had been denied him, and he took it to clear himself of the recent charges against his conduct during the Guiana voyage and later. His worst detractor has admitted that 'every word he spoke was literally true', though adds carpingly, 'but it was not the whole truth'.[1] Naturally; for to tell the whole truth would have been to accuse the King of such infamy as might well, amid the pent-up emotions of the crowd, stir thoughts of rebellion. Revolt and civil war he would never wish to foster; nor did he ever lose respect for the Crown, no matter who wore it. He dismissed any reference to James with 'But what have I to do with Kings, who am about to go before the King of Kings?'

Nor did he waste a word on his supposed 'treason' of seeking alliance with Spain fifteen years before, which had been given as the only reason for his execution now. That pretence was too patently absurd to be worth even mentioning. All there knew that he was being slaughtered at the request of Spain, and on the pretext that he had not kept his word to King James. To that last, he was determined to give the lie; and on an impulse he turned to Lord Arundel, who had helped to back his expedition to Guiana, and reminded him of their farewell on the decks of the *Destiny*, just as he was setting out, and of the promise that Arundel had then asked of him, on behalf of the King.

"Your Honour took me by the hand and said you would request me one thing, which was that whether I made a good voyage or bad, yet I should return again unto England; and I gave you my faith that I would."

"And so you did!" cried Lord Arundel, and to reach the crowd he called out in a great voice: "It is true. They were the last words I spake unto you!"

So Ralegh had his one witness to prove how he had given his faith, and kept it, in returning to the King who had kept no faith with him. There was a stir through the crowd at this spontaneous appeal, and its eager response, showing there was still honesty and generosity between men. They would have cheered, but that it was no moment for cheering, and many found relief instead in weeping; but Ralegh showed only his gratitude to Arundel with a friendly smile. Then he turned courteously towards the Sheriff for leave to speak 'but a word more, because I will not trouble Mr Sheriff too long'.

[1] Gardiner's *History*, Vol. III, p. 150.

For now at last was his opportunity to refute the old scandal that had so long troubled him, as none other could do—that he had rejoiced at Essex' death and puffed out tobacco 'in disdain of him'. It has surprised some critics that he should trouble about so personal a matter even at this hour, when the condemnation of him as a traitor was surely more important than the false belief that he had once acted like a cad.

But not to Ralegh. He wanted private persons to know that he had not 'crowded upon Essex' on the scaffold, but had left his official place there, although it was his duty to be present, the moment he had thought Essex wanted it, and had gone to the Armoury where Essex could not see him; and that ever since he had bitterly regretted this considerate act, for later, 'I heard he had a desire to see me, and be reconciled to me.'

Even now, and after nearly eighteen years, he could hardly speak without tears of that lost, last minute, when their antagonism could have melted in the flame of their natural friendship; for that it came naturally to them they had both discovered, surprisingly, in those few happy evenings together on each other's flagships; and, best of all, on their shared peak of triumph outside Cadiz. He and Essex might indeed have been friends, away from the Court, and in another world; as now perhaps they would be.

It was the only moment when he showed, even faintly, some emotion. An observer, Thomas Larkin, wrote just afterwards that 'in all the time he was upon the scaffold, nor before, there appeared not the least alteration in him, either in his voice or countenance; but he seemed as free from all apprehension as if he had come hither rather to be a spectator than a sufferer. Nay, the beholders seemed much more sensible than did he.'

That unfailing correspondent, Sir Dudley Carleton, went further. Remembering the trial he had watched in amazement fifteen years before at Winchester, he boldly asserted to his crony, John Chamberlain, that Ralegh's 'happiest hours were those of his arraignment and his execution'.

Later and more cynical critics have learned how to belittle this; to strike at the heart of his character by saying it was a jewel cracked by a flaw, and worn for show; that he saw his whole life as a drama (which it was, so how could he see it else?), and that he was not the great man that romantics suppose him, but a great actor, who would welcome even death in such dreadful form as

309

the supreme chance to show off. But Ralegh had learned that the love of show is the enemy of true quality, and to say, like his friend Fulke Greville, 'I know the world, and believe in God'; aware at last of the terrible 'odds betweene the earth and the skie'.

His earthly life had been a quest of more various aims than any man's; of honours and wealth and fine estates, to enjoy them himself and to leave to his family; yet he had never rested quiet in them, but had always left them to seek hardship and danger in new adventures. And now all were snatched from him, and from his wife and son. He had started English colonies in the North of America, but had never been allowed to go and settle their government; and others in the South, that were to be cravenly abandoned to Spain.

He had sought knowledge in every science, and had tried to bring it within the reach of all. He and his half-brother Humphrey Gilbert had planned to found a University in London for practical learning, a 'Queen Elizabeth's Academy' for naval and military training and the Arts of Navigation and shipbuilding, engineering and the making of maps and charts; and above all of history as a practical influence, so that 'all the noble exploits that ever were' should be 'continually kept in fresh remembrance', to prepare the pupils' minds for any later emergency. But Elizabeth had thought it unpractical to spend any money on it, so the best educational scheme of her day was dropped; and Ralegh could not know that it would bear fruit centuries later in England's Naval and Military Colleges. All his aims had in appearance been missed, all his schemes had failed.

But 'the soul cannot know her true aim till she has achieved it'.[1] Ralegh knew his in achieving it. It no longer counted that his nobler exploits were left unfinished, but only that he had started them; others would come after him to carry them on. And all lesser, personal aims had shrunk to nothing in his present knowledge of his true aim, to die in the peace of God.

He went to the edge of the scaffold and made his personal confession before that motley throng, with a deeper and humbler earnestness than he could summon in answering Dean Tounson. He asked them to 'all join with me in prayer to that great God of

[1] C. S. Lewis on Spenser's 'Faerie Queene' in *English Literature in the 17th Century*, p. 383.

Heaven whom I have grievously offended, being a man of all
vanity, who has lived a sinful life in such callings as have been
most inducing to it. Of a long time my course was a course of
vanity. I have been a sea-faring man, a soldier, and a courtier,
and in the temptations of the least of these there is enough to
overthrow a good mind and a good man. . . .'

The old street-song against him at the height of his courtier's
triumph so long ago, must have echoed in many minds:

> 'Ralegh doth Time bestride
> Yet uphill he cannot ride
> For all his bloody pride.'

There was none of that pride now, only a simple dignity and
humility as he owned to his offences to God, before all those
vagabonds and rascals, shopkeepers, nobles and gentlemen on
horseback and ladies in the windows, but all alike transfixed in
reverent silence. Time had at the last given him their love.

He told them that he died in the faith of the Church of England, hoping for salvation through our Saviour Christ; 'so I take
my leave of you all, making my peace with God. I have a long
journey to take, and must bid the company farewell.' This
last he said lightly and gladly, to remind them that they need
not weep for him, as many were doing, since 'All life is but a
wand'ring to find home'.

He told the Sheriffs that he was ready, and they cleared the
scaffold, leaving only the headsman and the Dean with Ralegh.
He took off his long gown and doublet, refusing any assistance,
but giving his hat and some money to the attendants from the
Gate-House; and bared his neck for the axe, so that one saw how
brown and weather-beaten was the upper part and how white
the lower. He braced his shoulders against the cold as he pulled
off these clothes, and flung back his head, which had bent forward as he talked to the crowd below; so that he looked even
taller and, strangely, younger. This was no pitiful shivering old
man when half undressed in the raw air, but alert and keen as a
vigorous youth. His face too, in repose, looked far younger; the
anxiously tormented frown was smoothed out, and his eyes had
lost the restless glitter that had so often flashed into them of late.
They shone indeed, but with a clear serenity. The crowd saw,
and were awed by it.

Ralegh had called to the headsman to let him feel the edge of the axe to see if it were sharp and good. The man hesitated, but Ralegh, still with that easy, pleasant air, asked him as a courtesy, 'I pray thee let me see it,' so the headsman gave it him, and he felt along the edge and nodded his approval, smiling at the Sheriff as he remarked, 'This is a sharp medicine, but it is a physician for all diseases.' The headsman knelt and begged his forgiveness, and Ralegh put both hands on his shoulders and assured him of it; and then told him, 'When I stretch forth my hands, despatch me.' He refused to be blindfolded, saying, 'Think you I fear the shadow of the axe, when I fear not the axe itself?'

He lay down with his head on the block, and Dean Tounson, officious to the end, asked him if he would not lie facing east, for our Lord's rising? But Ralegh dismissed him with the quiet reminder, "so that the heart be right, it is no matter which way the head lieth", and Dr Tounson at last left him in peace, to pray in silence for a moment. Then he stretched out his hands in signal for the blow, but the headsman was trembling all over, and could not strike. Ralegh gave him an instant to recover and then again made the signal; but again the man, quite unnerved, failed to give the blow. Hysteria quivered through the crowd as the tension grew, and they struggled and craned on tiptoe to see if some miracle had come to prevent the sacrifice. It was checked by Ralegh's firm voice ringing out sharply in his last word of command: 'What dost fear? Strike, man, strike!'

It compelled the man to obey him. The axe fell; then fell again. A deep groan arose and swelled from the multitude, as they watched the star of the Elizabethans fall at last.

Ralegh's body 'never shrank nor moved' under the twice repeated blows. The second blow had severed the head, and the executioner held it up to show the people as of wont; but he dared not call out the accustomed formula as ordered, 'This is the head of a traitor!' Instead, a voice shouted from the thick of the crowd, 'We have not another such head to be cut off!'

The Sheriffs tried hurriedly to disperse them, but they hung about in little groups, some sobbing, others murmuring that they might all as well be dead as live under a King who could butcher the paragon of Englishmen as a compliment to the Spanish Ambassador. Many had the whole course of their lives changed by this day; among them such famous men as Sir John Eliot and John Pym. They were as 'deeply impressed' as the rest of their contemporaries by Ralegh's courage, though 'frivolity, lightness and gaiety' were unlikely to appeal to these two earnest, rising M.P.s, who were later to rouse the Puritan party against the tyranny of the Sovereign's arbitrary power. The crying need for that was driven into them by what they had just witnessed; the King, they agreed, had harmed himself irreparably by sacrificing 'so great a wise man as Sir Walter Ralegh'; James would have done far better for himself if he had bought off Spain's demand for blood with 100,000 crowns. So much they dared say low to each other, while Pym silently resolved that the only hope of safeguarding Englishmen was to transfer power from the King to Parliament—though he did not foresee that in leading this demand he would also lead all England into Civil War.

Sir John Eliot, gentler and with more regard for persons, as yet knew only that he could no longer bear his career as a follower of Buckingham, the favourite of such a King; he was thankful that he had been appointed to succeed 'Sir Judas' Stukeley shortly as Vice-Admiral of Devon, since all Devon men had spewed Stukeley out of even their formal business meetings. Eliot would be proud to serve the sea in Ralegh's own county, and escape from the Court he now loathed. But he too could not guess whither his change of heart would bring him, as forerunner of the Rebellion that Pym would engineer; it lead him to the Tower, where he would sicken for years, and die the 'straw death' in its darkness, that Ralegh had thanked God he had been spared.

At this moment Eliot could only think and talk of 'our Ralegh', as he called him when he wrote of all the terrible preparations for death 'presented to his eye', and behind them, unseen, 'the more cruel expectation of his enemies. And what did all this work on the resolution of our Ralegh? Made it any impression of weak fear, to distract his reason? Nothing so little did that great soul suffer. His mind became the clearer, as if already it had been freed from the cloud and oppression of the body.'

Another, an unknown man in the crowd, had this same impression so strongly that he thought he had seen a vision; and perhaps he had, of the 'Summer's Nightingale' that Ralegh had kept in his bosom, from his glorious youth to his tragic old age.

The man who had seen his joy walked back entranced by the vision, and wrote the verse on it that has been quoted ever since.

> 'Great Heart! who taught thee so to die?
> Death yielding thee the Victory!
> Where took'st thou leave of life? If here,
> How could'st thou be so far from Fear?
> But sure thou died'st and quit'd'st the state
> Of Flesh and Blood before that Fate.
> Else what a Miracle were wrought,
> To triumph both in Flesh and Thought!
> I saw in every Stander-by
> Pale Death; Life only in thine Eye.
> Farewell! Truth shall this Story say,
> We died; Thou only lived'st that Day.'

*   *   *

Ralegh's head was put in a red velvet bag and taken away with his body in a black coach. On the same day Lady Ralegh wrote to her kinsman, Sir Nicholas Carew, in spelling so wild that it had better be translated: "The Lords have given me his dead body though they denied me his life. This night he shall be brought you with two or three of my men. Let me hear presently. God hold me in my wits."

The body was buried in front of the Communion table at St Margaret's, Westminster; the head was embalmed, and kept by his widow till she died, twenty-nine years later; and then by his son Carew until his death, when it was buried with him.

Lady Ralegh made passionate appeals to be allowed to keep her husband's library; had the books been rare, she would have dutifully given them to the King, but as he could easily get them elsewhere, she begged she might treasure Ralegh's own copies. Of greater value were the globes and scientific instruments, one of which last had cost him a hundred pounds. The most precious to her were the charts and maps he had made himself, and his manuscripts, never printed, some on all the seaports of the world, and on the 'Art of War'. But the Commissioners of the King's warrant pounced on them all indiscriminately, with the excuse of their being 'small use to Sir Walter's wife'. But they themselves made no use of them; and all his unprinted writings were lost. They also seized his last ship, the *Destiny*, and all the stores and splendid fittings that it still held, though they paid back to her the bare sum she had herself put into it from the sale of her own estates.

She and her young son were saved from penury by her husband's friends and relatives. They sent Carew to Oxford, and then to Court. But the sight of him gave a nasty twinge to James' strange conscience; he cried out that the youth had appeared like 'the ghost of his father'. James' instinct was right; our greatest living historian has shown how 'the ghost of Ralegh pursued the House of Stuart to the scaffold'.[1]

[1] G. M. Trevelyan, *History of England*, p. 389.

INDEX

316

INDEX

Edwards, Philip, 206-7
El Dorado, 96, 100, 203, 287
Eliot, Sir John, 313
Elizabeth I, Queen, and Philip II of Spain, 11-12, 34, 39-47; executes Mary Queen of Scots, 11; confronts Lord Grey with Ralegh, 22-23; receives Essex at Court, 32 *et seq.*; her looks, 34-5; her various favourites, 35-6; quarrel with Essex, 37; the Armada, 38-57; her navy, 50-1; reviews army at Tilbury, 54; names Virginia, 60-1; her sexual jealousy, 71-2; her friendship, 72-3; capture of the Great Carrack, 85-6; bestows authority on expedition to Guiana, 95; orders Essex to stay in Ireland, 120; his arrest, 120; contributes personally to defence expenditure, 130; advancing age and disillusionment, 134-6; visit to Penshurst, 138; increasing weakness and fears, 141-2; summons her last Parliament, 143; desperate state of finances, 144; abolishes some Monopolies, 146-7; her 'Golden Speech', 148; acknowledges James as successor, 159; Ralegh at her funeral, 149
Elizabeth II, Queen, 60
Elizabeth, Princess, daughter of James I, 213, 219-20, 229-30
Elwes, Sir Gervase, 242, 246
Essex, Second Earl of, 12, 31-3, 36, 59, 62-3, 71, 73-4, 81, 88, 106, 108-12, 115, 117-25, 134, 137, 142, 170, 184, 309
Essex, Third Earl of, 222, 228, 233-234, 244, 246-7

Fayal, 118
Fenton, Viscount, 273
Feria, de, 39
Fitton, Mary, 138
Flores, 118
Frederick, Elector Palatine, 229-30, 250
Frobisher, Martin, 15, 43, 53, 75-6, 108

Gascoigne, George, 15-16, 18

Gaudy, Sir Francis, 193, 291
Gilbert, Sir Humphrey, 15, 17-20, 22, 35, 60-1, 169, 310
Gomera, 273-5, 277
Gondomar, Count, 238, 257-8, 260-261, 271, 273, 287-9, 301
Gowrie, Earl of, 157
Greene, Richard, 88
Greenwich, 298
Greville, Fulke, 310
Grenville, Sir Richard, 13, 43, 60-1, 114-15, 132, 295
Grey, de Wilton, Lord, 21
Grey, de Wilton, son of above, 198-200
Guiana, 95, 97-8, 103-5, 107, 257-259, 296

Harcourt, Robert, 259
Harrington, Sir John, 72, 136, 142, 159, 191
Hariot, Thomas, 29, 50, 60, 87
Harvey, Gabriel, 88
Harvey, Sir George, 180
Hastings, Captain, 271
Hatfield, 58, 93
Hatton, Sir Christopher, 24, 36, 57, 72
Hatton, Lady (m. Sir Edward Coke), 173, 243, 264-6, 301
Hawkins, Sir John, 29, 42, 44, 50, 84, 108, 194, 286
Hay, Lord, 188, 223
Hayes Barton, 17, 25-6, 65
Hele, Serjeant, 177-8
Henry, Prince of Wales, 212-14, 216-226, 228-34, 259
Henry III of France, 71
Henry IV of France, 125, 143, 208
Henry VII, King, 140
Henry VIII, King, 33, 49, 67-8, 236
Horta, 118-19
Howard, Lord Charles, 51, 53-4, 210, 300
Howard, Frances, see Carr, Countess of Somerset
Howard, Lord Henry, 161-2, 177, 194, 210, 228, 240, 242-3, 246, 300
Howard, Lord Thomas, 111-13, 115, 119, 123

Infanta, 219, 290

James I, King, and Elizabeth's funeral, 159; fear of Ralegh, 160-161; hatred of tobacco, 162, 211; first meeting with Ralegh, 162; desire for peace with Spain, 164, 209; insistence on Divine Right, 172; postpones date of Ralegh's execution, 194; his capriciousness and macabre humour, 197-200; doubts his popularity, 208; reprieves Ralegh, 209; his jealousy 211, 236; devotion to his children, 213; *Basilikon Doron*, 214; the 'King's Evil', 215; growing estrangement from Prince Henry, 216-19, 222; oppresses the Papists, 220; befriends Robert Carr, 222-248; marriage of Princess Elizabeth, 229-31; supports Carr's divorce, 233; uses Prerogative to save Carr, 246; befriends George Villiers, 241, 247 *et seq.*; signs order for Ralegh's release, 248; aversion to the sight of swords, 251; relations with Gondomar, 257-8, 260-1, 271, 274, 288; supports Sir John Villiers' marriage to Coke's daughter, 264-5; neglect of the navy, 267; anxious to proclaim Ralegh a traitor, 274; betrayal of Ralegh to Spaniards, 283, 287; promises to send Ralegh to Spain for execution, 289; dilemma over accusing Ralegh, 290-2; accepts Bacon's solution, 293; signs warrant for Ralegh's execution, 302
James, C. W., 171n
Jamestown, 261
Jarnac, Battle of, 15
Jeffries, Judge, 172, 175
John of Gaunt, 11
Jones, Inigo, 252
Jonson, Ben, 230, 252-3

Kerr, *see* Carr
Keymis, Lawrence, 87, 99, 104, 183, 260, 267, 274-5, 277-8, 280-5
Kinsale, 143, 270
Knollys, 12, 19
Kyd, 88

Lambarde, William, 139-40

Lanzarote, 272-3
Larkin, Thomas, 309
Le Clerc, 298
Leicester, Earl of, 13, 16, 19, 33, 35-8, 49, 54-5, 57-8, 78-80
Lettice, Lady Leicester, 12, 33, 59
Lewis, C. S., 310n
Lisbon, 12, 62, 83
Lismore Castle, 64-5, 165, 268

Macdonell, Sir John, 175n, 181n
Magnus, Sir Philip, 259n, 289 and n
Markham, Sir Griffin, 198-200
Marlowe, Christopher, 88-9
Mary Queen of Scots, 11-12, 45, 48-50, 56, 70-2, 78-80, 86
Mary Tudor, 13, 17, 40, 46, 56, 58, 77, 141, 168
Medici, Catherine de, 15, 34
Medina Sidonia, Duke of, 45-6, 52, 110
Montcontour, Battle of, 15
More, Sir George, 245
Morice, James, 172n
Mountjoy, Lord, *see* Blount, Charles
Murray, Sir Davis, 231-2

Naunton, Sir Robert, 22-3, 27, 90
Newfoundland, 18, 60
Northumberland, Earl of, 87, 161, 220
North-West Passage, 18

Oriel, 14
Orinoco, River, 96-8, 100, 102, 257, 277, 280
Ormonde, Earl of, 21, 23-4, 54
Overbury, Sir Thomas, 192, 228, 232-4, 238-48, 251
Oxford, 14, 315
Oxford, Seventeenth Earl of, 28, 138
Oxford, Eighteenth Earl of, 264

Parma, Duke of, 45, 51-2
Pembroke, Lord, 200
Perrot, Lady Dorothy, 36
Perrot, Sir John, 15, 63, 67-8
Perrot, son of Sir John, 19, 36
Philip II of Spain, 11-13, 17, 34, 39-42, 44-5, 50, 55-6, 71
Plymouth, 18, 19, 51, 110, 288
Popham, Chief Justice, 177, 181-3, 190, 192, 195, 223

INDEX

Trevelyan, G. M., 172, 315n
Trinidad, 95-6, 100, 103, 105
Tyrone, Earl of, 109, 120, 142-3, 269
Turner, Mistress, 242-3, 251

Valois, Isabel de, 39, 41
Venezuela, 258
Verde, Cape, 19
Vere, Edward de, *see* Oxford, Seventeenth Earl of,
Vere, Henry de, *see* Oxford, Eighteenth Earl of,
Vere, Sir Francis, 111, 115
Victoria, Queen, 134
Villiers, George, 241-2, 261-2, 264-265, 301-2
Villiers, Sir John, 264, 265
Virginia, 60-1

Waad, Sir William, 216, 218
Walsingham, Frances, 71
Walsingham, Sir Francis, 21
Warwick, Earl of, 140
Wedgwood, C. V., 173, 188n
Whiddon, Captain Jacob, 96
White, Captain John, 28, 60
William of Orange, 15
Williams, Sir Roger, 62-3
Winchester, 170-1, 176, 198, 210
Windsor Castle, 80
Winwood, Sir Ralph, 239-40, 242, 247, 261, 265-6, 286
Wolvesey Castle, 176
Woolf, Virginia, 155
Wotton, Sir Henry, 234, 253

Youghal, 50, 65

320